The Church
Sacrament of Salvation

The Didache Series
— PARISH EDITION —

The Didache

[DID-uh-kay]

The *Didache* is the first known Christian catechesis. Written in the first century, the *Didache* is the earliest known Christian writing outside of Scripture. The name of the work, "*Didache*," is indeed appropriate for such a catechesis because it comes from the Greek word for "teaching," and indicates that this writing contains the teaching of the Apostles.

The *Didache* is a catechetical summary of Christian sacraments, practices, and morality. Though written in the first century, its teaching is timeless. The *Didache* was probably written by the disciples of the Twelve Apostles, and it presents the Apostolic Faith as taught by those closest to Jesus Christ. This series of books takes the name of this early catechesis because it shares in the Church's mission of passing on that same Faith, in its rich entirety, to new generations.

Below is an excerpt from the *Didache* in which we see a clear example of its lasting message, a message that speaks to Christians of today as much as it did to the first generations of the Church. The world is different, but the struggle for holiness is the same. In the *Didache*, we are instructed to embrace virtue, to avoid sin, and to live the Beatitudes of our Lord.

My child, flee from everything that is evil and everything that is like it. Do not be wrathful, for wrath leads to murder, nor jealous nor contentious nor quarrelsome, for from all these murder ensues.

My child, do not be lustful, for lust leads to fornication, nor a filthy-talker nor a lewd-looker, for from all these adulteries ensue.

My child, do not be an interpreter of omens, since it leads to idolatry, nor an enchanter nor an astrologer nor a magical purifier, nor wish to see them, for from all these idolatry arises.

My child, do not be a liar, for lying leads to theft, nor avaricious nor conceited, for from all these thefts are produced.

My child, do not be a complainer, since it leads to blasphemy, nor self-willed nor evil-minded, for from all these blasphemies are produced.

Be meek, for the meek will inherit the earth.

Be long-suffering and merciful and guileless and peaceable and good, and revere always the words you have heard.[1]

The *Didache* is the teaching of the Apostles and, as such, it is the teaching of the Church. Accordingly, this book series makes extensive use of the most recent comprehensive catechesis provided to us, the *Catechism* of the Catholic Church. The *Didache* series also relies heavily on Sacred Scripture, the lives of the saints, the Fathers of the Church, and the teaching of Vatican II as witnessed by the pontificates of John Paul II and Benedict XVI.

---

1. Swett, Ben H. "The Didache (The Teaching)." © January 30, 1998. *http://bswett.com/1998-01Didache.html*

The Church
Sacrament of Salvation

Author: Dr. Scott Hahn
Publisher: Rev. James Socias

MIDWEST THEOLOGICAL FORUM
Woodridge, Illinois

Published in the United States of America by

Midwest Theological Forum
1420 Davey Road
Woodridge, IL 60517

Tel: 630-739-9750
Fax: 630-739-9758
mail@mwtf.org
www.theologicalforum.org

Author: Dr. Scott Hahn

Publisher: Rev. James Socias

Editor in Chief: Jeffrey Cole

Editorial Board: Rev. James Socias, Rev. Peter V. Armenio, Dr. Scott Hahn, Jeffrey Cole

Contributing Editors: Gerald Korson, Kevin Aldrich

Design and Production: Marlene Burrell, Jane Heineman of April Graphics, Highland Park, Illinois

Acknowledgements

Excerpts from the English translation of the *Catechism of the Catholic Church* for the United States of America, copyright © 1994, United States Catholic Conference, Inc.—Libreria Editrice Vaticana. Used with permission.

Excerpts from the English translation of the *Catechism of the Catholic Church: Modifications from the Editio Typica*, copyright © 1997, United States Catholic Conference, Inc.—Libreria Editrice Vaticana. Used with permission.

Scripture quotations are adapted from the *Revised Standard Version of the Bible*, copyright © 1946, 1952, 1971, and the *New Revised Standard Version of the Bible*, copyright © 1989, by the Division of Christian Education of the National Council of the Churches of Christ in the United States of America, and are used by permission. All rights reserved.

Excerpts from the *Code of Canon Law, Latin/English Edition*, are used with permission, copyright © 1983 Canon Law Society of America, Washington, DC.

Citations of official Church documents from Neuner, Josef, SJ and Dupuis, Jacques, SJ, eds., *The Christian Faith: Doctrinal Documents of the Catholic Church*, 5th ed. (New York: Alba House, 1992). Used with permission.

Excerpts from *Vatican II: The Conciliar and Post Conciliar Documents, New Revised Edition* edited by Austin Flannery, OP, copyright © 1992, Costello Publishing Company, Inc., Northport, NY, are used with permission of the publisher, all rights reserved. No part of these excerpts may be reproduced, stored in a retrieval system, or transmitted in any form or by any means—electronic, mechanical, photocopying, recording or otherwise, without express written permission of Costello Publishing Company.

Excerpts from *YouCat*, copyright © 2011, Ignatius Press, San Francisco. Used with permission.

Disclaimer: The editor of this book has attempted to give proper credit to all sources used in the text and illustrations. Any miscredit or lack of credit is unintended and will be corrected in the next edition.

Printed in USA

TABLE OF CONTENTS

TABLE OF CONTENTS

TABLE OF CONTENTS

ABBREVIATIONS USED FOR THE BOOKS OF THE BIBLE

OLD TESTAMENT

Genesis	Gn	Tobit	Tb	Ezekiel	Ez
Exodus	Ex	Judith	Jdt	Daniel	Dn
Leviticus	Lv	Esther	Est	Hosea	Hos
Numbers	Nm	1 Maccabees	1 Mc	Joel	Jl
Deuteronomy	Dt	2 Maccabees	2 Mc	Amos	Am
Joshua	Jos	Job	Jb	Obadiah	Ob
Judges	Jgs	Psalms	Ps	Jonah	Jon
Ruth	Ru	Proverbs	Prv	Micah	Mi
1 Samuel	1 Sm	Ecclesiastes	Eccl	Nahum	Na
2 Samuel	2 Sm	Song of Songs	Sg	Habakkuk	Hb
1 Kings	1 Kgs	Wisdom	Wis	Zephaniah	Zep
2 Kings	2 Kgs	Sirach	Sir	Haggai	Hg
1 Chronicles	1 Chr	Isaiah	Is	Zechariah	Zec
2 Chronicles	2 Chr	Jeremiah	Jer	Malachi	Mal
Ezra	Ezr	Lamentations	Lam		
Nehemiah	Neh	Baruch	Bar		

NEW TESTAMENT

Matthew	Mt	Ephesians	Eph	Hebrews	Heb
Mark	Mk	Philippians	Phil	James	Jas
Luke	Lk	Colossians	Col	1 Peter	1 Pt
John	Jn	1 Thessalonians	1 Thes	2 Peter	2 Pt
Acts of the Apostles	Acts	2 Thessalonians	2 Thes	1 John	1 Jn
Romans	Rom	1 Timothy	1 Tm	2 John	2 Jn
1 Corinthians	1 Cor	2 Timothy	2 Tm	3 John	3 Jn
2 Corinthians	2 Cor	Titus	Ti	Jude	Jude
Galatians	Gal	Philemon	Phlm	Revelation	Rev

GENERAL ABBREVIATIONS

AG — *Ad Gentes Divinitus* (Decree on the Church's Missionary Activity)

CA — *Centesimus Annus* (On the Hundredth Anniversary)

CCC — *Catechism of the Catholic Church*

CDF — Congregation for the Doctrine of the Faith

CIC — *Code of Canon Law* (*Codex Iuris Canonici*)

CPG — *Solemn Profession of Faith*: Credo of the People of God

CT — *Catechesi Tradendæ* (On Catechesis in our Time)

DCE — *Deus Caritas Est* (God is Love)

DD — *Dies Domini* (The Lord's Day)

DH — *Dignitatis Humanæ* (Declaration on Religious Freedom)

DoV — *Donum Vitæ* (Respect for Human Life)

DV — *Dei Verbum* (Dogmatic Constitution on Divine Revelation)

DS — Denzinger-Schonmetzer, *Enchiridion Symbolorum, definitionum et declarationum de rebus fidei et morum* (1985)

EV — *Evangelium Vitæ* (The Gospel of Life)

FC — *Familiaris Consortio* (On the Family)

GS — *Gaudium et Spes* (Pastoral Constitution on the Church in the Modern World)

HV — *Humanæ Vitæ* (On Human Life)

IOE — *Iura et Bona* (Declaration on Euthanasia)

LE — *Laborem Exercens* (On Human Work)

LG — *Lumen Gentium* (Dogmatic Constitution on the Church)

MF — *Mysterium Fidei* (The Mystery of Faith)

PH — *Persona Humana* (Declaration on Sexual Ethics)

PL — J.P. Migne, ed., *Patrologia Latina* (Paris: 1841-1855)

PT — *Pacem in Terris* (On Establishing Universal Peace)

QA — *Quadragesimo Anno* (The Fortieth Year)

RP — *Reconciliatio et Pænitentia* (On Reconciliation and Penance)

RH — *Redemptor Hominis* (The Redeemer of Man)

SC — *Sacrosanctum Concilium* (The Constitution on the Sacred Liturgy)

SRS — *Sollicitudo Rei Socialis* (On Social Concerns)

SS — *Spe Salvi* (In Hope We Are Saved)

USCCB — United States Conference of Catholic Bishops

VS — *Veritatis Splendor* (Splendor of the Truth)

Introduction

The eternal Father, by a free and hidden plan of His own wisdom and goodness, created the whole world. His plan was to raise men to a participation of the divine life. Fallen in Adam, God the Father did not leave men to themselves, but ceaselessly offered helps to salvation, in view of Christ, the Redeemer "who is the image of the invisible God, the firstborn of every creature" (Col 1:15). All the elect, before time began, the Father "foreknew and pre-destined to become conformed to the image of His Son, that he should be the firstborn among many brethren" (Rom 8:29). He planned to assemble in the holy Church all those who would believe in Christ. Already from the beginning of the world the foreshadowing of the Church took place. It was prepared in a remarkable way throughout the history of the people of Israel and by means of the Old Covenant.[1] In the present era of time the Church was constituted and, by the outpouring of the Spirit, was made manifest. At the end of time it will gloriously achieve completion, when, as is read in the Fathers, all the just, from Adam and "from Abel, the just one, to the last of the elect,"[2] will be gathered together with the Father in the universal Church....

All men are called to belong to the new people of God. Wherefore this people, while remaining one and only one, is to be spread throughout the whole world and must exist in all ages, so that the decree of God's will may be fulfilled. In the beginning God made human nature one and decreed that all His children, scattered as they were, would finally be gathered together as one (cf. Heb 1:2). It was for this purpose that God sent His Son, whom He appointed heir of all things, that He might be teacher, king and priest of all, the head of the new and universal people of the sons of God. For this too God sent the Spirit of His Son as Lord and Life-giver. He it is who brings together the whole Church and each and every one of those who believe, and who is the well-spring of their unity in the teaching of the apostles and in fellowship, in the breaking of bread and in prayers.

(*Lumen Gentium*, 2, 13)

---

1. Cf. S. Cyprianus, *Epist.* 64, 4: PL 3, 1017. CSEL (Hartel), III B, p. 720. S. Hilarius Pict., *In Mt.* 23, 6: PL 9, 1047. S. Augustinus, passim. S. Cyrillus Alex., *Glaph. in Gen.* 2, 10: PG 69, 110 A.
2. Cf. S. Gregorius M., *Hom. in Evang.* 19, 1: PL 76, 1154 B. S. Augustinus, *Serm.* 341, 9, 11: PL 39, 1499 s. S. Io. Damascenus, *Adv. Iconocl.* 11: PG 96, 1357.

Madonna with the Fish (of Tobias) by Raphael.

The Church
Sacrament of Salvation

Chapter 1
Introduction to the Church

God made the universe for his Church, including for you.

OPENING ACTIVITY

Incorporate into the class's Opening Prayer the Bible passage on Christ founding his Church (cf. Mt 16: 13-21).

Now when Jesus came into the district of Caesarea Philippi, he asked his disciples, "Who do men say that the Son of man is?" And they said, "Some say John the Baptist, others say Elijah, and others Jeremiah or one of the prophets." He said to them, "But who do you say that I am?" Simon Peter replied, "You are the Christ, the Son of the living God." And Jesus answered him, "Blessed are you, Simon Bar-Jona! For flesh and blood has not revealed this to you, but my Father who is in heaven. And I tell you, you are Peter, and on this rock I will build my church, and the powers of death shall not prevail against it. I will give you the keys of the kingdom of heaven, and whatever you bind on earth shall be bound in heaven, and whatever you loose on earth shall be loosed in heaven." Then he strictly charged the disciples to tell no one that he was the Christ. From that time Jesus began to show his disciples that he must go to Jerusalem and suffer many things from the elders and chief priests and scribes, and be killed, and on the third day be raised.

Afterwards, discuss what this passage reveals about who Jesus Christ is and what his "work" on earth was.

BASIC QUESTIONS

This chapter attempts to answer the following basic questions:

* What do we mean by "church"?
* What did the Church have to do with the creation of the universe?
* Why did God create human beings?
* What is salvation history?
* What are some ways the Church can be described?

CHAPTER 1
Introduction to the Church

The title of this book and chapter demand that we first answer one fundamental question: What do we mean by *church*?

If we think about it for a moment, we will recognize readily that the definition is not as simple as it might seem at first. The word pertains to religion and faith, usually to Christianity, but beyond that it has many different nuances in various contexts.

For example, we can speak of belonging to a church, of attending a church, or of a church that is located on a particular street corner in a particular town. We might say, "I go to church on Sundays," or "I am a member of the Catholic Church," or "my parents were married in St. Ann's Church." We also speak of what "the Church teaches," or of how "we are the church."

As Catholics, we routinely use the word "church" to describe all believers wherever they may be found, the local faith community, and the liturgical assembly (cf. CCC 752).

The truth is that all of these uses of the word "church" are rooted in a single meaning. For that meaning, we turn to Sacred Scripture, the Bible, the Word of God.

As Catholics, we routinely use the word "church" to describe all believers wherever they may be found, the local faith community, and the liturgical assembly (cf. CCC 752).

The Entire People of God:
"the People that God gathers in the whole world" (CCC 752).

A PEOPLE CALLED TOGETHER

In the Old Testament, the books of Sacred Scripture that relate the period of time between the creation of the world and the Birth of Jesus Christ, we read of how God gradually gathered his people into one body of faith. Inundated with sin, humanity had wandered far from God's friendship, and God sought to draw them back to him by gradually revealing himself to them, giving them a Law and a way of worship, and promising to send them a Redeemer.

As those who received and responded to this Divine Revelation began to form into a people, known as the people of Israel and later as the Jews, the Old Testament books begin to refer to this congregation by the Hebrew word *qahal*, which means "assembly" or "convocation." This was how the Book of Exodus describes the assembly of God's people as they gathered at the foot of Mount Sinai to receive the Law from God and to accept his *covenant*, or solemn agreement (cf. CCC 751).

Later, when the books of the Old Testament were translated into Greek, the Jewish scholars rendered the Hebrew word *qahal* as the Greek *ekklesia*, which also connotes a convocation but also has a more specific meaning as "the people called together" or "called out." The Apostles, as reflected in the New Testament writings, used the word *ekklesia* to refer to the assembly called together or convoked by Christ, i.e., the community of his followers. Another way of referring to the Church was *ekklesia kyriake* ("assembly of the Lord" or "convocation of those who belong to the Lord"), and from this phrase is derived the English word "church."

Fundamentally, then, "church" refers to the assembly of people called together by Christ.

Defining "Church"

Earlier we referred to three meanings of the word "church" as found in the *Catechism of the Catholic Church*. Let us examine those meanings a little more closely.

The entire People of God: In its broadest definition, the Church comprises "the universal community of believers,"[1] "the People that God gathers in the whole world" (CCC 752). In Catholic teaching, we include among the members of the Church all those who have died in faith, not just those still living on earth.

VOCABULARY

VOCABULARY

DIOCESE (ARCHDIOCESE)

A territorial jurisdiction of the Church, ordinarily governed by a bishop (or archbishop).

MYSTERY

Something that cannot be fully explained or understood, or whose meaning cannot be completely exhausted.

Focus Question 5:

"God created the universe for his Church." Explain.

Focus Question 6:

Did God have any need to create the universe or anything in it?

Focus Question 7:

What does it mean to "fill the earth and subdue it"?

Focus Question 8:

What is the main reason God created human beings?

VOCABULARY

CHRIST or MESSIAH

Literally, "the anointed one."

CREATION

God's bringing forth the universe and all its inhabitants into being out of nothing. Creation is good, yet it has been corrupted by sin.

The local Church: The Catholic Church is organized into territories or jurisdictions called *dioceses* and *archdioceses*, each headed by a bishop, a successor to the Apostles. Thus, we can refer to the Church in the Archdiocese of New York, for example.

Liturgical assemblies: Likewise, the very local communities of believers who gather for worship, most notably Sunday Mass, are churches, too. The community of faithful who worship at St. John's Church can refer to this community, or parish, as "our church." They can do the same with regard to their local diocese and to the Catholic Church as a whole: "our Church."

However, for the Christian believer, even this range of meanings does not fully define the concept of church. The Church is something much more. The Church is a *mystery* because it cannot be fully understood or explained. This mystery has a lot to do with some of the other ways in which the Sacred Scripture refers to the Church.

For example, one of the images, derived from the writing of St. Paul, to describe the Church is the *Mystical Body of Christ*. By becoming a member of the Church through the Sacrament of Baptism, we are incorporated into the Body of Christ.

For the balance of this chapter, we will survey how God began to form his people, his assembly, in preparation for the coming of his only Son, Jesus Christ, the Redeemer of the world.

THE CHURCH AND CREATION

About two thousand years ago, the Second Person of the Blessed Trinity —the Son or the Word—took on human nature. The result was the Incarnation of Jesus Christ, a Divine Person with both a divine nature and a human nature. The name Jesus means "Savior" or "he who saves"; his title, *Christ*, describes his role as the Messiah or "the anointed one"—in other words, "God's specially chosen one." During his public ministry, Jesus Christ established what he called his Church.

To understand why God became man and founded the Church, we have to go back even further than the Incarnation—not just to the beginning, at the creation of the universe, but even "before" the beginning, before time or

Reflection Nebula in the Constellation Orion (Martin Pugh-NASA).
God exists outside of time and space; he is his own principle of existence.

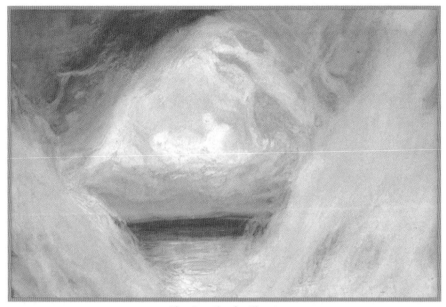

The Creation by Tissot.
"The heavens are telling the glory of God; and the firmament proclaims
his handiwork." (Ps 19: 1)

GUIDED EXERCISE
Conduct a think/pair/share to answer the
following question:

✠ What does it mean to say that Christ
created the universe for his Church?

First, *think* about your response to
the question, then discuss this with a
partner, then *share* your response with
the class.

FROM *YouCat*
Why did God create us?

**God created us out of free and
unselfish love.**

When a man loves, his heart overflows.
He would like to share his joy with
others. He gets this from his Creator.
Although God is a mystery, we can still
think about him in a human way and
say: Out of the "surplus" of his love
he created us. He wanted to share his
endless joy with us, who are creatures of
his love. (*YouCat* 2)

anything other than God even existed. As we read in our previous texts in this series, *Faith and Revelation* and *The Blessed Trinity*, God exists outside of time and space; he is his own principle of existence. He is infinitely happy—in beatitude—living his own Trinitarian life. The one God is a Trinity of Persons: Father, Son, and Holy Spirit.

God had no need whatsoever to create anything, but he created the universe nevertheless. He did it to share his goodness, truth, and beauty with creatures, beings that would never exist unless he brought them into existence. These creatures—i.e., everything in the material universe—by their very existence reflect in some way the power, intelligence, beauty, or other attributes of God. As the Book of Psalms puts it:

> **The heavens are telling the glory of God;
> and the firmament proclaims his handiwork. (Ps 19: 1)**

However, the vast majority of created things have no consciousness of God their Creator. Rather, they "tell the glory of God" by their very existence. The exception, as far as we know, is human beings. As the only conscious, rational beings in material creation, humans alone can see God's handiwork "in the things that have been made" (Rom 1: 20).

God did not stop at creating rational human beings. He also decided to share his own divine life with us so we could be in friendship with him and with one another. This communion in God is the deepest meaning of the Church, which is the gathering or assembly of God's people. This is the sense in which God created the universe for the Church (cf. CCC 759-760).

Because God is all-powerful, it might be easy for us to assume that if God wants every human person to share in his divine life, then that is exactly what will happen. Yet, in making human persons into rational beings, he also endowed us with freedom—free will, the power of self-determination, by which we use our intellect to choose how to think and act, whether for good or for evil. Each human person has the opportunity to accept God's offer of his divine life or to reject it through sin. So, although God earnestly desires that we enter into friendship with him and remain there forever, we have the power to choose otherwise.

Creation of the Animals
by Master Bertram.
The vast majority of created things have
no consciousness of God their Creator.

Focus Question 9:

How can the ideas of good creation and the Fall summarize the first three chapters of Genesis?

Focus Question 10:

What is communion?

Focus Question 11:

What does it mean to be created in the image and likeness of God?

VOCABULARY

COMMUNION

The state of being united together in friendship.

FROM *YouCat*

Does man have a special place in creation?

Yes. Man is the summit of creation, because God created him in his image (Gen 1:27).

The creation of man is clearly distinguished from the creation of other living things. Man is a *person*, which means that through his understanding and will he can decide for or against love. (*YouCat* 56)

The Creation, Ceiling Mosaic, Baptistry of St. John, Florence. Humanity is the pinnacle of God's creation for the simple reason that we resemble him.

Creation of Adam (detail) by Michelangelo. The world had been created for mankind, and mankind had been created for God.

THE CREATION OF HUMANITY

The first two chapters of the Book of Genesis, the first book of the Old Testament, use literary devices to tell the story of Creation. God made the material universe and saw that it was good; he then made the first humans, Adam and Eve, and deemed them to be "very good"—qualitatively superior to the rest of his creation. Adam and Eve were created in an intimate friendship with God, who made them stewards of his creation. They were created male and female, in a natural state of marriage. Made to mirror his image as creator, they were to be co-creators with God, who charged them to "be fruitful and multiply" and to "fill the earth and subdue it" (Gn 1:28). Thus, the marriage of man and woman was part of God's plan from the very beginning.

Note that the human person was the last being God created. God said, "Let us make man in our image, after our likeness" (Gn 1:26). Humanity is the pinnacle of God's creation for the simple reason that we resemble him. God made man and woman in his "own image," endowing them with the ability to understand and to reason, to make free choices, and to love. God's eternal plan was to draw them and all their descendants to himself in a relationship called *communion*, which means "united together in friendship." Created in communion with him, Adam and Eve would enjoy an intimate friendship with God in the paradise that he had created for them. The world had been created for mankind, and mankind had been created for God.

Image and Likeness

What does it mean to be made in the "image and likeness of God"? The term has several meanings, all of which pertain to our communion with God.

The first meaning is that we are made in the image and likeness of God because we are endowed with an immortal soul, a rational intellect, and a free will. God is eternal and therefore immortal; he is all-knowing and all-powerful. He thus possesses these attributes to perfection. Humans did not always exist—although we will exist forever, either in Heaven with God or separated from him in Hell—and we possess a limited but real intellect and freedom. We are the only beings on earth with these attributes. These attributes and powers make us able to consciously and freely unite ourselves with other persons, including God.

Another meaning of the "image and likeness" of God is that human relationships are intended to reflect the Blessed Trinity as a "community of persons." As we have seen, God's inner triune life is a loving communion of Father, Son, and Holy Spirit. In matrimony, the state in which God created Adam and Eve, a man and woman in love become "one flesh" and the result is new human life welcomed with love. Children are bonded as brothers and sisters. Because we are descended from one set of parents, all human beings are really part of one human family.

A third meaning is that of a familial relationship: To be in the "image and likeness" of God is to bear a resemblance to God. After Cain slew Abel, Adam became the father of Seth, a child "in his own likeness, after his image" (Gn 5: 3). Just as Seth received his nature from Adam his father, Adam received his nature from God his Father. Because we have the same nature as Adam and Eve, we also share in God's nature and are made in his image and likeness. All human beings are in this most basic sense not just children of Adam but children of God. Thus we are made for communion with one another and with God.

The dignity of human beings is that we are in the image of God. The tragedy of human life is that we can truly have the image of God and yet have lost his likeness; we can be alienated from God, just as a son or daughter can be estranged from his or her parents. We are also made to live in community with others—in an assembly, as it were.

Work and Worship

In Genesis, God worked for six days and rested on the seventh. Because we were created in God's image, humanity was also made for work and then rest.

Adam, who was given dominion over every living thing,[2] was to till and keep the garden in which God placed him. This was in keeping with God's original command to "subdue" the earth. Human work, therefore, has had special value from the very beginning of creation. Work is not a curse, even though it was eventually made harder because of Adam's sin. Just as God labored to bring creation into existence, we are called to work with creation in imitation of God.

The *Sabbath*, or seventh day, the day of rest, is the sign of God's love and desire for us. God gives himself as a Father to Adam, and Adam in turn is made to give of himself, as a son, back to God. The Sabbath was made in order to remind us that we are created out of God's love so that we may enter into communion with him. For Christians, this communion is expressed in our prayer, worship, and other appropriate activities on the Lord's Day. The Sabbath is not just for physical rest but also to rest in God.

Focus Question 12:
What is the significance of work?

Focus Question 13:
Why did God create the Sabbath?

VOCABULARY

MATRIMONY

The Sacrament of Marriage, by which a man and a woman, in accordance with God's design from the beginning, are joined in an intimate union of life and love, "so they are no longer two but one." Adam and Eve, our first parents, were created by God in a state of marriage.

SABBATH

The Sabbath—or seventh—day on which God rested after the work of the six days of creation was completed. In honor of Christ's Resurrection, Sunday, the new Sabbath, must include rest from servile labor and the worship of God as required by the Third Commandment.

Adam and Eve's Life of Toil
by Master Bertram.
Just as God labored to bring creation into existence, we are called to work with creation in imitation of God.

VOCABULARY

DEVIL

A fallen angel, who sinned against God by refusing to accept his reign; also called Satan or the Evil One.

FALL

Biblical revelation about the Original Sin which introduced sin in human history, as narrated in the Book of Genesis.

ORIGINAL SIN

Adam and Eve's abuse of their human freedom in disobeying God's command. As a consequence, they lost the grace of original holiness and justice, and became subject to the law of death; sin became universally present in the world; every person is born into this state of Original Sin. This sin separated mankind from God, darkened the human intellect, weakened the human will, and introduced into human nature an inclination toward sin.

SALVATION HISTORY

The gradual process by which God has redeemed sinful humanity.

Focus Question 14:
What is salvation history?

Focus Question 15:
How did Adam and Eve fall from grace?

Focus Question 16:
What two lies did the serpent tell Eve?

Focus Question 17:
What did Adam and Eve reject when they disobeyed God?

Focus Question 18:
What do we inherit from Adam and Eve?

The Fall of Man (detail) by Goltzius.
By disobeying God's command, they rejected their status as children of God.

SALVATION HISTORY

The third chapter of Genesis recounts the surprising and tragic fall from grace of our first parents. Although they had a perfect existence, they used their free will to sin by disobeying God due to their pride and the deception of the demonic serpent. As a consequence, they lost the grace of original holiness and justice, and became subject to the law of death; sin became universally present in the world; and every person is born into this state of Original Sin. This sin separated mankind from God, darkened the human intellect, weakened the human will, and introduced into human nature an inclination toward sin.

Although the generations succeeding Adam and Eve fell deeper and deeper into sin and, thus, ever further from God, he had a plan for restoring humanity to his friendship. The gradual process by which God redeemed fallen humanity is called *salvation history*.

Fall from Grace

God had forbidden Adam and Eve to eat the fruit of the Tree of the Knowledge of Good and Evil, lest they die. Then Eve was tempted to do so by Satan or the Devil, a fallen angel who sinned against God by refusing to accept his reign. Taking on the form of a serpent, he deceived Eve. "You will not die," he said. "For God knows that when you eat of it your eyes will be opened, and you will be like God, knowing good and evil" (Gn 3: 4-5). Satan insinuated both that God coveted his own knowledge and power and that Adam and Eve were not already "like God." So Eve took the fruit, and explaining Satan's promise to Adam, he ate of it, too. By disobeying God's command, they rejected their status as children of God. Like Satan, another created being, Adam and Eve had desired to usurp the role of creator. Losing communion with God's life is true death—a fate much worse than mere physical death, which would become another consequence of Original Sin.

As a result of the Fall, Adam and Eve lost their supernatural life and forfeited their communion with God, as well as the inheritance of that communion, which they would not be able to hand down to their children. What they did hand down was the burden of Original Sin, a state into which all their descendants would be born. Because of sin, the world had fallen far from the original design with which it was created.

BL. WILLIAM JOSEPH CHAMINADE AND THE FRENCH UNDERGROUND

he Church's missionary apostolate is not just about evangelizing those who have never heard of Christ. It is also about reevangelizing those who once knew him, or knew him poorly, but have abandoned him.

After the French Revolution at the end of the eighteenth century, the secular anti-Catholic government tried to do what countless political leaders have attempted during the two-thousand-year history of the Church: separate the Church from her hierarchy—the Pope and those bishops in communion with him—and control her for the benefit of the state.

Bl. William Joseph Chaminade, a native of Perigueux, France, was ordained a priest in 1785. Four years later the French Revolution toppled the monarchy and made war on the rest of the *ancien regime*, including the Church. Among the many measures meant to eradicate the old order, the new regime enacted the Civil Constitution of the Clergy, which required clergy to take an oath professing that the Church was an organ of the French government. Fr. Chaminade refused. As a result, he was forced to exercise his priestly ministry underground.

Many recognized Fr. Chaminade's extraordinary faith during this time of persecution. After the Civil Constitution of the Clergy was repealed in 1795, he was given the task of receiving back into the Church priests in his diocese who had taken the oath. He reconciled some fifty priests.

Two years later, the Directory, the name of a new revolutionary government, came to power. A price was put on Fr. Chaminade's head, so he fled to Spain for three years. There he founded the Society of Mary, a family of religious and laity.

He returned to France and began to reevangelize the country that had suffered so much under the tyrannies of the Revolution. In 1800 he received the title of "Missionary Apostolic" from Rome. He was going to be a new kind of missionary, one that reconverted those who had fallen away from the Church.

On December 8, 1800, the Feast of the Immaculate Conception, Fr. Chaminade gathered twelve young Catholics to form the Marian Sodality, which would become the basis of his new evangelization. "You are all missionaries," he told them, called to "multiply Christians." Fr. Chaminade strove to provide a solid religious formation to the members of his Sodality, hoping to make these groups the basis of the re-Christianization of France.

Soon the Sodality spread to cities across France. Fr. Chaminade encouraged groups of young men and women who, desiring greater dedication, made private vows and dedicated themselves to the apostolate of the Sodality without leaving their secular work. His followers, called Marianists, dedicated themselves to teaching and opened primary and secondary schools. They also established a network of schools for Christian education.

When the Marianists ventured to the United States, they established schools as well. To this day they continue to educate young people in the Faith.

Bl. William Chaminade died on January 22, 1850, and was beatified by Pope Bl. John Paul II on September 3, 2000.

Focus Question 19:
How was Bl. William's apostolic work different from most missionaries?

Focus Question 20:
What do political rulers often want to do to the Church?

CLOSURE
Summarize what the Church is in one concise paragraph.

ALTERNATIVE ASSESSMENT

Consider this mini-lesson on *anthropocentrism*.

- Anthropocentrism is the idea that human beings have a central importance in the universe.

- Our Catholic Faith agrees with this idea.
    - The first two chapters of Genesis present God creating human beings last and in God's own image.
    - The central idea of Christianity is that God became man in Jesus Christ.

- Historically, anthropocentrism seemed to be supported by the long-standing Ptolemaic scientific view of the cosmos that the earth was in the center and that all celestial bodies revolve around it.

- In the sixteenth century, the Ptolemaic view gave way to the Copernican view that the earth and other planets revolved around the sun. In addition,
    - Subsequently, astronomy discovered that our sun is one of billions of suns in our own galaxy and that there are billions of galaxies. In addition, the universe was discovered to be immensely old.

Continued

ALTERNATIVE ASSESSMENT
Continued

- Evolutionary biology suggested that human beings could have developed from earlier forms of life, according to natural processes, rather than directly created by God.

- Many people concluded this meant that human beings had no particular importance. We weren't the "center" of anything.

- However, modern science provides some clues that human beings may not be so peripheral.

  - The universe is old but not infinitely old. It had a definite start some 13.7 billion years ago.

  - The very many initial conditions of the universe at the time of its creation were all incredibly fine-tuned in such a way that life, including human beings, could exist. Science calls this "anthropic fine-tuning."

- The following anthropocentric conclusions are reasonable (but certainly debatable):

  - God created the universe out of nothing 13.7 billion years ago.

  - God set up the universe so that human life could develop.

  - As far as we know, man is the only material being capable both of knowing and appreciating the complexity, order, and beauty of the universe and of seeing its origin in God.

  - As far as we know, due to his freedom, man is the only creature capable of committing grave sins, and so, is the only one in need of a redeemer.

  - Because man seemingly is the only creature capable of appreciating God and the only one in need of salvation, it does not seem unreasonable that God would become man in order to redeem him.

The Expulsion of Adam and Eve from Paradise by West.

CONCLUSION

The Church fundamentally is the assembly of people called together by Christ. It is predated and made possible by God's gathering of his people throughout salvation history, in which they were slowly prepared for the coming of his Son our Savior, Jesus Christ.

Immediately after the sin of Adam and Eve, God promised he would send a Redeemer to save humanity. As we will read in the next chapter, God would follow up this promise with a number of solemn agreements with those who believed in him in order to help form them into his faithful people—and eventually into his Church, which would welcome all of humanity.

DISCUSSION QUESTIONS

1. In what Old Testament context is the idea of "church" rooted?

2. Describe several meanings for the word "church."

3. "God created the universe for his Church." Explain.

4. Did God have any need to create the universe or anything in it?

5. What is the main reason God created human beings?

6. How can the ideas of good creation and the Fall summarize the first three chapters of Genesis?

7. What does it mean to be created in the image and likeness of God?

8. What is salvation history?

9. How did Adam and Eve fall from grace?

ENDNOTES – CHAPTER 1

1. Cf. 1 Cor 15:9; Gal 1:13; Phil 3:6.
2. Cf. Gn 1:28, 2:15.

The Church
Sacrament of Salvation

Chapter 2
God Prepares for His Church

From the beginning, man's vocation has been to live in truth and holiness as a son of God with dominion over creation.

OPENING ACTIVITY

Incorporate into the class's Opening Prayer this reading of the Annunciation of the Incarnation of Jesus Christ.

In the sixth month, the angel Gabriel was sent from God to a town of Galilee called Nazareth, to a virgin betrothed to a man named Joseph, of the house of David, and the virgin's name was Mary. And coming to her, he said, "Hail, full of grace! The Lord is with you." But she was greatly troubled at what was said and pondered what sort of greeting this might be. Then the angel said to her, "Do not be afraid, Mary, for you have found favor with God. Behold, you will conceive in your womb and bear a son, and you shall name him Jesus. He will be great and will be called Son of the Most High, and the Lord God will give him the throne of David his father, and he will rule over the house of Jacob forever, and of his Kingdom there will be no end." (Lk 1: 26-38)

BASIC QUESTION

✠ What were the promises and covenants that God established with Adam, Noah, Abraham, Moses, and David?

KEY IDEAS

The key ideas of this chapter are:

✠ After the Fall of Adam and Eve, God promised to send a Redeemer.

✠ God made a covenant with Noah that he would never again destroy the world by flood.

✠ God made a covenant with Abraham that he would make him the father of a nation and bless every nation through him.

✠ Through Moses, God created a covenant with the nation of Israel to be his son with the Israelites a priestly people obeying the Ten Commandments.

✠ God promised that David's kingly heirs would be sons of God, with the Temple on Mount Zion as the nation's spiritual center, and wisdom the nation's new law.

CHAPTER 2
God Prepares for His Church

Review of Chapter 1:

✠ Fundamentally, the Church refers to the assembly called together by Christ, forming the People of God.

✠ God created humanity out of love so that we might share in his divine life. He created us in his image and likeness, endowing us with free will, a rational intellect, and an immortal soul so that we might choose to remain in his love and friendship.

✠ After our first parents sinned and lost his friendship, God promised to send a Redeemer and began to implement his plan of salvation.

The process by which God redeems fallen humanity is called salvation history. One way of following the events of salvation history is to see them as a series of promises and covenants—solemn agreements that involve mutual commitments between God and man.

In this chapter, we will examine the promises and covenants of God and how they were a preparation for the New Covenant he would establish in Jesus Christ through the institution of his Church.

THE PROMISE AFTER THE FALL

God richly blessed our first parents and gave them dominion over the earth. He made them in his own image and likeness, giving them intellect and free will so that they could freely choose to return his love for them in obedience to his will. Instead, they chose sin and lost the communion and friendship with God they had previously enjoyed. This tragic event is referred to as the Fall of Humanity, the Fall of Adam and Eve, or simply as the Fall.

The Garden of Eden by Field.
God richly blessed our first parents and gave them dominion over the earth.

After confronting Adam and Eve about their sin, God turned to Satan, the serpent, and told him, "I will put enmity between you and the woman, and between your seed and her seed; he shall bruise your head, and you shall bruise his heel" (Gn 3: 15). "This passage in Genesis is called the *Protoevangelium* ('first gospel'): the first announcement of the Messiah and Redeemer, of a battle between the serpent and the Woman, and of the final victory of a descendant of hers" (CCC 410). Although this promise was not fully understood by the Jewish people in Old Testament times, we can see in the light of the Gospel that the "woman" is the Blessed Virgin Mary, and her "seed" who will "bruise the head of the serpent" is Jesus Christ, who eventually would come to redeem the world and defeat sin and death.

This promise, which came as a direct and immediate reply from God to that first sin, is the beginning of God's gathering, or rather "re-gathering," of his people into what would someday become his Church. This regathering remains an invitation to which each individual person must choose to respond (cf. CCC 761).

The effects of Original Sin on the children of Adam and Eve bore bitter fruit in the murder of their first son, Abel, by their second son, Cain, and by the countless sins which have followed. Humanity as a whole tumbled out of control into the grips of sin and away from their loving God and Creator. Only God could save them from the evil consequences of their evil choices.

THE COVENANT WITH NOAH

Several generations after Adam and Eve, humanity had spiraled deeper into sin and self-destruction—so much so that the entire world was corrupt.

To help remedy this, the Book of Genesis tells us, God decided to destroy the world, saving only a man named Noah and his family. Of all the people of the world, Noah alone had remained faithful and righteous. God commanded Noah to build an Ark, a large boat, where his family and pairs of all the creatures of the earth would live and remain safe during the forty days and forty nights that God planned to send rain upon the earth.

The rains came, and the earth was flooded. After the waters had subsided and the Ark found dry land, Noah and his family left the Ark and offered God their praise and thanksgiving. God then made a covenant with humanity through Noah:

> I will never again curse the ground because of man, for the imagination of man's heart is evil from his youth; neither will I ever again destroy every living creature as I have done. (Gn 8: 21)

God also renewed his command to Adam and Eve to have dominion over creation, but with an added stipulation that no person may murder another, since every person is made in the image of God:

> Every moving thing that lives shall be food for you; and as I gave you the green plants, I give you everything. Only you shall not eat flesh with its life, that is, its blood. For your lifeblood I will surely require a reckoning; of every beast I will require it and of man; of every man's brother I will require the life of man. Whoever sheds the blood of man, by man shall his blood be shed; for God made man in his own image. (Gn 9: 3-6)

Yet, the effects of Original Sin remained even among Noah's own family, and within a few generations humanity had returned to its sinful ways. Nevertheless, there were still righteous men and women who walked the earth.

Focus Question 1:

What is the *Protoevangelium*?

Focus Question 2:

From the Christian perspective, who is the "seed" mentioned in the *Protoevangelium*?

VOCABULARY

PROTOEVANGELIUM

God's first promise that he would send a Redeemer, a "seed" of Eve who would bruise the head of the serpent, the Devil (Gn 3: 15).

Noah Sacrificing After the Deluge by West.
The effects of Original Sin remained even among Noah's own family.

Focus Questions 3:

What is a covenant?

Focus Question 4:

What covenant did God make with Noah?

Focus Question 5:

Why is it striking that God promised Abraham countless offspring?

Focus Question 6:

What was the sign of the covenant with Abraham?

GUIDED EXERCISE

After reading this section, discuss the following questions as a class:

✴ What are all the possible reasons why a good and loving God might give Abraham such a horrible test?

✴ What are all the reasons why Abraham might have cooperated?

✴ What is the most likely answer to each question?

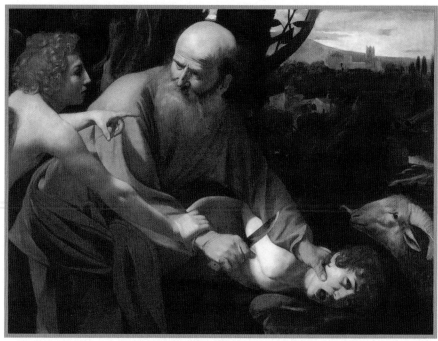

The Sacrifice of Isaac by Caravaggio.
Christians from the earliest times have understood the sacrifice of Isaac as a foreshadowing of the sacrifice of Christ.

Abraham, Sarah, and the Angel
by Provost.
Abraham believed what God had promised. When Sarah was about ninety years old, God gave Abraham and Sarah a son, Isaac.

"...I will multiply your descendants as the stars of heaven and as the sand which is on the seashore...." (Gn 22:17)

THE COVENANT WITH ABRAHAM

One of these was Abram, who would become one of the most important figures in history. God called Abram to a special mission. Renaming him Abraham, God told him to leave his native city of Ur to found a new nation.

> Now the LORD said to Abram, "Go forth from your country and your kindred and your father's house to the land that I will show you. And I will make of you a great nation, and I will bless you, and make your name great, so that you will be a blessing. I will bless those who bless you, and him who curses you I will curse; and in you all the families of the earth shall be blessed." (Gn 12: 1-3)

But Abraham and his wife Sarah were already old—he was seventy-five, and she was already sixty-five—and Sarah had never been able to conceive a child. How was he to become the father of a great nation when he would have no descendants? Nevertheless, Abraham believed what God had promised and left his homeland with his wife, his nephew, their servants, and their possessions.

Years later, when Sarah was about ninety years old, God gave Abraham and Sarah a son, Isaac. God instructed Abraham to observe a sign of their covenant with him: Their men would undergo *circumcision*, the surgical removal of the male foreskin.

Abraham and Isaac

When Isaac was a young man, God gave Abraham an incomprehensible and seemingly inhuman test. God told Abraham to bring his son to the land of Moriah, and on a mountain he would show him, to offer him as a burnt sacrifice (cf. Gn 22: 2). Abraham loved Isaac, who was also the basis of God's promises to him. Yet, Abraham obeyed.

On the way up the mountain, Isaac carried the wood for the sacrifice. He innocently asked his father where the lamb was for the offering. Abraham said, "God will provide himself the lamb" (Gn 22: 3, 6-8).

When the time came, Isaac did not resist but instead was obedient, trusting in God, just like Abraham. At the last moment, an angel appeared and said to Abraham, "Do not lay your hand on the lad or do anything to him; for now I know that you fear God, seeing you have not withheld your son, your only son" (Gn 22: 12). Then Abraham saw a ram that was caught by its horns in a thicket, so he took it and offered it to God. Just as Abraham said, God indeed provided the sacrifice.

Because of Abraham's fidelity, God renewed his covenant promises:

> By myself I have sworn, says the LORD, because you have done this, and have not withheld your son, your only son, I will indeed bless you, and I will multiply your descendants as the stars of heaven and as the sand which is on the seashore. And your descendants shall possess the gate of their enemies, and by your descendants shall all the nations of the earth bless themselves, because you have obeyed my voice. (Gn 22: 16-18)

Christians from the earliest times have understood the sacrifice of Isaac as a foreshadowing of (or a "type" for) the sacrifice of Christ, and we can see a number of parallels between this story and the story of Christ's Crucifixion.

ISAAC	CHRIST
A father offers his beloved son.	The Father offers his beloved Son.
The son submits to the father's will.	The Son submits to the Father's Will.
Isaac carries the wood for his own sacrifice.	Christ carries the wood of his own Cross.
God himself provides the sacrifice.	God provides himself as the perfect sacrifice.
The sacrifice takes place on Mount Moriah.	Jerusalem, where Christ was sacrificed, was founded at the location of Mount Moriah.

Abraham's son Isaac had a son named Jacob, also named Israel. Jacob had twelve sons, and the descendants of these sons would become known as the Twelve Tribes of Israel. One of these sons, Joseph, was the favorite of Jacob. Out of jealousy, his older brothers sold Joseph into slavery, telling Jacob he had been killed by wild animals in the wilderness. Joseph ended up in Egypt, where he became a favorite in the court of the pharaoh, the Egyptian king (called "Pharaoh" when referring to a specific individual). His wisdom and ability to interpret dreams helped Pharaoh make plans to store up grain for a coming famine.

Joseph's family migrated to Egypt to survive the famine and were reunited with him after Joseph, whom they did not recognize, revealed who he was. The Egyptians at first welcomed the children of Israel because of their appreciation of Joseph, but generations later they became resentful as the Hebrews grew in population. Worried that the Israelites might eventually rise up against him, a later pharaoh declared them slaves and ordered the killing of all newborn male Hebrew children.

GUIDED EXERCISE

Work with a partner to put in your own words all the things that God promised to Abraham

Focus Question 7:

How did the Israelites become captives in Egypt?

Joseph and His Brethren Welcomed by Pharaoh by Tissot. Joseph's wisdom and ability to interpret dreams helped Pharaoh make plans to store up grain for a coming famine.

Focus Question 8:
Why did Moses flee Egypt?

VOCABULARY

ARK OF THE COVENANT

An ornate box that held the tablets of the Law (Ten Commandments), the rod of Aaron, and some manna; it represented God's throne on earth.

GENTILES

The non-Jewish people of the world.

MANNA

A kind of bread "from Heaven" given by God to the Hebrews as their daily food to sustain them during their years of wandering in the desert.

MONOTHEISM

The belief that there is only one God.

PASSOVER (*Pasch, Pascha*)

A Jewish feast commemorating the deliverance of their firstborn males from death by the blood of the lamb sprinkled on the doorposts while in bondage in Egypt; the angel of death passed over their homes, allowing them to leave Egypt for the Promised Land. This was a type of the sacrificial Passion and Death of Jesus Christ, saving men from bondage to sin. The Eucharist celebrates Christ's Passover.

PLAGUES ON EGYPT

Any of the ten torments God sent upon the people of Egypt in an effort to convince Pharaoh to let the Israelites go free. The plagues were: river turned to blood; frogs; lice; flies; sick animals; boils; hail; locusts; darkness; and the death of every firstborn child.

Focus Question 9:
What belief would set the people of Israel apart from all other peoples?

Moses and the Burning Bush by Raphael.
Appearing to Moses, God calls the Israelites "my people."

THE COVENANT WITH MOSES

Moses was a newborn at the time of the Pharaoh's command to slaughter the male Hebrew infants. To save the life of Moses, his mother hid him in a reed basket and set him afloat in the River Nile. The baby was found by Pharaoh's daughter, who reared him in the royal household, while his actual mother secretly taught him his heritage.

When Moses was grown, he saw an Egyptian taskmaster beating a Hebrew slave. In anger, Moses killed him. Fearing Pharaoh's punishment, Moses fled Egypt, finding refuge in the land of Midian with Jethro, the high priest. There, Moses settled into his new life of tending the flocks and eventually married Jethro's daughter, Zipporah.

When Moses was eighty years old, with the Israelites still in bondage in Egypt, God appeared to Moses in a burning bush, saying:

> The cry of the people of Israel has come to me, and I have seen the oppression with which the Egyptians oppress them. Come, I will send you to Pharaoh that you may bring forth my people, the sons of Israel, out of Egypt. (Ex 3: 9-10)

Note how God already is calling the Israelites "my people." He also calls them the "sons of Israel," acknowledging his people as the descendants of Jacob. As he calls them out of Egypt, he will assemble them and unite them even more closely to himself and to one another.

Moses initially was hesitant to fulfill his mission.

> "If I come to the people of Israel and say to them, 'The God of your fathers has sent me to you,' and they ask me, 'What is his name?' what shall I say to them?" So God revealed his name to Moses: "I AM WHO I AM." (Ex 3: 13-14)

God was one—there is only one God. This belief set God's people apart from all the other nations of the world that worshiped many gods. *Monotheism* was the defining faith of the Israelites, and those sons and daughters of Israel who had been influenced by the paganism of the Egyptians and other cultures would have to learn to put aside the temptation to worship false idols.

Pharaoh refused to give in to Moses' demand for the Israelites' freedom, so God sent a series of ten miraculous plagues over Egypt. The final plague involved the killing of every firstborn son, the same punishment that Pharaoh had imposed on the Israelites. The firstborn of the Israelites were spared, however; God had instructed his people to sacrifice a spotless lamb and splash some of its blood over their doorposts. The blood of the lamb was a sign of faith that would prevent the plague from affecting Israelite households. This event is known as the Passover, and its annual observance has been a major Jewish feast ever since.

Pharaoh finally relented. The Israelites departed Egypt, crossing the Red Sea to safety and withstanding one final assault from Pharaoh's pursuing army. Entering the Sinai wilderness, they began a forty-year sojourn of trials and hardships toward the "Promised Land," the land of Canaan in the present-day Middle East that God had promised them.

In that desert, when the Israelites became hungry, God sent them *manna* from Heaven, a bread-like substance that they collected each morning. This manna became known as their "bread from heaven" (Ex 16: 4); it served as a sign of God's faithfulness and presence among them, and it was their food that sustained them on their journey.

God appeared on Mount Sinai and called Moses to him in order to give him the Law, including the Ten Commandments, as a sign of his covenant. God told Moses to tell the Israelites:

> If you will obey my voice and keep my covenant, you shall be my own possession among all peoples; for all the earth is mine, and you shall be to me a kingdom of priests and a holy nation. (Ex 19: 3-5)

Israel collectively was to be God's firstborn son among the nations. There was only one God, and he would have only one people. Israel would have the task of bringing all the other nations into the family of God. The condition of the covenant was encoded in the laws we know as the Ten Commandments, which would govern his holy nation.

Yet, a covenant is a two-way agreement, and so the people had to accept the terms of the covenant. They had to receive it and respond to it positively as an act of the will. Moses read aloud all of the laws Israel was to follow, and the Israelites gave a resounding "yes" to what God was asking of them: "All that the LORD has spoken we will do, and we will be obedient" (Ex 24: 7).

Immediately after the covenant was made, God called Moses to spend another forty days with him on Mount Sinai. There God gave Moses the stone tablets on which he had written the Commandments, as a reminder to Israel of the permanence of the covenant. God also gave Moses detailed instructions for building the *Tabernacle*, a moveable tent that would be used as a temple for the Israelites as they journeyed to the Promised Land. At the center of the Tabernacle was to be placed the *Ark of the Covenant*—an ornate box covered in gold containing the stone tablets of the Ten Commandments and other relics. This would serve as God's throne and the place where God himself would dwell among his people.

Sanctified by the presence of God in the Tabernacle, the entire assembly or *qahal* of Israelites was to serve God as a kingdom of priests, with God as their king. This status as a kingdom of priests and a holy nation meant that Israel was to serve as a witness and beacon to all the *Gentiles*, the non-Jewish peoples of the world: "I will give you as a light to the nations, that my salvation may reach to the end of the earth" (Is 49: 6). This was a unique and glorious calling, but it depended on Israel's continuing obedience.

Focus Question 10:
How did the tenth plague turn the tables on Pharaoh?

Focus Question 11:
How did God feed the Israelites in the desert?

Focus Question 12:
What would the nation of Israel be if they kept the Mosaic covenant?

Focus Question 13:
What was the basic law God gave the Israelites on Mount Sinai?

Focus Question 14:
What did the people of Israel promise God?

Moses Receives the Tablets of Stone by Zeferino da Costa. Israel would have the task of bringing all the other nations into the family of God.

VOCABULARY

CHRIST

Greek for "anointed." This is used in reference to Christ because he accomplished perfectly the divine mission of priest, prophet, and king, signified by his being "anointed" as Christ. The Hebrew word for this is *messiah*.

CONSECRATION

The act of separating someone or something apart as holy and devoted for a particular purpose. Israelite kings of the Old Testament were consecrated by being anointed with sacred oil. Today, we refer to the consecration of individuals to the priesthood, the religious life, or to ministry as a bishop; in the context of the Mass, we also refer to the consecration of the bread and wine by which it becomes the Body and Blood of Christ.

LEVITES

The priestly class of Israel, members of the tribe of Levi.

MOUNT ZION

The hill on which the oldest part of Jerusalem was built. A poetic name for the city of Jerusalem.

Focus Question 15:
How did God respond to the Israelites for worshiping the golden calf?

Focus Question 16:
Why did Israel want a king?

Focus Question 17:
What is the Hebrew name meaning "anointed"?

Focus Question 18:
How was David both a king and a priest?

God's promise with David was unconditional and permanent.

However, while Moses was on Mount Sinai, the people of Israel fell into idolatry. They fashioned a golden calf, which all except the Levites, one of the Twelve Tribes, worshiped. As punishment, God established a different order of priests. Whereas the Israelites were to have been a priestly nation, now the Levites alone would serve as priests. Because Israel had shown that it could not overcome the temptation of worshiping the gods of other nations, they were given a second set of laws (found in the Book of Deuteronomy) intended to keep Israel separate from the other nations. Israel was far from ready to be that light to the Gentiles.

THE PROMISE TO DAVID

When Israel finally entered the Promised Land, Jacob's descendants began a long cycle characterized by faithfulness to the covenant accompanied by victory in battle followed by a relapse into idolatry and military losses.

The Israelites longed for the power, wealth, and stability that other nations enjoyed and so they asked for a king whom they hoped would provide these things. Although there was a provision for selecting a king in Deuteronomy, God was always to be *the* king of Israel. God chose the Israelite king, Saul, through his prophet, Samuel.

Samuel anointed Saul's head with oil—an action previously reserved for the ordination of priests—and declared him to be God's chosen. The oil was a visible sign of Saul's *consecration*. It is significant that the Hebrew word *messiah* and the Greek word *christ* both mean "the anointed one." The *messiah* was to be the one anointed and chosen by God to be the leader and savior of his people.

> When Saul became corrupted by power, God told his prophet Samuel to anoint David, a young shepherd of Bethlehem. "The spirit of the LORD came mightily upon David from that day forward" (1 Sm 16: 13).

When David became king, he unified the tribes of Israel and defeated their pagan neighbors. He established a political and religious capital for Israel in Jerusalem, a city near the center of Israel that none of the Twelve Tribes had claimed as its own. Wearing the robes of a priest, David himself led the

King David Playing the Zither by Celesti.
Wearing the robes of a priest, David himself led the procession of the Levite priests carrying the Ark of the Covenant into the city.

procession of the Levite priests carrying the Ark of the Covenant into the city. When it was put in its resting place, David offered the sacrifices. As the primary form of worship, David established the *thank offering*, a sacrifice that included unleavened bread and wine, made in gratitude for God's deliverance. Previously, the Israelites had offered only animal sacrifices to God.

God then made these promises to David:

> I will raise up your offspring after you, who shall come forth from your body, and I will establish his kingdom. He shall build a house for my name, and I will establish the throne of his kingdom for ever. I will be his father, and he shall be my son....And your house and your kingdom shall be made sure for ever before me; your throne shall be established for ever. (2 Sm 7: 12-16)

By this promise, God was renewing his covenant with Israel through David. Once again, we can see the language of family being used. Under the Mosaic covenant, Israel collectively was to be God's firstborn son. Under the Davidic promise, David's heir was God's son. God's promise with David was unconditional and permanent.

God's promises to David had several facets:

✠ David's heirs would be great kings.

✠ God would establish a royal Davidic dynasty.

✠ The king of Israel would not only be the son of David, but the son of God, as Adam was, and Israel as a whole was supposed to be.

✠ The king of Israel was to rule the Twelve Tribes and all the nations, leading the entire world in worship of and obedience to God.

✠ Jerusalem, and particularly Mount Zion, would be Israel's—and the world's—spiritual center, the place of pilgrimage for both the Israelites and all the nations.

✠ The Temple was the visible sign of the covenant and of God's kingdom. It would be God's permanent dwelling place and a "house of prayer for all peoples." A son of David would build the Temple.

After David's death, his son Solomon became king, and the kingdom became an empire. All the neighboring nations sought out Solomon to make alliances with him and to worship the God of Israel.

Unfortunately, the wise king Solomon became foolish, imposing high taxes on the Twelve Tribes, taking hundreds of pagan wives and concubines, and allowing them to turn him toward idolatry. This unfaithfulness by Solomon and many of his successors led to national disunity, attacks by pagan neighbors, and finally destruction. The Northern Kingdom was destroyed by the Assyrians in 722 BC. In 597 BC, Babylon sacked Jerusalem and destroyed the Temple, slaughtering the royal family and sending the remaining citizens into exile.

The challenge for the Israelites in the coming centuries would be maintaining their faith, despite the seeming hopelessness of their situation. Through a series of prophets, who appeared both while Israel was in exile and when the Hebrew people finally returned to Canaan, the Israelites were repeatedly called back to the ways of God. This exile helped deepen the faith of the nation and solidified their hope in God's promise of an everlasting kingdom—one that would be truly universal and ruled by the heir of David who would be the Messiah.

Through the prophets, God began to reveal more and more about the Redeemer. He also indicated he would make a "new covenant" with his

Focus Question 19:
How long did God promise David his "throne" would last?

Focus Question 20:
What did God say the relationship would be between God and David's son?

Focus Question 21:
What is the importance of Jerusalem in the Davidic covenant?

GUIDED EXERCISE

Work with a partner to tie each of the secondary characteristics of the Davidic Covenant to the Catholic Faith. Share findings with the class.

The Idolatry of Solomon (detail) by Conca. Unfaithfulness by Solomon and many of his successors led to national disunity and finally destruction.

Focus Question 22:
What did the Assyrians and Babylonians do to Israel?

Focus Question 23:
What was one thing the Israelites desired after their exile?

Focus Question 24:
What did the prophet Jeremiah say about a "new covenant"?

CLOSURE
Summarize in one sentence each the most important promise of each of the four covenants discussed in this chapter.

ALTERNATIVE ASSESSMENT
Review together the passage from Luke printed in the Opening Activity for this chapter. Then discuss the meaning of the various Old Testament references in light of the material presented in this chapter.

Some phrases to consider:

✖ The house of David

✖ Son of the Most High

✖ The throne of David his father

✖ He will rule the house of Jacob forever

✖ Of his Kingdom there will be no end

Jeremiah Lamenting the Destruction of Jerusalem by Rembrandt.

All the covenants and promises of the Old Testament were a preparation for the New Covenant to be established in Christ.

people, a covenant unlike any he had made before. As the prophet Jeremiah wrote:

> Behold, the days are coming, says the LORD, when I will make a new covenant with the house of Israel and the house of Judah, not like the covenant which I made with their fathers when I took them by the hand to bring them out of the land of Egypt, my covenant which they broke, though I was their husband, says the LORD.

> But this is the covenant which I will make with the house of Israel after those days, says the LORD: I will put my law within them, and I will write it upon their hearts; and I will be their God, and they shall be my people.

> And no longer shall each man teach his neighbor and each his brother, saying, "Know the LORD," for they shall all know me, from the least of them to the greatest, says the LORD; for I will forgive their iniquity, and I will remember their sin no more. (Jer 31: 31-34)

This "new covenant" with God would surpass the old covenant with Israel. It would involve a law written on the hearts of his people, and an intimate knowledge of God himself. Most importantly, God would forgive the sins of humanity.

CONCLUSION

All the covenants and promises of the Old Testament were a preparation for the New Covenant to be established in Christ. This New Covenant, which would last for all eternity, involved the founding of his Church and the calling together of all of God's people into one body, one communion of faith.

In Chapter 3, we will go deeper into the New Testament to show how these covenants and promises were fulfilled in Jesus Christ and his Church, which together comprise the Kingdom of God, and perfected in the New Covenant.

DISCUSSION QUESTIONS

1. What is the *Protoevangelium*?

2. What is a covenant?

3. What covenant did God make with Noah?

4. What covenant did God make with Abraham?

5. What covenant did God make with Moses?

6. What is the name meaning "anointed"?

7. How was David both a king and a priest?

8. What promises did God make to David?

9. What did the prophet Jeremiah say about a "new covenant"?

The Church
Sacrament of Salvation

Chapter 3
The Church in Light of the Covenants

To better understand the Church we need to understand the promises and covenants that God made with Adam, Noah, Abraham, Moses, and David.

CHAPTER 3
The Church in Light of the Covenants

OPENING ACTIVITY

Incorporate these brief parables of the Kingdom of God (or, in St. Matthew's Gospel, Kingdom of Heaven) into the class's Opening Prayer.

The Kingdom of Heaven is like a grain of mustard seed which a man took and sowed in his field; it is the smallest of all seeds, but when it has grown it is the greatest of shrubs and becomes a tree, so that the birds of the air come and make nests in its branches. (Mt 13: 31-32)

The Kingdom of Heaven is like leaven which a woman took and hid in three measures of flour, till it was all leavened. (Mt 13: 33)

The Kingdom of Heaven is like treasure hidden in a field, which a man found and covered up; then in his joy he goes and sells all that he has and buys that field. (Mt 13: 44)

The Kingdom of Heaven is like a merchant in search of fine pearls, who, on finding one pearl of great value, went and sold all that he had and bought it. (Mt 13: 45-46)

The Kingdom of Heaven is like a net which was thrown into the sea and gathered fish of every kind; when it was full, men drew it ashore and sat down and sorted the good into vessels but threw away the bad. So it will be at the close of the age. The angels will come out and separate the evil from the righteous, and throw them into the furnace of fire; there men will weep and gnash their teeth. (Mt 13: 47-50)

Afterwards, have the students write for a few minutes on what they think one of the parables means.

Review of Chapter 2:

✠ Immediately after the Fall of Adam and Eve, God promised to send a Redeemer, the "seed" of the woman who would bruise the head of the serpent.

✠ With Noah, God made a covenant never to destroy the earth again; he also renewed his command for humanity to take stewardship of the earth and all its creatures.

✠ The great nation promised to Abraham was first realized in the people of Israel.

✠ In the time of Moses, God called his people to assemble at the Tabernacle, which served as a kind of portable Temple during their years wandering in the wilderness. The Tabernacle was the place of God's presence among his people.

✠ King David united Israel. God promised David a permanent Temple as a sign of his presence, "a house of prayer for all peoples"; Israel would lead the entire world toward the worship of God and obedience to God. His heirs would be considered sons of God.

✠ The prophet Jeremiah spoke of a "new covenant" that God would establish with his people.

God's aim in salvation history was and remains to restore the communion—the intimate friendship—between man and himself that was broken by Original Sin. In this chapter, we will try to describe the way God completed the plan he chose from the beginning. The Church is God's ultimate way of uniting himself with humanity. We also will show how the Church founded by Christ completes the covenants and promises of the Old Testament.

The Church is both the means and the goal of God's plan: prefigured in creation, prepared for in the Old Covenant, founded by the words and actions of Jesus Christ, fulfilled by his redeeming Cross and his Resurrection, the Church has been manifested as the mystery of salvation by the outpouring of the Holy Spirit. She will be perfected in the glory of Heaven as the assembly of all the redeemed of the earth (cf. Rev 14: 4). (CCC 778)

THE SAVIOR AND KING IS BORN

In the *Protoevangelium* in Genesis, as we saw, God promised he would send a Redeemer. The Incarnation marks the imminent fulfillment of this promise made by God.

We learn early on in the Gospels that the child Jesus was from the tribe of Judah, which was the tribe of David. The genealogies presented in the Gospels of St. Matthew and St. Luke affirm that Christ was a direct descendant of David through both Joseph and Mary.

When God sent the Archangel Gabriel to the Virgin Mary, the young woman of Nazareth whom he had selected for the purpose of conceiving and bearing the Redeemer, the angel told Mary that the child she would conceive would

Annunciation by Poussin.
The Virgin Mary, a young woman of Nazareth, was selected by God to conceive and bear the promised Redeemer.

BASIC QUESTIONS

- ✠ What is the purpose of the Incarnation?
- ✠ What is the Kingdom of God?
- ✠ Where did the Church get its hierarchical structure?
- ✠ How does Christ save?
- ✠ What is the "food" of the kingdom of God?
- ✠ How did Christ fulfill the covenants and promises made with Adam, Noah, Abraham, Moses, and David?

KEY IDEAS

The key ideas of this chapter are:

- ✠ In the Incarnation, the Son of God became man so that men might receive adoption as sons of God.
- ✠ The Kingdom of God is Jesus Christ and his Church: It is God and redeemed humanity in restored communion.
- ✠ Christ gave his Church its hierarchical structure, with the Apostles and their successors the bishops.
- ✠ Jesus Christ, as the Lamb of God, died on the Cross to save us from our sins and to make us children of God.
- ✠ The food Christ gives is himself, the Bread of Life, the Eucharist.
- ✠ Christ fulfilled the Old Testament covenants and promises.

Focus Question 1:
What is God's aim in regard to fallen humanity?

Focus Question 2:
Why has God limited himself in the means he can employ in our salvation?

Focus Question 3:
What does the name "Jesus" mean?

Focus Question 4:
What does "Son of the Most High" mean?

Focus Question 5:
What is the "house of Jacob"?

Focus Question 6:
What is the aim of our redemption?

be named Jesus and would be "called the Son of the Most High." In addition, "the Lord God will give to him the throne of his father David, and he will reign over the house of Jacob for ever." Finally, "of his kingdom there will be no end" (Lk 1: 31-33).

The name *Jesus* means "he saves" or "savior." Jesus will reign over the Chosen People, that is, the "house of Jacob" or the heirs of the promise given to Abraham, forever. Jesus is the "anointed one," the Messiah or the Christ. Even the wise men from the East, who had come seeking Jesus after they had seen the star announcing his Birth, recognized the Christ child as a king, despite the fact he was born to simple parents in the most impoverished of circumstances.

Christ came as a king and heir of David, but his kingdom was not what most of the Jewish people were expecting.

THE KINGDOM OF GOD

The Kingdom of God was a key theme of the public ministry of Christ. He preached about the Kingdom often, and he pointed to his works as evidence of the Kingdom. The "good news" ("gospel") of salvation he preached is summarized early in the Gospel of St. Mark: "The time is fulfilled, and the Kingdom of God is at hand; repent, and believe in the gospel" (Mk 1: 15).

To state that the Kingdom is "at hand" means that it is present or imminent. Christ invites everyone to respond to the good news of salvation through their reception of the Gospel message and their repentance, by which they can enter his Kingdom.

Christ also spoke as though the Kingdom of God (or, as Matthew's Gospel calls it, the Kingdom of Heaven) was something that existed in the future, or that had not yet arrived in its fullness. The Kingdom that Christ came to proclaim is something of a mystery in itself.

What is this Kingdom, then? To understand what the Kingdom of God is, we must first take note of what it is *not*.

Focus Question 7:

What did many *hope* the Kingdom of God meant?

Focus Question 8:

What is the Kingdom of God?

Focus Question 9:

What kind of stories did Christ use to teach about the Kingdom?

VOCABULARY

KINGDOM OF HEAVEN

It is the state of communion between God and humanity; it is the something to which Christ calls every person to respond and enter through faith and repentance; it is the Church herself.

PARABLE

A fictitious narrative or allegory (usually of something that might naturally occur) used to illustrate and explain moral or spiritual principles.

"All this Jesus said to the crowds in parables; indeed he said nothing to them without a parable. This was to fulfil what was spoken by the prophet: 'I will open my mouth in parables, I will utter what has been hidden since the foundation of the world.'"
(Mt 13: 34-35)

Contrary to the hopes of many Jews, the Kingdom of God is not an earthly kingdom with immense civil authority and legions of soldiers. Many Jews of the time probably believed the Messiah would be some kind of military leader sent by God to drive their Roman conquerors out of Israel and to reestablish Israel as a great empire. Many Jews expected the Messiah to be a beloved and esteemed king who would unite the people the way David had done in his day. But this was not God's plan.

Speaking in Parables

When Christ did speak of the Kingdom, he often did so in *parables*, brief stories or comparisons that illustrate some aspect of the Kingdom. His preaching as a whole can be seen as describing what the Kingdom of God is like and how we are to live in it.

In the Parable of the Sower (cf. Mt 13: 3-9), Christ revealed his mission of proclaiming the Kingdom to all mankind—he is the sower who sows the Word. All are called by Christ to be part of this Kingdom, but as Christ explained in the Parable of the Treasure Buried in a Field (cf. Mt 13: 44) and the Parable of the Pearl of Great Price (cf. Mt 13: 45), we have to be willing to give up everything to follow him.

The Parable of the Wheat and the Weeds or Tares (cf. Mt 13: 24-30, 37-43) gives us an explanation of why, even though his Kingdom has arrived, there coexists good and evil. Although Christ has sown good seed, the Devil has planted seed of his own—weeds that are meant to ruin the work of Christ the sower. Christ allows both to grow side-by-side until the time of judgment at the end of the world. He does so for the sake of the good seed—the wheat that represents the faithful—rather than seeking to selectively pull up the weeds before the "harvest," which might result in some of the wheat being destroyed as well. In the parable, young wheat is indistinguishable from a weed called tares, and the two can be distinguished only at the harvest when

Parable of the Hidden Treasure by Tissot.
"The kingdom of heaven is like treasure hidden in a field, which a man found and covered up; then in his joy he goes and sells all that he has and buys that field." (Mt 13: 44)

they can be separated. To seek to eradicate these weeds before they had a chance to grow and show their true nature would have been foolhardy for a farmer. So Christ judges people once they have been allowed the chance to show themselves to be wheat or weeds.

In the Parable of the Mustard Seed (cf. Mt 13: 31-32) and the Parable of the Leaven (cf. Mt 13: 33), Christ highlights the way that the heavenly Kingdom is present in the world. Although it will start out small in appearance, the Kingdom will grow on earth until it has spread throughout the world and brought the Gospel to all humanity. The Kingdom is also present in the world like yeast, sanctifying it from within by continuing the work of Christ.

What, then, is this Kingdom? In the first of his three-volume book *Jesus of Nazareth*, Pope Benedict XVI summarizes three dimensions or interpretations of the Kingdom of God, all of which have developed from Christian reflection since the time of the Apostles:

- The Kingdom of God is Christ himself present among us.
- The Kingdom of God is present in the hearts of the faithful who receive and respond to the Gospel message.
- The Kingdom of God is the Church, or rather draws near to the Church community as she grows in holiness on her journey toward her ultimate perfection in Heaven.

All three can be seen as harmonious: The Kingdom of God is Christ, and those who embrace the Gospel message become part of the Mystical Body of Christ. This Kingdom, then, can be seen as the regathering or convocation of God's people as Christ draws all people to himself. Like the mustard seed, the Church begins small and grows to tremendous size; like the leaven, the faithful of the Church witness and influence others around them such that the world gradually is transformed and increasingly made holy. That is why the *Catechism of the Catholic Church* refers to the Church as "the Reign of Christ already present in mystery" (CCC 763; *LG*, 3).

A Kingdom both Visible and Invisible

The Kingdom of God exists perfectly only in Heaven, but it is also present here and now in an imperfect way. That is part of its mystery, a mystery that is sometimes expressed by stating that the Kingdom of God is "here, but not yet." It is still "in development" on earth, a work in progress. It is the task of the Church and her faithful to help advance the Kingdom of God on earth toward the fulfillment and perfection for which she is destined.

Unlike an earthly kingdom that has defined boundaries, ornate palaces, and physical signs of its existence and power, the Kingdom of God, the Church, is present invisibly, as a spiritual reality, within the hearts of its people—the faithful who welcome the good news of redemption and, thus, are part of the Mystical Body of Christ, a term we introduced in Chapter 1 and will explore further in later chapters.

The Kingdom of God, the Church, is the state of communion or unity of friendship between God and human beings that God intended from Creation. This unity, broken by sin, was reinstituted on earth through the Incarnation of Christ, who became one of us in order to redeem us. By taking on our humanity, he identified himself with our human condition and set about to reverse the ill effects that sin had caused for the entire human race.

In the very act of uniting us, he begins to call us into assembly, inviting us to become one with him in his Church. The assembly of the faithful and the structure of the Church constitute the visible presence of the Church on earth.

Focus Question 10:

In what way is the Church like the mustard seed or the leaven in the parables of Christ?

GUIDED EXERCISE

Have the students work with a partner to read the Parable of the Sower with the following question in mind:

- How is the Parable of the Sower an example of God respecting the freedom, even the twisted freedom, of fallen humanity?

A sower went out to sow. And as he sowed, some seeds fell along the path, and the birds came and devoured them. Other seeds fell on rocky ground, where they had not much soil, and immediately they sprang up, since they had no depth of soil, but when the sun rose they were scorched; and since they had no root they withered away. Other seeds fell upon thorns, and the thorns grew up and choked them. Other seeds fell on good soil and brought forth grain, some a hundredfold, some sixty, some thirty.

When any one hears the word of the kingdom and does not understand it, the evil one comes and snatches away what is sown in his heart; this is what was sown along the path. As for what was sown on rocky ground, this is he who hears the word and immediately receives it with joy; yet he has no root in himself, but endures for a while, and when tribulation or persecution arises on account of the word, immediately he falls away. As for what was sown among thorns, this is he who hears the word, but the cares of the world and the delight in riches choke the word, and it proves unfruitful. As for what was sown on good soil, this is he who hears the word and understands it; he indeed bears fruit, and yields, in one case a hundredfold, in another sixty, in another thirty." (Mt 13: 3-9, 19-23)

Share responses with the class.

Focus Question 11:

What is the invisible and visible presence of the Church on earth?

VOCABULARY

MYSTICAL BODY OF CHRIST

The faithful People of God, who in a supernatural way become one body, with Christ as its head. The faithful are united together in Christ's Mystical Body; that is, we are brought into communion with one another through our communion with Christ. For this reason, St. Paul refers to Christ as the head of the Mystical Body: "He is before all things, and in him all things hold together. He is the head of the body, the church" (Col 1: 17-18). As the Mystical Body of Christ, the Church extends throughout time Christ's work of salvation.

FROM *YouCat*

To whom does Jesus promise "the kingdom of God"?

God wills "all men to be saved and to come to the knowledge of the truth" (1 Tim 2: 4). The "kingdom of God" begins in those who allow themselves to be transformed by God's love. In Jesus' experience these are above all the poor and the lowly.

Even people unaffiliated with the Church find it fascinating that Jesus, with a sort of preferential love, turns first to those who are socially marginalized. In the Sermon on the Mount, it is the poor and the sorrowing, the victims of persecution and violence, all those who seek God with a pure heart, all who seek his mercy, his justice, and his peace, who have prior access to the kingdom of God. Especially invited are sinners also: "Those who are well have no need of a physician, but those who are sick; I came not to call the righteous, but sinners" (Mk 2: 17). (*YouCat* 89)

Focus Question 12:
Who were Christ's disciples?

Focus Question 13:
Who were Christ's Apostles?

Focus Question 14:
Why did the Apostles appoint successors?

Focus Question 15:
Why did Christ establish a hierarchy?

CHRIST CALLS THE TWELVE APOSTLES

By his preaching, miracles, works of healing, and exorcisms, Christ attracted great crowds comprising men and women of all ages and backgrounds. This growing community of disciples gathered around Christ offers the first glimpses of the Church taking shape. We can note both the invisible spiritual communion between the disciples and Christ as well as the visible form of the community itself.

Christ appointed twelve Apostles "to be with him, and to be sent out to preach and have authority to cast out demons" (Mk 3: 14-15). He established them as leaders within the community of disciples.

It was only to the Apostles that Christ explained the deeper meanings of his parables. Much of his teaching in the Gospels was given to the Apostles alone. In doing this, Christ was equipping these twelve men to provide the foundation of his Church. At the Last Supper, Christ revealed more explicitly the role that his Apostles would play in the kingdom.

> You are those who have continued with me in my trials; as my Father appointed a kingdom for me, so do I appoint for you that you may eat and drink at my table in my kingdom, and sit on thrones judging the twelve tribes of Israel. (Lk 22: 28-30)

In this passage, Christ clearly connected the kingdom of the Church with the restoration of the kingdom of Israel, which he entrusted to the Twelve Apostles. This task of leading the Church would last until the end of time, long beyond the lifetime of the Apostles. In time, the Apostles would appoint successors to fulfill their responsibilities as shepherds as well as to serve newly formed communities in the ever-expanding Church (cf. CCC 765).

Christ told the Apostles they were to lead the Church by living lives of service to the faithful (cf. Lk 22: 25-27) and in communion with God. In later chapters, we will look further at the structure of the Church and its teaching authority.

Calling of the Apostles (detail) by Ghirlandaio.
Christ established the Apostles as leaders within the growing community of disciples.

The Last Supper (detail) by Carducci.
The sacrificial Passover lamb symbolized the Israelites' deliverance from slavery.

THE NEW PASSOVER

At the start of his public ministry, Christ was proclaimed by St. John the Baptist to be "the Lamb of God, who takes away the sin of the world" (Jn 1: 29). For Jews, the image of the lamb was intimately tied to the Passover lamb, the symbol of Israel's salvation from slavery in Egypt in the time of Moses.

Recall that the blood of the sacrificed lamb was sprinkled on the doorposts of the Israelites' homes to protect them from the tenth plague of Egypt, the death of the firstborn sons. It was this plague that finally convinced Pharaoh to free the captive Israelites. Since that time, Jews have celebrated the feast of Passover, which includes a meal of lamb to remind them of how God rescued them from their oppression.

Just as the sacrificial Passover lamb symbolized the Israelites' deliverance from slavery, a new lamb would have to be sacrificed and shed its blood in order to deliver humanity from their slavery to sin. Christ, the Lamb of God, was that sacrificial lamb.

During the Israelites' sojourn in the desert, God fed his people manna from Heaven. Christ referred to this manna when he called himself "the living bread which came down from heaven" (Jn 6: 51) and "the bread of life":

> I am the bread of life. Your fathers ate the manna in the wilderness, and they died. This is the bread which comes down from heaven, that a man may eat of it and not die. (Jn 6: 48-50)

Christ gives himself to his Church in the Sacrament of the Eucharist, by which we partake of his true Body and Blood. He instituted this great Sacrament at the Last Supper, which began as a Passover meal:

> And he took bread, and when he had given thanks he broke it and gave it to them, saying, "This is my body which is given for you. Do this in remembrance of me." And likewise the cup after supper, saying, "This cup which is poured out for you is the new covenant in my blood." (Lk 22: 19-20)

VOCABULARY

DISCIPLE

Literally, "one who follows." Sometimes in Scripture the term is applied to the Twelve Apostles; at other times, and more generally, it refers to the entire crowd of Christ's followers and believers.

TWELVE APOSTLES

Also, "the Twelve" or "the Apostles," they assisted Christ in his public ministry and were Christ's chosen witnesses of his Resurrection and the foundation on which the Church is built. The Apostles were the first bishops of the Church.

FROM *YouCat*

Why did Jesus call apostles?

Jesus had a large circle of disciples around him, both men and women. From this circle he selected twelve men whom he called APOSTLES (Lk 6: 12–16). The apostles were specially trained by him and entrusted with various commissions: "He sent them out to preach the kingdom of God and to heal" (Lk 9: 2). Jesus took only these twelve apostles with him to the Last Supper, where he gave them the command, "Do this in remembrance of me" (Lk 22: 19b).

The apostles became witnesses of Jesus' Resurrection and guarantors of the truth about him. They continued Jesus' mission after his death. They chose successors for their ministry: the bishops. To this day, the successors of the apostles exercise the authority conferred by Jesus: They govern and teach and celebrate the liturgy. The cohesiveness of the apostles became the foundation for the unity of the CHURCH (APOSTOLIC SUCCESSION). Preeminent once again among the Twelve was Peter, on whom Jesus bestowed special authority: "You are Peter, and on this rock I will build my Church" (Mt 16: 18). From Peter's special role among the apostles developed the papal ministry. (*YouCat* 92)

Focus Question 16:

How did Christ compare himself with the manna in the desert?

Focus Question 17:

How is Christ related to the lamb of Passover?

Focus Question 18:

How did Christ inaugurate the New Covenant?

Focus Question 19:

What did Christ mean by "do this in remembrance of me"?

Focus Question 20:

According to tradition, how is the Church like the New Eve?

Communion of the Apostles by Signorelli.
By commanding his Apostles to "do this in remembrance of me,"
he made his Apostles the priests of the New Covenant.

VOCABULARY

EUCHARIST

The Sacrament by which bread and wine are consecrated by a priest and become the true Body and Blood of Christ, which the faithful consume in Holy Communion; more broadly, Eucharist, which means "thanksgiving," refers to the Catholic Mass itself.

SACRAMENT

An efficacious sign of grace, instituted by Christ and entrusted to the Church, by which divine life is dispensed to us through the work of the Holy Spirit; specifically, any of the Seven Sacraments of the Catholic Church: Baptism, Eucharist, Penance, Confirmation, Matrimony (Marriage), Holy Orders, and Anointing of the Sick; more generally, any signs or means through which we receive grace from God (for example, the Church as the "Sacrament of Salvation"). In the Eastern Catholic Churches, the Sacraments are called "mysteries."

By telling his Apostles to "do this in remembrance of me," Christ instituted the Sacrament of the Eucharist. This first celebration of the Mass, the "new Passover," inaugurates the "new covenant" prophesied by the prophet Jeremiah. Like the thank offering in the time of David, the Eucharist became the memorial sacrifice of the New Covenant.

In the Eucharist, Christ is present among us in a unique way. Like the Tabernacle carried by the Israelites through the wilderness, Christ is present to us in this Sacrament and in the tabernacle within our churches where the consecrated bread of the Eucharist is reserved. By commanding his Apostles to "do this in remembrance of me," he made his Apostles the priests of the New Covenant and empowered them to consecrate the Eucharistic bread and wine, transforming them as he did into his true Body and Blood. In this way, through the Church he established, Christ remains intimately present among us until the end of the world.

Blood and Water

Christ, the Lamb of God, completed his Passover through his Passion and Death on the Cross. St. John's Gospel tells us that as Christ's lifeless body hung from the Cross, a Roman soldier pierced his side with a lance. Immediately Blood and water flowed forth.

According to Church tradition, this Blood and water from the side of Christ represents the Church itself:

> "The origin and growth of the Church are symbolized by the blood and water which flowed from the open side of the crucified Jesus."[1] "For it was from the side of Christ as he slept the sleep of death upon the cross that there came forth the 'wondrous sacrament of the whole Church.'"[2] As Eve was formed from the sleeping Adam's side, so the Church was born from the pierced heart of Christ hanging dead on the cross.[3] (CCC 766)

After his Resurrection, Christ explained to the Apostles that it was necessary that he should suffer death in order to fulfill the plan of his Father:

> Then he opened their minds to understand the scriptures, and said to them, "Thus it is written, that the Christ should suffer and on the third day rise from the dead, and that repentance and forgiveness of sins should be preached in his name to all nations." (Lk 24: 44-47)

Through the Church he established, Christ remains intimately present among us until the end of the world.

This task given to the Apostles was to continue Christ's proclamation of the kingdom. As the kingdom of Christ present in the world, the Church imitates her founder by calling mankind to conversion and repentance. Through the ministry of the Church, Christ continually offers the salvation and reconciliation of the Cross to men and women in every age.

THE CHURCH FULFILLS THE COVENANTS AND PROMISES

Briefly let us review how the promises and covenants of the Old Testament with regard to the regathering of God's people are fulfilled in the establishment of the Church in the New Covenant.

The Church fulfills the promise made after the fall of Adam and Eve. Our original communion with God was lost by the disobedience of Adam and Eve. It is offered to us once more through Christ, who was "obedient unto death, even death on a cross" (Phil 2: 8). For this reason, Christ is sometimes called the "New Adam" because his obedience reversed the effects of Adam's disobedience.

> For as by one man's disobedience many were made sinners, so by one man's obedience many will be made righteous. (Rom 5: 19)

The restoration of humanity's communion with God, accomplished through Christ's Death and Resurrection, marked the fulfillment of his promise made after the Fall in the *Protoevangelium*. Our new communion with God is found in his regathered assembly, the Church, through which we obtain redemption from our sins.

The Church fulfills the covenant with Noah. Rather than destroy sinful humanity again, God saves us. Just as God saved Noah and his family by gathering them into the Ark during the great Flood, God saves his people today by gathering them into the Church. Just as the floodwaters in the time of Noah destroyed iniquity, through Christ the waters of the Sacrament of Baptism, administered through his Church as the means for obtaining salvation and entering his Kingdom, wash away our sins.

The Church fulfills the covenant with Abraham. As part of his covenant, God promised to make Abraham "the father of a multitude of nations" and told him that "kings shall come forth from you" (Gn 17: 5, 6). He also told Abraham that "by your descendants shall all the nations of the earth bless themselves" (Gn 22: 18). This call began the remote preparation for the Church.

The promise of a universal blessing is fulfilled in Jesus Christ, "the son of Abraham" (Mt 1: 1). The sacred mission of the Church founded by Christ extends God's blessings throughout the world by continuing to proclaim the Gospel message of repentance and serving as a source of God's grace through the Sacraments. By carrying out her mandate to "make disciples of all nations," the Church calls all people to unite in the one Kingdom of God.

The Church fulfills the covenant with Moses. The *qahal* or assembly of the Israelites at Mount Sinai is fulfilled in the Church, the assembly of the People of God. The first Christian community, by referring to itself as "church," clearly understood that they were the heirs to that assembly. The identification of the Twelve Apostles with the Twelve Tribes of Israel also denotes the status of the Church as the new People of God.

Just as God liberated the children of Israel from slavery, so, too, does he liberate us from sin through the redemption of Christ. He gave his Law and

FROM *YouCat*

Why is Jesus Christ the Lord of the whole world?

Jesus Christ is Lord of the world and Lord of history because everything was made for his sake. All men were redeemed by him and will be judged by him.

One to whom we bend the knee in worship; he is *with us* as Head of his Church, in which the kingdom of God begins even now; he is *ahead of us* as Lord of history, in whom the powers of darkness are definitively overcome and the destinies of the world are brought to perfection according to God's plan; he *comes to meet us* in glory, on a day we do not know, to renew and perfect the world. We can experience his nearness especially in God's Word, in the reception of the SACRAMENTS, in caring for the poor, and wherever "two or three are gathered in my name" (see Mt 18: 20). (*YouCat* 110)

Focus Question 21:
What is one way Christ fulfills the promise God made after the Fall of Adam and Eve?

Focus Question 22:
What is one way Christ fulfills the covenant with Abraham?

Noah Releases the Dove, Mosaic. Rather than destroy sinful humanity again, God saves us.

Focus Question 23:
What is one way Christ fulfills the covenant with Moses?

Focus Question 24:
What is one way Christ fulfills the promises to David?

VOCABULARY

TEMPLE OF THE HOLY SPIRIT
A title of the Church used by St. Paul; it highlights the relationship between the Church and the Old Testament Temple in Jerusalem.

The Savior by Juanes.
Christ identified himself as the true Temple. The Temple is Christ's Body, and his Body is one with the Church.

covenant through Moses to show the Israelites how to live as his people as a sign of the future gathering of all nations (cf. CCC 762). In his New Covenant, Christ perfects the Law of Moses by teaching that love for God and neighbor is the greatest commandment.

God set apart the nation of Israel to become "a kingdom of priests and a holy nation" (Ex 19: 6). This part of the covenant is fulfilled in the New Covenant in the Church, which is called to "make disciples of all nations, baptizing them in the name of the Father and of the Son and of the Holy Spirit, teaching them to observe all that I have commanded you" (Mt 28: 20-24). The Church reaches beyond the children of Israel and embraces people of all nations, cultures, and backgrounds who respond to the Gospel message of Christ. We will see in a later chapter how each Christian, by virtue of Baptism and the call to be holy, also shares in the priestly ministry of Christ, so that the Church is truly a "kingdom of priests and a holy nation."

As we saw earlier, the Tabernacle that served as a sign of the presence of God among his people while the Israelites wandered in the desert is fulfilled in the Eucharist, where Christ is truly present among us in his real Body and Blood.

The Church fulfills the promises to David. Christ fulfilled God's promise to David of an everlasting kingdom. Jesus Christ is an heir to his throne, born of his tribe and of his direct line of descendants; his kingdom is the Church itself, the People of God.

A son of David was to build "a house for my name," a Temple. Solomon built the first Temple of Jerusalem, which signified God's presence and dwelling place among his people. During his public ministry, Christ identified himself as the true Temple: indeed, "something greater than the Temple [at Jerusalem]" (Mt 12: 6). He also predicted his own Resurrection by describing the true Temple as his own Body: "Destroy this temple, and in three days I will raise it up" (Jn 2: 19). The Temple is Christ's Body, and his Body is one with the Church.

St. Peter further describes the Church as a temple or "house of God":

> You are...members of the household of God, built upon the foundation of the apostles and prophets, Christ Jesus himself being the cornerstone, in whom the whole structure is joined together and grows into a holy temple in the Lord; in whom you also are built into it for a dwelling place of God in the Spirit. (Eph 2: 20-22)

The Church is the new and everlasting temple, the temple of the Holy Spirit, built by Christ as a sign of his presence, a house of prayer for all the nations.

David also was promised that his descendants would be called "sons of God," which is fulfilled in the adoption of the baptized, the members of the Church, as sons and daughters of God.

CONCLUSION

God's plan of salvation was indeed a "plan," and every one of his acts or steps in the process of his self-revelation prepared the way for the coming of Christ and the establishment of his Kingdom, the Church on earth. Gradually calling together his faithful through his covenants and promises in order to form them as a people, God "in the fullness of time" sent his Son to preach the good news of the Kingdom and to institute the Church under the New Covenant. This Church is charged with continuing his mission of gathering people of all nations into one body in faith.

ST. AUGUSTINE: "THE OLD TESTAMENT IS REVEALED IN THE NEW"

 t. Augustine is one of the most important saints and theologians of the Catholic Church. His thought permeates many of the doctrines developed since his time, and aside from the Bible, he is one of the most frequently cited sources within official Church documents.

St. Augustine's contributions to the study of Scripture are especially important, for he sought to understand the inner unity of God's plan of salvation. He was a master of *typology*, the discernment of the Old Testament foreshadowing of New Testament realities (cf. CCC 128). As he once stated, "The New Testament is concealed in the Old, and the Old Testament is revealed in the New."

Augustine was born in AD 354 in North Africa. His mother, St. Monica, was a devout Christian. Augustine excelled in law, literature, and philosophy. Whatever Christian beliefs and practices he had learned as a child, however, he soon ignored or forgot. As a young adult, he lived an immoral life and soon began to follow the heretical teachings of Manichæism.

St. Augustine and St. Monica by Scheffer.

By thirty, Augustine established himself as a brilliant teacher of rhetoric. Even so, he became increasingly restless. In AD 383, he took a position in Milan, Italy. There he met Ambrose, a bishop who would later be declared a saint and Doctor of the Church. Like Augustine, Ambrose possessed a powerful intellect and a love for truth; but unlike Augustine, he also had peace.

Through the example and patient instruction of Ambrose, Augustine gradually came to see the truth of the Catholic Faith, and, in AD 387, to the great joy of his mother, he at last became a Christian. Upon his return to North Africa, Augustine was ordained a priest, and in AD 395, he became the Bishop of Hippo (in modern-day Algeria). Over the next three and a half decades, Augustine dedicated himself to the pastoral care of his diocese, preaching thousands of homilies and fighting heresies within the Church.

St. Augustine died in AD 430, at the age of seventy-five, and was soon proclaimed a saint. In AD 1298, Pope Boniface VIII named St. Augustine a Doctor of the Church in recognition of his innumerable contributions to Christian thought. His feast day is August 28.

FROM *YouCat*

What is unique about the People of God?

The founder of this people is God the Father. Its leader is Jesus Christ. Its source of strength is the Holy Spirit. The entryway to the People of God is Baptism. Its dignity is the freedom of the children of God. Its law is love. If this people remains faithful to God and seeks first the kingdom of God, it changes the world.

In the midst of all the peoples on earth, there is one people that is like no other. It is subject to no one but God alone. It is supposed to be like salt, which adds flavor; like yeast, which permeates everything; like light, which drives away the darkness. Anyone who belongs to the People of God must count on coming into conflict with people who deny God's existence and disregard his commandments. In the freedom of the children of God, however, we have nothing to fear, not even death. (*YouCat* 125)

St. Augustine Reading the Epistle of St. Paul by Gozzoli.
"*Credo ut intelligam, intelligo ut credam.*"
"I believe that I might understand, and understand that I might believe."

CLOSURE

Summarize the content of this chapter in five succinct sentences (there are five sections).

ALTERNATIVE ASSESSMENT

Discuss the validity of the statement that heads this chapter:

To better understand the Church we need to understand the covenants and promises that God made with Adam, Noah, Abraham, Moses, and David.

Moses on Mount Sinai by Gerome.
In his New Covenant, Christ perfects the Law of Moses by teaching that love for God and neighbor is the greatest commandment.

In the next chapter, we will look at the remarkable events of Pentecost and how it gave birth to the evangelizing mission of the Church.

DISCUSSION QUESTIONS

1. What is the purpose of the Incarnation?
2. What is the Kingdom of God?
3. What kind of stories did Christ use to teach about the Kingdom?
4. What is the invisible and visible presence of the Church on earth?
5. Who were Christ's Apostles?
6. Why did Christ establish a hierarchy?
7. How did Christ compare himself with the manna in the desert?
8. How did Christ inaugurate the New Covenant?
9. What is one way Christ fulfills the covenant with Moses?
10. What is one way Christ fulfills the promises to David?

The Church is the new and everlasting temple, the temple of the Holy Spirit.

ENDNOTES – CHAPTER 3

1. *LG* 3, cf. Jn 19:34.
2. *SC* 5.
3. Cf. St. Ambrose, *In Luc.* 2, 85-89; PL 15, 1666-1668.

The Church
Sacrament of Salvation

The Holy Spirit enlightens and empowers the Church to fulfill the apostolic mission given her by Christ.

OPENING ACTIVITY

Free write for a few minutes on anything in your past experience that was very hard for you to learn. It could be a fact, a skill, or even a life lesson. What was it? Why was it difficult? Did you actually finally learn it? If so, how?

This activity is meant to make you consider how the Apostles, who were given the task of heading the Church, "learned" how to do this.

BASIC QUESTIONS

This chapter attempts to answer the following basic questions:

✠ What is the significance of the Great Commission for the Church?

✠ Why did Christ appear to the Apostles after the Resurrection?

✠ What did the Apostles do for the Church while waiting for the Holy Spirit?

✠ What is the significance of Pentecost for the Church?

KEY IDEAS

The key ideas of this chapter are:

✠ Just as at the Incarnation the Father sent Christ into the world to redeem it, after the Resurrection Christ commissioned the Apostles to go to the entire world to preach the Gospel in order to save it.

✠ Christ gave the Apostles final instructions during the forty days after the Resurrection to prepare them for their task of making disciples, baptizing, and teaching Divine Revelation.

✠ The Apostles, led by Peter, created a new Apostle to take Judas's place.

✠ Pentecost was an outpouring of the Holy Spirit on the Church, which gave her the power to evangelize.

CHAPTER 4
The Early Church Through Pentecost

Review of Chapter 3:

✠ Christ fulfills the promise of a Redeemer made in the *Protoevangelium* of Genesis.

✠ Christ is a king, but of a Kingdom not of this world, the Kingdom of God. This Kingdom of God is a mystery: It is the state of communion between God and humanity; Christ calls every person to enter his kingdom through faith and repentance; his kingdom is the Church herself.

✠ Christ established the Church during his public ministry on earth. He announced that the Kingdom of God was "at hand"; he formed his Apostles as her first leaders, with St. Peter as head of the Church; he empowered them and commissioned them to continue his work of redemption; he instituted the New Passover (Mass), the priesthood, and the Sacraments in order to sanctify his people and remain present among them.

✠ The covenants God made with Noah, Abraham, and Moses, along with the promises he made to Adam and David, all helped prepare the way for the New Covenant in Christ and the foundation of his Church. All these promises and covenants are fulfilled in Christ and the Church he established.

In this chapter, we will look at the experiences of the Apostles and the faithful of Christ from the time of the Resurrection of Christ to the descent of the Holy Spirit at Pentecost, which marks the beginning of the public ministry of the Church.

THE RESURRECTION

In the Old Testament, we can see how the process of gathering and forming the Jews into a people in preparation for the coming Messiah and the promised redemption was a long process. It took centuries for the ancient People of God to be brought along by God's Revelation to a point where they were ready to receive the Son of God into their midst—and even then imperfectly, for many rejected him.

In a somewhat similar manner, it took time for the Apostles to understand more fully who Christ was and what he wanted them to do. Their questions throughout the Gospels reveal a knowledge of Christ and his mission that unfolded only gradually and that remained incomplete at the time of Christ's Death. Even at the Resurrection, the meaning of the Kingdom of God had not fully dawned on them. They needed something more to help them understand the truth that Christ was trying to teach them and to carry out the sacred mission Christ had in mind for them. They needed the guidance of the Holy Spirit.

The Crucifixion and Death of Jesus Christ had greatly confused the Apostles and disciples. Earlier that week, they had triumphantly entered Jerusalem with Christ. Enthusiastic crowds lined their path, laying down palm branches before him and honoring him with their cheers and prayers: "Hosanna! Blessed is he who comes in the name of the Lord, even the king of

Appearance Behind Locked Doors by Duccio.
Christ told them to be at peace because of what he had accomplished.

Focus Question 1:
Were the Apostles expecting Christ to rise from the dead?

Focus Question 2:
What is one reason Christ offered his Apostles peace?

Focus Question 3:
What power did Christ give his Apostles in the Upper Room?

GUIDED EXERCISE

Work with a partner to analyze Christ's appearance to the Apostles in the Upper Room (cf. Jn 20: 19-23) to articulate exactly what Christ said and did in that encounter. Use bullet points for precision. For example:

✴ He appeared out of nowhere since the "doors were shut."

Focus Question 4:
What is the Great Commission?

Israel!" (Jn 12: 13). Then, a few days later, after celebrating the Passover meal with his Apostles, Christ was betrayed and arrested, and on the following day, tried, sentenced, scourged, put to death by crucifixion, and sealed in a tomb. All the Apostles but one abandoned him for fear of being arrested themselves. Judas, who betrayed Christ, hung himself afterward.

Grief-stricken and remorseful for their lack of loyalty, the Apostles hid in the same Upper Room where they had shared Christ's Last Supper. Then reports came from the women who had gone to anoint the body of Christ: They had seen Christ alive, and his tomb was empty! Skeptical at first, Peter and John ran to investigate. Finding the tomb indeed empty, they tried to make sense of it.

> On the evening of that day, the first day of the week, the doors being shut where the disciples were, for fear of the Jews, Jesus came and stood among them and said to them, "Peace be with you." When he had said this, he showed them his hands and his side. Then the disciples were glad when they saw the Lord. Jesus said to them again, "Peace be with you. As the Father has sent me, even so I send you." (Jn 20: 19-21)

Why did Christ offer them "peace"? The disciples were confused and anxious, and initially a bit frightened at the sight of Christ. Christ told them to be at peace because of what he had accomplished: He had restored the friendship between God and humanity. Because he was God, Christ not only wished them peace, but also instilled in them peace of mind and heart.

Christ later gave them a commission. A commission is an order to do something with the authority and power to actually carry it out. Christ sent the Apostles into the world the way the Father had sent him. Later this task would become even more explicit in what is termed the *Great Commission*:

> All authority in heaven and on earth has been given to me. Go therefore and make disciples of all nations, baptizing them in the name of the Father and of the Son and of the Holy Spirit, teaching them to observe all that I have commanded you. (Mt 28: 19-20)

The Disbelief of St. Thomas (detail) by Tissot.
The disciples were confused and anxious, and initially a bit frightened at the sight of Christ.

Focus Question 5:

Why did the Apostles need further instruction after the Resurrection?

Focus Question 6:

How did Christ restore Peter's leadership?

Focus Question 7:

What was the goal of the forty-day preparation Christ gave the Apostles?

FROM *YouCat*

What is the task of the Church?

The CHURCH'S task is to make the kingdom of God, which has already begun with Jesus, germinate and grow in all nations.

Wherever Jesus went, heaven touched earth: the kingdom of God was inaugurated, a kingdom of peace and justice. The CHURCH serves this kingdom of God. She is not an end in herself. She must carry on what Jesus started. She should act as Jesus would act. She continues the sacred signs of Jesus (the SACRAMENTS). She hands on Jesus' words. That is why the Church, for all her weakness, is a formidable bit of heaven on earth. (*YouCat* 123)

Christ's Charge to Peter (detail) by Raphael.
Christ wanted Peter to exercise his primacy in the Church.

During one post-Resurrection appearance, Christ also gave the Apostles the power to forgive sins. Breathing on them, he said, "Receive the Holy Spirit. If you forgive the sins of any, they are forgiven; if you retain the sins of any, they are retained" (Jn 20:22-23). By instituting the Sacrament of Penance in this way, Christ gave his Apostles, the priests of the New Covenant, the way of conferring his grace of forgiveness upon the faithful; and a way for the faithful to confess their sins and receive that grace, the fruit of their repentance, made available by his act of Redemption.

FORTY DAYS OF INSTRUCTION

Even though Christ had taught his Apostles many things, including explicitly instructing them that he would be rejected and put to death by crucifixion, but would rise from the dead on the third day, they were still confused by what had happened. This is why Christ continued teaching the Apostles for forty days after his Resurrection, appearing to them and "speaking of the Kingdom of God" (Acts 1:3).

One of the matters Christ attended to was related to his Resurrection gift of peace. Peter was still dejected from having denied Christ three times, as the Lord had predicted. When he and some of the Apostles had been fishing on the Sea of Galilee all night without catching anything, Christ appeared on the shore but they did not recognize him. He told them to lower their nets and they caught a huge number of fish. Peter then recognized it was the Lord.

When they came to shore, they saw that Christ had built a charcoal fire and was roasting some fish.

> When they had finished breakfast, Jesus said to Simon Peter, "Simon, son of John, do you love me more than these?" He said to him, "Yes, Lord; you know that I love you." He said to him, "Feed my lambs." A second time he said to him, "Simon, son of John, do you love me?" He said to him, "Yes, Lord; you know that I love you." He said to him, "Tend my sheep." He said to him the third time, "Simon, son of John, do you love me?" Peter was grieved because he said to him the third time, "Do you love me?" And he said to him, "Lord, you know everything; you know that I love you." Jesus said to him, "Feed my sheep." (Jn 21:15-17)

Notice Christ's charity in gently reminding Peter of his sin. At the same time, Christ purifies Peter of it through his "grief." Simultaneously, Christ assured Peter of his confidence in him to be the Good Shepherd for his flock, his Church. Christ wanted Peter to exercise his primacy in the Church and to act as his vicar or "representative."

During the forty days of post-Resurrection instruction, Christ told the Apostles:

> You shall receive power when the Holy Spirit has come upon you; and you shall be my witnesses in Jerusalem and in all Judea and Samaria and to the end of the earth. (Acts 1:8)

Christ was drawing for them a verbal map of the ancient kingdom of David. Jerusalem was David's capital city. Judea was the tribal territory of David that surrounded Jerusalem. Samaria was the land to the north where the rest of the tribes of Israel were located. "The ends of the earth" represented all the Gentile nations that David had brought under his control. It also indicated that Christ intended the Church to fulfill God's promise to David: that his kingdom would encompass the whole world.

The Ascension by Copley. Christ ascended into Heaven before their very eyes, having completed his mission on earth.

The Apostles were being given the Great Commission of Christ—to evangelize all the peoples who were once part of the old kingdom of David, reclaiming them for the restored kingdom, which is the Church.

The Apostles and all those who assisted them were to "make disciples of all nations." They were to baptize them in the name of the Blessed Trinity. They were also to teach them to observe all that Christ commanded (cf. Mt 28: 19-20). This teaching includes the entire Deposit of Faith found in Divine Revelation, part of which would subsequently be written down in the New Testament. It includes the observation of the entire moral law as restored and completed by Christ and which can be summarized in the New Law of Love: to love one another with a sacrificial love. It would take more than human memory to always recall and preserve without error these teachings. This is where the Holy Spirit came in.

As the forty days came to an end, Christ instructed the Apostles:

> "[S]tay in the city [of Jerusalem], until you are clothed with power from on high." Then he led them out as far as Bethany, and lifting up his hands he blessed them. While he blessed them, he parted from them, and was carried up into heaven. And they returned to Jerusalem with great joy, and were continually in the temple blessing God. (Lk 24: 49-53)

Christ ascended into Heaven before their very eyes, having completed his mission on earth. According to the Book of Acts, the Apostles momentarily stood there, amazed, until an angel of God appeared and told them:

> Men of Galilee, why do you stand looking into heaven? This Jesus, who was taken up from you into heaven, will come in the same way as you saw him go into heaven. (Acts 1: 11)

Christ would indeed come again to judge the world at the end of time. Until then, the Apostles had work to do: Leading the Church that Christ had founded, and taking his message to the ends of the earth.

Focus Question 8:
Is the moral law part of the teachings of the Apostles?

Focus Question 9:
Did the Apostles use the New Testament in their teaching?

VOCABULARY

GREAT COMMISSION
Name given to Christ's commission to the Apostles to teach, baptize, and make disciples of all nations.

FROM *YouCat*

Why do we hand on the faith?

We hand on the faith because Jesus commands us: "Go therefore and make disciples of all nations" (Mt 28: 19).

No genuine Christian leaves the transmission of the faith exclusively to specialists (teachers, pastors, missionaries). We are Christ for others. This means that every genuine Christian would like God to come to other people, too. He says to himself, "The Lord needs me! I have been baptized and confirmed and am responsible for helping the people around me to learn about God and 'to come to the knowledge of the truth'" (1 Tim 2: 4b).

Mother Teresa used a good comparison: "Often you can see power lines running alongside the street. Unless current is flowing through them, there is no light. The power line is you and I! The current is God! We have the power to allow the current to flow through us and thus to generate the light of the world—JESUS—or to refuse to be used and, thus, allow the darkness to spread." (*YouCat* 11)

Focus Question 10:
What is the Ascension?

Focus Question 11:

Why did Christ create twelve Apostles?

Focus Question 12:

Who was responsible for the replacement of Judas?

Focus Question 13:

What was St. Peter's criterion for selecting a new Apostle?

VOCABULARY

APOSTOLIC SUCCESSION

The process by which the leadership of the Church has been passed down in a direct line from the original Twelve Apostles through the bishops of the Church.

Focus Question 14:

How was the selection of St. Matthias the beginning of Apostolic Succession?

Focus Question 15:

Why were there so many foreign-language-speaking Jews in Jerusalem fifty days after Passover?

Focus Question 16:

What did Pentecost traditionally commemorate?

Focus Question 17:

What two similes did Luke use to describe the descent of the Holy Spirit?

Focus Question 18:

What immediate power did the Holy Spirit give the disciples of Christ?

"Charismatic gifts" are gifts of the Holy Spirit to build up the Church.

CREATING AN APOSTLE

Before they could do so, however, the Apostles had to wait until they were "clothed with power from on high," as Christ had promised.

As we saw in the previous chapter, the Twelve Apostles represented the Twelve Tribes of Israel, and they were to preside over the restored People of God in his kingdom, the Church. Yet, by the time of the Resurrection, they numbered only eleven: Judas, one of the original Apostles, had betrayed Christ and had taken his own life in despair (cf. Mt 27: 3-5).

To restore their number to twelve, St. Peter, as head of the Church, took the initiative to replace Judas. He laid down these criteria for selecting this new Apostle as he called for an election for a replacement:

> So one of the men who have accompanied us during all the time that the Lord Jesus went in and out among us, beginning from the baptism of John until the day he was taken up from us—one of these men must become with us a witness to his resurrection. (Acts 1: 21-22)

A disciple named Matthias, who had been with Christ from the beginning, was selected to take Judas's place among the Twelve. Just as the Apostles now "enrolled" a new Apostle (cf. Acts 1: 26), they would later appoint many more bishops to act in their places so that Christ's commission would continue to be carried out after their deaths. This was the beginning of *Apostolic Succession*, as bishops handed on to other bishops the authority that originated with Christ and the Apostles.

With their number now complete, the Apostles continued in prayer.

THE DAY OF PENTECOST

Ten days after Christ's Ascension into Heaven, the Apostles were again gathered together with Mary and other disciples in the Upper Room, about a hundred and twenty souls in all.

At the time, Jerusalem was filled with faithful Jews from all over the world who had come to celebrate the feast of Pentecost. This feast was celebrated on the fiftieth day after the Passover (the word *Pentecost* is taken from the Greek word for "fifty"). It commemorated the giving of the Law to Moses on Mount Sinai. The Apostles were there in the Upper Room when something extraordinary happened:

> [S]uddenly a sound came from heaven like the rush of a mighty wind, and it filled all the house where they were sitting. And there appeared to them tongues as of fire, distributed and resting on each one of them. And they were all filled with the Holy Spirit and began to speak in other tongues, as the Spirit gave them utterance. (Acts 2: 1-4)

The transformation of the Apostles was immediate. They became like new men. They spoke out boldly, proclaiming the Gospel to all who would listen, unafraid of the consequences of bearing such bold witness. This ability is a gift of the Holy Spirit, as the *Catechism* points out:

> So that she can fulfill her mission, the Holy Spirit "bestows upon [the Church] varied hierarchic and charismatic gifts, and in this way directs her."[1] "Henceforward the Church, endowed with the gifts of her founder and faithfully observing his precepts of charity, humility and self-denial, receives the mission of proclaiming and establishing

Pentecost by Van Der Werff.
The day of Pentecost marks the beginning of the Church's public ministry in the world.

Focus Question 19:
What was the immediate effect of Pentecost on the Church?

FROM *YouCat*

What happened on Pentecost?

Fifty days after his Resurrection, the Lord sent the Holy Spirit down from heaven upon his disciples. The age of the CHURCH began.

On Pentecost the Holy Spirit transformed fearful apostles into courageous witnesses to Christ. In a very short time, thousands had themselves baptized: it was the birthday of the Church. The miracle of the languages on PENTECOST shows that the Church is there for all peoples from the very beginning: She is universal (the Latin term for the Greek *kat' holon*, catholic) and missionary. She speaks to all men, overcomes ethnic and linguistic barriers, and can be understood by all. To this day the Holy Spirit is the "soul" of the Church, the essential principle of her life. (*YouCat* 118)

among all peoples the Kingdom of Christ and of God, and she is on earth the seed and the beginning of that kingdom."[2] (CCC 768)

"Hierarchic gifts" have to do with the exercise of leadership in the Church. For example, the Apostles were the shepherds of the Christian faithful and Peter was the leader of the Apostles. Later the Apostles would appoint deacons to assist them, and later bishops. "Charismatic gifts" are gifts of the Holy Spirit to build up the Church. We see one of them right away when those to whom the disciples preach to can hear them in their own languages.

> Now there were dwelling in Jerusalem Jews, devout men from every nation under heaven. And at this sound the multitude came together, and they were bewildered, because each one heard them speaking in his own language. And they were amazed and wondered, saying, "Are not all these who are speaking Galileans? And how is it that we hear, each of us in his own native language?" (Acts 2: 5-8)

St. Peter stood up and began to address the crowd, proclaiming to them that the long-awaited Messiah had come. It was Christ, crucified and resurrected from the dead, who now sits at the right hand of God the Father in Heaven. Upon hearing this, the people asked St. Peter and the rest of the Apostles what they must do to be saved. St. Peter responded by urging them to repent and to be baptized.

The day of Pentecost marks the beginning of the Church's public ministry in the world. The Apostles took up Christ's commission to be his witnesses and to baptize men and women from every nation. On the day of Pentecost alone, 3,000 people were baptized and became Christians. But this was only the beginning of the mission. From Jerusalem, the Gospel message would go out to all the nations, to Jews and Gentiles alike. Filled with the power of the Holy Spirit, the Church on earth would continue to grow in numbers and in fervor.

St. Peter Preaching by Masolino.
"And Peter said to them, 'Repent, and be baptized every one of you in the name of Jesus Christ for the forgiveness of your sins; and you shall receive the gift of the Holy Spirit.'" (Acts 2: 38)

THE MEANING OF THE DESCENT OF THE HOLY SPIRIT

Before his Ascension, Christ had promised his Apostles that he would be with them always, and at Pentecost, he fulfilled his promise. Through the gift of the Holy Spirit, Christ gave life to the Church and united it to himself. It was the Holy Spirit who empowered the Apostles to preach the Gospel to the multitudes. It was the Holy Spirit who opened the hearts of those who heard the Good News, and it was the Holy Spirit who revealed the Church as Christ's instrument of salvation for the entire world.

> "When the work which the Father gave the Son to do on earth was accomplished, the Holy Spirit was sent on the day of Pentecost in order that he might continually sanctify the Church."[3] Then "the Church was openly displayed to the crowds and the spread of the Gospel among the nations, through preaching, was begun."[4] As the "convocation" of all men for salvation, the Church in her very nature is missionary, sent by Christ to all the nations to make disciples of them.[5] (CCC 767)

As we will explore in later chapters, the Holy Spirit is like the "soul" of the Mystical Body of Christ, giving life to the Church and guiding its actions. The Holy Spirit continues to work within the Church in many different ways.

✷ **Through the Pope and the bishops.** The Holy Spirit assists the Pope and the bishops, the successors of the Apostles, in their role of governing, sanctifying, and proclaiming the Gospel in the Church.

✷ **In Sacred Scripture.** The Holy Spirit inspired the human authors of the Bible. Even though the Bible is made up of books written by different authors, the ultimate author of Scripture is the Holy Spirit. This is why we say that the Bible is inspired and without error. The Holy Spirit also guides the Church in infallibly interpreting the words of Sacred Scripture.

✷ **In the Sacraments.** The Holy Spirit gives life to new members of the Church through Baptism, incorporating them into the Mystical Body of Christ. In each of the Seven Sacraments, the Holy Spirit works to give growth and healing to all the members of the Church.

✷ **In the Gifts of the Holy Spirit.** These seven supernatural gifts render us attentive to the will of God and to the actual graces that he sends us to follow his will. Recall that the gifts of the Spirit are wisdom, understanding, knowledge, counsel, fortitude, piety, and fear of the Lord.

✷ **In the Fruits of the Holy Spirit.** These are the supernatural works that a person is enabled to perform with the assistance of the Holy Spirit. The twelve fruits of the Spirit are charity, generosity, joy, gentleness, peace, faithfulness, patience, modesty, kindness, self-control, goodness, and chastity.

✷ **Through special graces.** The Holy Spirit also gives the faithful special graces, called *charisms*, so that they are able to contribute to the task of building up the Church. For example, one person may be given the *charism* of teaching the Faith so that others can easily understand it.

ST. STEPHEN, THE FIRST MARTYR

Through the work of the Apostles and disciples, the Gospel of Christ spread to many new believers in those first days of the Church. Nevertheless, there was significant opposition. The Jewish authorities had assumed that Christ's Death would scatter his followers and silence his message. After the events of Pentecost, however, it became clear that this was not the case. The Christian community was growing by the day. Even after they were imprisoned by the authorities and beaten, the Apostles refused to stop preaching about Jesus Christ.

A man named Stephen, a Christian convert and a deacon in the Church, was taken before the Jewish authorities and accused of blasphemy. Just as at the trial of Christ, false witnesses were

St. Peter Consecrates Stephen as Deacon by Fra Angelico.

brought forward to testify against him. St. Stephen did not hold his tongue. Filled with the Holy Spirit, he began to preach, explaining how the Scriptures showed Christ to be the promised Messiah. He added that just as his accusers' ancestors had opposed the Holy Spirit by persecuting the prophets, they themselves had betrayed and murdered Christ (cf. Acts 7: 51-52). Stephen's audience became enraged, and they took him out of the city and stoned him to death.

St. Stephen was the Church's first martyr, meaning witness: that is, put to death for witnessing his faith in Jesus Christ.

The martyrdom of St. Stephen marked the beginning of a tremendous persecution of the Church in Jerusalem. Many of the Christians fled to the surrounding regions, where they continued to spread the Gospel. Those who did not leave were imprisoned. The persecution by the Jewish leaders was only the first of many similar persecutions during the first several centuries of Christianity.

Of all the saints honored and celebrated by the Church, martyrs hold a special place. Martyrs are the ultimate witnesses to the truth of the Faith, "bearing witness even unto death." All Christians are called to live in imitation of Christ. Those who are given the grace of martyrdom imitate Christ in the fullest way possible, by dying like Christ died, out of love: "Greater love hath no man than this" (Jn 15: 13).

St. Stephen's feast day is December 26.

Focus Question 21:
What enraged the Jewish authorities about Stephen's preaching?

Focus Question 22:
What is a martyr?

FROM *YouCat*

Martyr (from Greek *martyria* = witness, testimony):

A Christian martyr is a person who is ready to suffer violence or even to be killed for Christ, who is the truth, or for a conscientious decision made on the basis of faith.

The deacon Stephen was the first Christian martyr. On account of his commitment to the truth of the Gospel, he was stoned to death outside the gates of the city of Jerusalem between AD 36 and 40. (p. 248)

Stoning of St. Stephen by Rembrandt. The martyrdom of St. Stephen marked the beginning of a tremendous persecution of the Church in Jerusalem.

CLOSURE

Summarize in one paragraph the activity of the Church from the Resurrection through Pentecost.

ALTERNATIVE ASSESSMENT

Have a class discussion on *teenagers as missionaries* using the following questions:

✠ What would it mean for teenagers to be missionary-minded?

✠ Why are teens generally not missionary-minded?

✠ If teens were to be so, who would most reasonably be the objects of their missionary activities?

✠ What would be required for teens to be enthusiastic missionaries?

Appearance on the Mountain in Galilee by Duccio.
"And lo, I am with you always, to the close of the age." (Mt 28:20)

CONCLUSION

Throughout the Old Testament, we see God forming his people into an assembly; throughout the life and ministry of Christ, we see him forming the faithful into a Church to continue his work of redemption. From the earliest days after the Ascension, we see the Church in action, spreading the Gospel and carrying out Christ's work under the guidance of the Holy Spirit.

In the next chapter, we will study the history of the Church as the first Apostles and evangelists took the Gospel message far and wide and won countless converts even in the face of hardships and persecutions.

DISCUSSION QUESTIONS

1. What power did Christ give his Apostles in the Upper Room?
2. What is the Great Commission?
3. Why did the Apostles need further instruction after the Resurrection?
4. What is the Ascension?
5. What was St. Peter's criterion for selecting a new Apostle?
6. What immediate power did the Holy Spirit give the disciples of Christ?
7. Name and describe six ways in which the Holy Spirit is active in the Church today.
8. What enraged the Jewish authorities about Stephen's preaching?

From the earliest days after the Ascension, we see the Church in action, spreading the Gospel and carrying out Christ's work under the guidance of the Holy Spirit.

ENDNOTES – CHAPTER 4

1. *LG* 4.
2. *LG* 5.
3. *LG* 4; cf. Jn 17:4.

4. *AG* 4.
5. Cf. Mt 28:19-20; *AG* 2, 5-6.

The Church
Sacrament of Salvation

Chapter 5
The Apostolic Church

The Apostles were completely faithful to Christ's command to "make disciples of all nations," but they only began the work.

CHAPTER 5
The Apostolic Church

Review of Chapter 4:

✠ After his Resurrection, Christ continued to appear to his Apostles, instructing them and conferring upon them powers to continue his mission on earth. He gave them the power to forgive sins and commissioned them to preach and make disciples of all nations through the Sacrament of Baptism. He promised to send the Holy Spirit who would give them "power from on high." He also promised he would be with them until the end of the world.

✠ The election of St. Matthias to replace Judas was the first act of Apostolic Succession, which continues in an unbroken line to our present-day bishops.

✠ After the Holy Spirit descended upon the Apostles at Pentecost, they received the promised power and gift to preach the Gospel boldly, winning many converts.

✠ The Holy Spirit, who is like the soul of the Mystical Body of Christ, continues to work within the Church through the authority of the Pope and bishops, in Scripture, in the Sacraments, and through the many gifts, fruits, and charisms with which he endows the faithful.

The *Apostolic Church* refers to the Church during the lifetime of the Apostles.

Specifically, it means the period from Pentecost, when the Holy Spirit began the Apostles' evangelization, until the death of St. John, the last Apostle, in about AD 100. "Evangelization" simply means *telling the good news*. During this time, the Church moved from being an entirely Jewish to a predominantly Gentile phenomenon. It went from the leadership of the Apostles to leadership by the bishops appointed by them. And its scope enlarged from Judea and Galilee to the greater Roman Empire and beyond. Part of this history is recorded in St. Luke's Acts of the Apostles and can be gleaned from the Epistles and the Book of Revelation.

In this chapter we will look at some of the developments of the Church during the Apostolic period and get to know some of the Apostles better.

OPENING ACTIVITY

Read 2 Cor 11:24-27 below, St. Paul's catalogue of his suffering for the sake of the Gospel.

Then free write for a few minutes on whichever of the following questions most pertain to you:

✠ What contradictions have you faced to live your faith?

✠ What sufferings would you be willing to endure for your faith?

✠ If you are not presently interested in facing any difficulties for the Faith, is there anything else you really believe in that you would be willing to face hardships for, and if so, what?

BASIC QUESTIONS

This chapter attempts to answer the following basic questions:

✠ Why has it been supremely important to know what the Apostles taught?

✠ What did the Church decide about Gentile Christian converts?

✠ What are some important things to know about some of the Apostles?

KEY IDEAS

The key ideas of this chapter are:

✠ It has always been important to know what the Apostles taught because they faithfully transmitted what Christ taught them.

✠ Led by the Holy Spirit and under the direction of St. Peter, the Apostles at the Council of Jerusalem decided that Gentile converts to Christianity did not need to follow the Mosaic Law.

Continued

ST. PAUL, A LIGHT FOR THE GENTILES

In Chapter 4, we read about the martyrdom of St. Stephen. Scripture tells us that a man named Saul was involved in the stoning of St. Stephen (cf. Acts 7: 58-8: 1). This Saul was a relentless persecutor of the Church, spending his time seeking out and arresting anyone who professed faith in Christ.

Saul, who was a Roman citizen, grew up in Tarsus where he received a pagan classical education. But Saul was also a strict Pharisee, educated in the Jewish faith by the renowned teacher Gamaliel. Saul approved of the murder of St. Stephen and felt it was his God-given duty to destroy what he considered a heretical Jewish sect.

Saul was "still breathing threats and murder against the disciples of the Lord" (Acts 9: 1) when he had a dramatic conversion. While on the road to Damascus, where he intended to persecute Christians who had fled there, the risen Christ appeared to him:

The Conversion of St. Paul by Murillo.
Once Jesus Christ revealed himself to Saul, he took the name Paul.

[S]uddenly a light from heaven flashed about him. And he fell to the ground and heard a voice saying to him, "Saul, Saul, why do you persecute me?"

And he said, "Who are you, Lord?" And he said, "I am Jesus, whom you are persecuting; but rise and enter the city, and you will be told what you are to do." (Acts 9: 3-6)

Once Jesus Christ revealed himself to Saul, he took the name Paul and poured all of his zeal into defending and spreading the Christian Faith, especially to the Gentiles, that is, pagans outside the Holy Land. God chose him, in fact, for a specific mission: "I have set you to be a light for the Gentiles, that you may bring salvation to the uttermost parts of the earth" (Acts 13: 47).

In his Second Letter to the Corinthians, St. Paul describes the hardships that he endured during his journeys:

> Five times I have received at the hands of the Jews the forty lashes less one. Three times I have been beaten with rods; once I was stoned. Three times I have been shipwrecked; a night and a day I have been adrift at sea; on frequent journeys, in danger from rivers, danger from robbers, danger from my own people, danger from Gentiles, danger in the city, danger in the wilderness, danger at sea, danger from false brethren; in toil and hardship, through many a sleepless night, in hunger and thirst, often without food, in cold and exposure. (2 Cor 11: 24-27)

St. Paul completed three missionary journeys through Gentile lands throughout the Roman Empire and brought countless new believers to Christ. He founded a number of new Christian churches and provided vital guidance and encouragement to the churches that had been founded by the Twelve. He is the author of most of the "wisdom" books of the New Testaments, the Epistles.

St. Paul was finally arrested and taken to Rome, where he was imprisoned and put to death around AD 64. Because he was a Roman citizen, however, St. Paul was spared the torture of crucifixion and was beheaded instead.

KEY IDEAS
Continued

✠ St. Peter was the rock or foundation on which Christ built the Church; Christ made St. Paul the Apostle to the Gentiles; St. John, the beloved disciple, wrote a Gospel and Revelation; St. Matthew, the former tax collector, wrote a Gospel in Aramaic; "Doubting Thomas" may have evangelized India; and St. James "the Lesser," a "brother" of the Lord, became head of the Church in Jerusalem.

Focus Question 1:
What is the Apostolic Church?

Focus Question 2:
What is evangelization?

Focus Question 3:
Why is the Apostolic period so important in the development of the Church?

Focus Question 4:
What kind of education did Saul have?

Focus Question 5:
Why was Saul so much against Christianity?

Focus Question 6:
What mission did Christ give St. Paul?

Focus Question 7:
What were some of St. Paul's accomplishments?

Ananias Laying Hands on Saul,
Byzantine Mocaic.

FROM *YouCat*

Why did Jesus call apostles?

Jesus had a large circle of disciples around him, both men and women. From this circle he selected twelve men whom he called APOSTLES (Lk 6:12–16). The apostles were specially trained by him and entrusted with various commissions: "He sent them out to preach the kingdom of God and to heal" (Lk 9:2). Jesus took only these twelve apostles with him to the Last Supper, where he gave them the command, "Do this in remembrance of me" (Lk 22:19b).

The apostles became witnesses of Jesus' Resurrection and guarantors of the truth about him. They continued Jesus' mission after his death. They chose successors for their ministry: the bishops. To this day, the successors of the apostles exercise the authority conferred by Jesus: They govern and teach and celebrate the liturgy. The cohesiveness of the apostles became the foundation for the unity of the Church (APOSTOLIC SUCCESSION). Preeminent once again among the Twelve was Peter, on whom Jesus bestowed special authority: "You are Peter, and on this rock I will build my Church" (Mt 16:18). From Peter's special role among the apostles developed the papal ministry. (*YouCat* 92)

Focus Question 8:

What question had to be decided in the early Church about the Gentiles?

VOCABULARY

APOSTLE

(from the Greek apostolos = messenger, envoy): in the New Testament initially the term for the twelve men who were called by Christ to be his closest collaborators and witnesses. Paul, too, was privileged to consider himself an Apostle called by Christ. (*YouCat*, p. 20)

APOSTOLIC CHURCH

The early Church during the lifetime of the Apostles.

PREACHING TO ALL NATIONS

Jesus Christ was a Jew, a member of a distinctive people. They followed the Law of Moses, had special dietary rules, worshiped in the Temple and in synagogues, and observed the Sabbath, and their men were circumcised. Yet, Christ also commanded that the Apostles make disciples of all nations. What would this mean for Gentiles who converted? Would these Gentiles need to become Jews as well?

St. Philip Baptizing the Ethiopian (detail) by Rembrandt.
An angel led the Apostle Philip to make the eunuch the first Gentile Christian.

St. Philip Baptizes the Ethiopian

From the Roman perspective, the nation of Ethiopia represented one of the farthest corners of the earth. The Acts of the Apostles records how a eunuch, who was the Queen of Ethiopia's treasurer, was reading the Old Testament Scriptures. Because he was a eunuch, the Jewish Law forbade him from becoming a member of the Chosen People (Dt 23: 1). An angel, however, led the Apostle Philip to make him the first Gentile Christian.

> But an angel of the Lord said to Philip, "Rise and go toward the south to the road that goes down from Jerusalem to Gaza." This is a desert road. And he rose and went. And behold, an Ethiopian, a eunuch, a minister of Candace, the queen of the Ethiopians, in charge of all her treasure, had come to Jerusalem to worship and was returning; seated in his chariot, he was reading the prophet Isaiah. (Acts 8: 26-28)

In those days, people often read aloud even when they were alone, so St. Philip could hear what the Ethiopian was reading.

> And the Spirit said to Philip, "Go up and join this chariot." So Philip ran to him, and heard him reading Isaiah the prophet, and asked, "Do you understand what you are reading?" And he said, "How can I, unless someone guides me?" And he invited Philip to come up and

sit with him. Now the passage of the scripture which he was reading was this: *As a sheep led to the slaughter or a lamb before its shearer is dumb, so he opens not his mouth. In his humiliation justice was denied him. Who can describe his generation? For his life is taken up from the earth.* And the eunuch said to Philip, "About whom, pray, does the prophet say this, about himself or about some one else?" Then Philip opened his mouth, and beginning with this scripture he told him the good news of Jesus. (Acts 8: 29-35)

Showing how Christ fulfilled the Scriptures was always the early Christians' most effective argument.

And as they went along the road they came to some water, and the eunuch said, "See, here is water! What is to prevent my being baptized?" (Acts 8: 36)

Led by the Holy Spirit, Philip agreed and baptized the Ethiopian. He became the first recorded Gentile convert to Christianity after the Resurrection.

The Vision of St. Peter

The question of Gentile converts also arose in the context of circumcision and Jewish dietary laws. The answer was given to St. Peter in a vision:

[Peter] saw the heaven opened, and something descending, like a great sheet, let down by four corners upon the earth. In it were all kinds of animals and reptiles and birds of the air. And there came a voice to him, "Rise, Peter; kill and eat." But Peter said, "No, Lord; for I have never eaten anything that is common or unclean." And the voice came to him again a second time, "What God has cleansed, you must not call common." (Acts 10: 10-16.)

Christ was calling together a new People of God, one that was united not by ethnicity or the Old Covenant, but rather by his Holy Spirit. Immediately after he received this vision, Peter went to meet Cornelius, a Roman centurion who wanted to learn about Christ. After Peter preached to his household, the Holy Spirit descended upon them before they were baptized. This showed Peter he should baptize them just as they were. As Peter explained later:

You yourselves know how unlawful it is for a Jew to associate with or to visit any one of another nation; but God has shown me that I should not call any man common or unclean. (Acts 10: 28)

The Council of Jerusalem

Nevertheless, some Jewish Christians remained convinced that Gentile converts had to become Jews by being circumcised and following the Law of Moses, since circumcision was a sign of God's covenant with Abraham. St. Paul was completely opposed to this. An assembly of the Apostles and the Church's elders (in Greek, *presbyteros*, from which we get the word "priest") was convoked in Jerusalem in order to decide the matter once and for all.

After much heated discussion, St. Peter stood up among the Apostles and essentially put an end to the debate.

"Brethren, you know that in the early days God made choice among you, that by my mouth the Gentiles should hear the word of the gospel and believe. And God who knows the heart bore witness to them, giving them the Holy Spirit just as he did to us; and he made no distinction between us and them, but cleansed their hearts by faith. Now therefore why do you make trial of God by putting a yoke upon the neck of the disciples which neither our fathers nor we have

VOCABULARY

EVANGELIZATION
The "telling of the good news," the preaching of the Gospel throughout the world and the lived witness of the faithful Christian life.

Focus Question 9:
Why do we know the Ethiopian eunuch was not a Jew?

Focus Question 10:
What part did Philip play in converting the Ethiopian?

Baptism of a Centurion by Corneille. Christ was calling together a new People of God.

Focus Question 11:
How did St. Peter decide that Jewish dietary laws no longer applied to Christians?

Focus Question 12:
How did St. Peter decide Gentiles did not need to be circumcised before Baptism?

Focus Question 13:
What was the first Church Council?

Focus Question 14:
What question did the Council of Jerusalem decide?

Focus Question 15:
Who defined the Church's teaching at this council?

Focus Question 16:
What did the Council decide?

FROM *YouCat*

What significance does the New Testament have for Christians?

In the NEW TESTAMENT God's REVELATION is completed. The four Gospels according to Matthew, Mark, Luke, and John are the center-piece of Sacred Scripture and the most precious treasure of the Church. In them the Son of God shows himself as he is and encounters us. In the Acts of the Apostles we learn about the beginnings of the Church and the working of the Holy Spirit. In the letters written by the apostles, all facets of human life are set in the light of Christ. In the Book of Revelation we foresee the end of the ages.

Jesus is everything that God would like to tell us. The entire Old Testament prepares for the Incarnation of God's Son. All of God's promises find their fulfillment in Jesus. To be a Christian means to unite oneself ever more deeply with the life of Christ. To do that, one must read and live the Gospels. Madeleine Delbrêl says, "Through his Word God tells us what he is and what he wants; he says it definitively and says it for each individual day. When we hold our Gospel book in our hands, we should reflect that in it dwells the Word that wants to become flesh in us, desires to take hold of us, so that we might begin his life anew in a new place, at a new time, in a new human setting." (*YouCat* 18)

been able to bear? But we believe that we shall be saved through the grace of the Lord Jesus, just as they will." And all the assembly kept silence. (Acts 15: 7-12)

The declaration of the Council—defined by St. Peter and later confirmed by St. James, the bishop of Jerusalem—was then sent out to Gentile Christians everywhere. With the controversy now settled, the Apostles returned to their task of evangelization, proclaiming the Gospel to the ends of the earth.

This assembly is referred to today as the Council of Jerusalem (AD 51). It is here that we find the first instance of a Pope officially defining a teaching of the Church.

Ordaining of the Twelve Apostles by Tissot.
"And he went up on the mountain, and called to him those whom he desired; and they came to him. And he appointed twelve, to be with him, and to be sent out to preach…"
(Mk 3: 13-14)

PORTRAITS OF THE APOSTLES

While the missionary work of St. Paul is mentioned the most in Sacred Scripture, the other Apostles were active in spreading the Gospel message as well. Using available evidence from Scripture, history, and tradition, we can follow the Apostles' lives from Christ's invitation to follow him to their eventual deaths in order to see the unique roles to which God called them. Here are portraits of some of the better known Apostles, with some details of their lives coming from traditional accounts.

St. Peter

St. Peter was the fisherman whom Christ called to be a fisher of men. Peter's defining moment came when Christ asked the Apostles, "Who do men say that I am?" and Simon replied, "You are the Christ" (Mt 16: 13-16). Then Christ gave Peter his new name, *Cephas*, an Aramaic word meaning "rock." In Greek it is *Petros*, from which we get *Peter*.

> **You are Peter, and on this rock I will build my Church….I will give you the keys of the Kingdom of Heaven, and whatever you bind on earth will be bound in heaven, and whatever you loose on earth will be loosed in heaven. (Mt 16: 18-19)**

In this commissioning, Christ used three metaphors that help to define St. Peter's future role in the Church:

✠ **His new name, *Rock*,** signified that St. Peter would be the foundation of the Church that Christ would establish.

✠ **The keys** indicated that St. Peter would be both the leader in this Church and Christ's own representative. He was the "prime minister" in the New Davidic Kingdom with the power of the keys.

✠ Finally, **the power of binding and loosing** granted St. Peter the authority to make decisions in Christ's Church.

Christ bestowed this leadership on St. Peter. He would be the final authority within the community of believers, an office that would later be known as the Holy See, the papacy.

Eventually traveling to Rome, St. Peter helped to establish and nourish the Christian community in the very heart of the Roman Empire. There, he suffered martyrdom. That is why each bishop of Rome becomes the successor of St. Peter, the Pope, the head of the Catholic Church. Tradition has it that St. Peter was crucified around AD 64—upside-down, as he said he was unworthy to die as Christ had—about the same time that St. Paul was martyred.

St. John

St. John was mending his fishing nets with his brother James when Christ called him (cf. Mt 4: 21; Mk 1: 19). St. John was the "disciple whom Jesus loved," the way he refers to himself in his Gospel. St. John sat beside our Lord at the Last Supper (cf. Jn 13: 23) and was the only Apostle with the courage to stay with Christ during the Crucifixion, where he stood at the foot of the Cross with Mary, the Mother of Jesus (cf. Jn 19: 26). There, Christ asked St. John to care for his Mother and gave St. John to the Blessed Mother as her son.

St. John the Evangelist by Borovikovsky. St. John has the distinction of being the last of the Apostles to die and the only Apostle not to suffer martyrdom.

St. Paul lists John as one of the pillars of the early Christian community (cf. Gal 2: 9), and the Acts of the Apostles shows John present at some of the most important events in the life of the early Church.[1]

St. John has the distinction of being the last of the Apostles to die and the only Apostle not to suffer martyrdom, although he did endure much persecution. During the reign of the Roman Emperor Domitian, St. John was exiled to the isle of Patmos off the coast of present-day Turkey. There he wrote the Book of Revelation (or Apocalypse). In Revelation, St. John addressed the early Christian communities and encouraged them to be steadfast in their faith and not to identify with the pagan world that was personified by the Roman Empire.

After his death, devotion to the Apostle John spread from the city of Ephesus where, according to an ancient tradition, he worked for many years and died during the reign of Emperor Trajan.

Focus Question 17:
What was the significance of the new name Christ gave Simon?

Focus Question 18:
What was the power of the keys Christ gave Peter?

Focus Question 19:
Why is the bishop of Rome the Pope?

FROM *YouCat*

How can we tell what belongs to the true faith?

We find the true faith in Sacred Scripture and in the living Tradition of the Church.

The NEW TESTAMENT developed out of the faith of the Church. Scripture and Tradition belong together. Handing on the faith does not occur primarily through documents. In the early Church it was said that Sacred Scripture was "written on the heart of the Church rather than on parchment." The disciples and the APOSTLES experienced their new life above all through a living fellowship with Jesus. The early Church invited people into this fellowship, which continued in a different way after the Resurrection. The first Christians held fast "to the apostles' teaching and fellowship, to the breaking of the bread and to the prayers" (Acts 2:42). They were united with one another and yet had room for others. This is part of our faith to this day: Christians invite other individuals to come to know a fellowship with God that has been preserved unaltered since the times of the apostles in the Catholic Church. (*YouCat* 12)

Focus Question 20:
How is John referred to in his Gospel?

Focus Question 21:
What was one way John showed his love for Christ?

Focus Question 22:
What did John write?

Focus Question 23:

What is unique about St. Matthew's Gospel?

GUIDED EXERCISE

Perform a focused reading on the section "St. Matthew," using the following question:

✠ What does St. Matthew teach us about the salvation of sinners?

In a focused reading, you read the focus question first, then read the selection with the question in mind, then reread the question, then attempt to answer the question.

GUIDED EXERCISE

After St. Thomas declared his faith in the Resurrection of Christ, Jesus replied to him, "Have you believed because you have seen me? Blessed are those who have not seen and yet believe" (Jn 20:29).

Do a think/pair/share on the following question:

✠ What do you think Christ meant by this comment?

Doubting Thomas by Strozzi.
"My Lord and my God!"

Focus Question 24:

What is the meaning of St. James the Lesser being called a "brother" of Our Lord?

St. Matthew

The Gospels introduce St. Matthew simply as "the tax collector," and it was while on the job that he received his call from Christ. He may have practiced his profession in Capernaum. If so, he might have met Christ and the other Apostles when they were visiting St. Peter's home.

At first glance, a tax collector seems an unlikely choice for an Apostle. Tax collectors were hated by the Jews as public sinners because they worked for the Romans and had a reputation for being dishonest.

The choice of St. Matthew emphasizes the universality of Christ's call. Christ showed through his call of St. Matthew that the Church was to be a refuge for sinners, a means to repentance and forgiveness of sins. As Christ said:

> Those who are well have no need of a physician, but those who are sick; I came, not to call the righteous, but sinners. (Mk 2: 17)

The Gospel relates that St. Matthew, following the call of Christ, underwent a complete conversion, immediately leaving his profession and becoming a disciple.

According to the historian Eusebius, St. Matthew's apostolic mission was directed primarily to the Jews. His Gospel is the only one written in Aramaic, the common language spoken in Palestine during Christ's time. Tradition holds that St. Matthew's Gospel was written to accommodate the Jewish people. He corroborates many details of Christ's life and words with Old Testament quotations.

St. Thomas

St. Thomas's name comes from an Aramaic word meaning "paired" or "twin." The New Testament often refers to him by the Greek word *Didymus* ("twin"), although the reason for this nickname is unknown.

On the day of the Resurrection, St. Thomas was absent when Christ appeared to the Apostles. He therefore refused to believe in the Resurrection, saying, "Unless I see in his hands the print of the nails, and place my finger in the mark of the nails, and place my hand in his side, I will not believe" (Jn 20: 25). This is why he is sometimes popularly known as "Doubting Thomas."

When Christ reappeared eight days later, St. Thomas was present. Christ told him, "Put your finger here, and see my hands; and put out your hand, and place it in my side; do not be faithless, but believing" (Jn 20: 27). St. Thomas then made a profession of faith in the Risen Lord: "My Lord and my God!" (Jn 20: 28).

Sources such as the historian Eusebius[2] claim that St. Thomas evangelized the Parthians in present-day Iran and Turkmenistan; others suggest that he established the Church in India and was martyred there. The Malabar Christians of India claim St. Thomas as their evangelizer. When Portuguese explorers arrived in India in the fifteenth century, they were amazed to find a very old Christian community there, traditionally tracing its founding to St. Thomas.

St. James the Lesser

The other Apostle named James, James the Lesser, came from Nazareth and was the son of Alphaeus and Mary. His Mother may have been Mary, the wife of Clopas, who stood at the Cross with the Mother of Jesus (cf. Jn 19: 25). St. James was most likely related to Christ (cf. Mt 13: 55; Mk 6: 3) as he was called a "brother" of Our Lord, which in the custom of the time was a title given to all close male relatives.

After Pentecost, St. James became the head of the Church in Jerusalem. He was known as one of the most devout Jews in that city, which gave weight to his support for Gentile Christians not having to adopt the Mosaic Law.

The Epistle of St. James shows us a very concrete and practical Christianity. The teachings of Christ must be put into practice, above all, in love of neighbor and in service to the needy. St. James teaches that works are the normal fruit of a living faith.

> A man is justified by works and not by faith alone....For as the body apart from the spirit is dead, so faith apart from works is dead. (Jas 2: 24, 26)

The Jewish historian and contemporary of Christ, Flavius Josephus, wrote in his book *Jewish Antiquities* that St. James was handed over for death by stoning by the High Priest Ananias in AD 62.

St. Andrew, the "First-Called"

Christians of Eastern Europe today revere St. Andrew as the Apostle who first evangelized the region now known as Russia and the Balkans. Because Andrew was the first Apostle chosen by Christ, he is sometimes known as "Andrew the First-Called." St. Andrew was also the brother of St. Peter, and it was Andrew who brought Peter to meet Christ.

Andrew was from Bethsaida, and worked as a fisherman along with Peter. He was first a disciple of St. John the Baptist, but immediately followed Christ when he was called to do so.

After Pentecost, legend has it that St. Andrew traveled throughout Asia Minor, along the region of the Black Sea, and made his way to the hills of the present-day city of Kiev in Ukraine. Pointing out the surrounding hills, he reportedly told his new converts, "See these hills? Upon these hills shall shine forth the beneficence of God, and there will be a great city here, and God shall raise up many churches." He established a church there before moving on to present-day Russia. Then he traveled to Byzantium, in modern Turkey, founded a church there, and served as its first bishop. Byzantium later was renamed Constantinople and became a major center of Christianity. He is also said to have evangelized the modern areas of Georgia, Cyprus, and Romania.

St. Andrew endured much in the way of suffering and rejection during his missionary journeys, even surviving an effort to stone him. He baptized many pagans and worked miracles among the people. He finally came to the city of Patra, in present-day Greece, and is said to have converted almost everyone to the Christian Faith. One he could not convert, however, was the prefect Aegeatos, who ordered that Andrew be executed by crucifixion, tied to the cross rather than nailed. It is said he was crucified on an X-shaped cross at his request as he thought himself unworthy to die as Christ did. His feast is November 30.

CALLED TO BE APOSTLES

The lives of the Apostles reveal the power that the grace of Jesus Christ gives to those called to evangelize. This mission, however, is not only for the Apostles or their successors—bishops, priests, and deacons, who make up the hierarchical Church. All of the Church's members are called to build up the Body of Christ, each one in ways specific to his or her state of life.

Focus Question 25:
What office did St. James hold in the Church later?

The Martyrdom of St. Andrew
by Murillo.

FROM *YouCat*

Why is the Church not a democratic organization?

Democracy operates on the principle that all power comes from the people. In the Church, however, all power comes from Christ. That is why the Church has a hierarchical structure. At the same time, however, Christ gave her a collegial structure as well.

The *hierarchical* element in the Church consists in the fact that Christ himself is the one who acts in the Church when ordained ministers, by God's grace, do or give something that they could not do or give by themselves, in other words, when they administer the SACRAMENTS in Christ's place and teach with his authority. The *collegial* element in the Church consists in the fact that Christ entrusted the entire faith to a group of twelve apostles, whose successors govern the Church, with the Pope, the Petrine ministry presiding. Given this collegial approach, councils are an indispensable part of the Church. Yet even in other administrative bodies of the Church, in synods and councils, the manifold gifts of the Spirit and the universality of the Church throughout the world can be fruitful. (*YouCat* 140)

Pentecost by Juan de Flandes. After Pentecost, the Church grew quickly.

The whole Church is apostolic...in that she is "sent out" into the whole world...."The Christian vocation is, of its nature, a vocation to the apostolate as well." Indeed, we call an apostolate "every activity of the Mystical Body" that aims "to spread the Kingdom of Christ over all the earth."[3] (CCC 863)

Those of us who are incorporated into the Mystical Body of Christ have been given the task of proclaiming the Gospel to all mankind, both through our words and our witness of the Christian life. Through our communion with Christ, especially in the frequent reception of the Eucharist, Christ continues to work in us to draw those around us into the Catholic Church, in which alone subsists his one, holy, catholic, and apostolic Church.

CONCLUSION

After Pentecost, the Church grew quickly. The Apostles—including an additional Apostle, St. Paul, who was called by the Risen Christ himself—began to preach the Gospel as Christ commanded, first in Judea and later in surrounding regions and throughout the world. St. Paul led the primary evangelization efforts in Gentile lands, greatly expanding the reach of the Gospel message. The Church survived despite great persecutions and hostility from Gentiles and Jews alike. Her survival itself presents strong evidence of the guidance and presence of the Holy Spirit in the Church.

In our next chapter, we will delve in more detail into the structure and teaching authority of the Church.

DISCUSSION QUESTIONS

1. Why is the Apostolic period so important in the development of the Church?

2. What mission did Christ give St. Paul?

3. What question had to be decided in the early Church about the Gentiles?

4. How did St. Peter decide that Jewish dietary laws no longer applied to Christians?

5. How did St. Peter decide Gentiles did not need to be circumcised before Baptism?

6. What did the Council of Jerusalem decide about Gentiles?

7. What was the significance of the new name Christ gave Simon?

8. Why is the bishop of Rome the Pope?

9. Who is called to be an apostle?

ENDNOTES – CHAPTER 5

1. Cf. Acts 3:1-4, 11; 4:13, 19-20; 8:14-15.
2. Cf. *Church History*, 3. I.
3. *AA* 2.

The Church
Sacrament of Salvation

Chapter 6
Authority in the Church

The Church hierarchy leads by serving her members.

CHAPTER 6
Authority in the Church

OPENING ACTIVITY

Think for a moment about how service and leadership are connected. Consider some of the leadership roles in society that are in some way a form of service to others: Teacher, police officer, soldier, and health-care worker might be some of these roles that come to mind.

Now think of the Pope, the bishop of your diocese, and the priest(s) and deacon(s) who serve your parish. How do their roles involve both leadership and service? Write a brief essay on this subject.

BASIC QUESTIONS

This chapter attempts to answer the following basic questions:

✠ What is the nature of leadership in the Church?

✠ Why does the Church have a hierarchy?

✠ What does the hierarchy of the Church do?

KEY IDEAS

The key ideas of this chapter are:

✠ The Pope and bishops, with the help of priests and deacons, exercise a servant leadership.

✠ Christ gave the Church a hierarchical authority to teach, rule, and sanctify all her members.

Review of Chapter 5:

✠ St. Paul, who was converted by the Risen Christ himself, became one of the greatest missionary preachers of the early Church. He was key in taking the Gospel into Gentile lands and converting non-Jews to the Gospel.

✠ The controversy over whether Gentile converts had to first become Jews through circumcision and the keeping of dietary laws was decided by St. Peter and the Apostles at the Council of Jerusalem.

✠ Each of the Apostles went forth preaching the Gospel fearlessly as Christ had commanded. Nearly all died martyrs for the Faith.

In this chapter, we will examine the basis of authority in the Church, which is vested in the hierarchy and the Magisterium.

VISIBLE AND INVISIBLE

As mentioned earlier in this text, part of the mystery of the Church as founded by Christ is that it is an invisible reality and visible society. It is both human and divine: Human members make up the Mystical Body of Christ, who is its head.

> The Church is in history, but at the same time she transcends it. It is only "with the eyes of faith"[1] that one can see her in her visible reality and at the same time in her spiritual reality as bearer of divine life. (CCC 770)

The Kingdom of God exists and grows mysteriously in the hearts of those who respond to the call of Christ to be incorporated into his Body, the Church, through Baptism. As one body, united in faith, the members of the Church work and cooperate to help make the Kingdom of God manifest on earth as it journeys toward its ultimate perfection in Heaven. The Church on earth is active as a community striving to live in faith, hope, and charity in the midst of the world.

At the same time, the Church necessarily has a visible structure. As humans living in the world, we rely on physical and visible signs to convey invisible realities. God established a visible structure to the Church in order to communicate his truth and grace to all humanity (cf. CCC 771).

The Kingdom of God, after all, is all about truth. When Christ was on trial and being questioned by Pontius Pilate, the two men had this telling exchange after Pilate asked Christ, "Are you the King of the Jews?":

> Jesus answered, "My kingship is not of this world; if my kingship were of this world, my servants would fight, that I might not be handed over to the Jews; but my kingship is not from the world."

> Pilate said to him, "So you are a king?" Jesus answered, "You say that I am a king. For this I was born, and for this I have come into the world, to bear witness to the truth. Every one who is of the truth hears my voice."

> Pilate said to him, "What is truth?" (Jn 18: 36-38)

What Is Truth? (detail) by Nikolai Gay
Christ shows us the way to holiness and how to live in truth.

Focus Question 1:
What challenge facing the Church today is characterized by Pontius Pilate's question, "What is truth?"

Focus Question 2:
How does the Church help the Kingdom of God to grow on earth?

Christ came "to bear witness to the truth" so that every person might respond and become part of his Kingdom. Christ called himself "the way, and the truth, and the life" (Jn 14: 6), for he shows us the way to holiness and how to live in truth, so that we may attain eternal life. He is our model of holiness. He also entrusted the Church with the responsibility to teach the faithful, indeed the world, his way of life and truth (cf. CCC 2037). In teaching this way of life and truth, the Church helps the Kingdom to grow on earth.

Pilate's response, "What is truth?" appropriately characterizes the challenge facing the Church today and in all generations. There are many in the world who, like Pilate, doubt that there is such a thing as objective truth or that such truth can ever be known with certainty. The presence of such doubt and cynicism in the world only points up more dramatically the divine wisdom on the establishment of the Church: Christ wanted a visible structure of Church authority to govern the faithful and communicate his truth and grace so that all believers may come to imitate him in holiness.

THE HIERARCHICAL CHURCH

A human community needs human leadership. In appointing the Apostles to lead his Church, with St. Peter as the "rock" upon which the Church would be built, Christ provided for just such leadership. These human leaders would not be left to their own devices, however; in addition to the formation and instruction Christ himself provided them during his public ministry and during his post-Resurrection appearances, Christ also sent the Holy Spirit to guide the Church and preserve her from moral and doctrinal error.

St. Peter Enthroned (detail) by Cima.
In the Church, those in authority serve the members by teaching and sanctifying them.

The Church Hierarchy

The structure of authority and governance in the Church is called her *hierarchy*, a term that comes from the Greek word *hierarchia*, meaning "sacred order." In the Church, those in authority—the Pope and those bishops, priests, and deacons in communion with him—serve the members by teaching and sanctifying them.

Focus Question 3:
What is the Church's hierarchy?

Focus Question 4:
What does hierarchy mean?

Focus Question 5:
Describe the difference between the common priesthood of the faithful and the ministerial priesthood.

Focus Question 6:
What is the origin of the hierarchy of the Church?

VOCABULARY

COMMON PRIESTHOOD OF THE FAITHFUL
The priesthood of Christ that is shared by all the baptized, who are called to seek holiness and to give their very lives in service to God.

HIERARCHY
The order of teaching authority in the Church, given such authority by Christ himself, with the Pope as its head, followed by bishops, priests, and deacons; from the Greek *hierarchia* ("sacred order"). It is also an order of service, in which the higher orders serve the lower orders.

LAITY
Lay persons of the Church, who do not receive the Sacrament of Holy Orders or take religious vows.

MINISTERIAL PRIESTHOOD
The ministry exercised by those men called to serve as bishops and priests in the Church. Their ministry is one of service to the faithful of the Church.

We read earlier in the text of how God told Moses his people would become "a kingdom of priests" (Ex 19: 6). This promise is fully realized in the Church. It may surprise you to consider that every member of the Church is a "priest." By virtue of Baptism, every member of the Church is called to seek personal holiness, to offer to God all the work, prayers, and sacrifices of ordinary life, and to serve as a witness of faith to others, thereby helping them to grow in holiness as well. This consecration of our lives is priestly work, and through it we share in the priestly office of Christ. Everyone who is baptized, then, is a member of this *common priesthood of the faithful*. We are, as God promised, a kingdom of priests.

> **But you are a chosen race, a royal priesthood, a holy nation, God's own people, that you may declare the wonderful deeds of him who called you out of darkness into his marvelous light. (1 Pt 2: 9)**

From among this common priesthood, some men are called to receive the Sacrament of Holy Orders, by which they are ordained to serve all the faithful by the authoritative proclamation of the Word of God, the administration of the Sacraments, and in the pastoral leadership of the faithful. These men form the *ministerial priesthood* and the hierarchy of the Church. Members of the faithful who do not receive Holy Orders and who do not belong to a religious state approved by the Church are commonly called lay persons, or simply the *laity*.

The hierarchy of bishops, priests, and deacons was developed while the Twelve Apostles were still alive. Through the Sacrament of Holy Orders, they passed down their authority and their traditions, so that the Church would continue on the course Christ had set for it.

Christ commanded the Apostles and their successors to exercise their authority in imitation of his own spirit of service. At the Last Supper, Christ said to his Apostles:

> **The kings of the Gentiles exercise lordship over [their people]; and those in authority over them are called benefactors. But not so with you; rather let the greatest among you become as the youngest, and the leader as one who serves....I am among you as one who serves. (Lk 22: 25-27)**

The hierarchy of bishops, priests, and deacons was developed while the Twelve Apostles were still alive.

Pope Francis and the College of Cardinals.
One of the Pope's titles is "Servant of the Servants of God."

Pope Francis Greets the Family of God in St. Peter's Square.
The Pope is the apostolic successor of St. Peter and he shares Peter's authority to rule the Church.

VOCABULARY

POPE
Successor of St. Peter; bishop of Rome; supreme pontiff of the Catholic Church. The Pope exercises a primacy of authority as Vicar of Christ and shepherd of the whole Church; he receives the divine assistance promised by Christ.

COLLEGIALITY
The principle that all the bishops of the Church with the Pope at their head form a single "college," which succeeds in every generation the "college" of the Twelve Apostles, with Peter at their head, which Christ instituted as the foundation of the Church.

INFALLIBILITY
Immunity from error and any possibility of error. The gift of the Holy Spirit to the Church whereby the Magisterium can definitively proclaim a doctrine in faith or morals without error. The Church possesses this character as promised by Christ, as does the Pope as defined by the Twentieth Ecumenical Council (Vatican I, 1870).

Although we refer to the various offices of the ministerial priesthood as a hierarchy, we ought not to think of the priests and bishops as "higher" than lay persons in the sense of dominance or control. The Church hierarchy is not one of domination, but of service. Christ's own dramatic example of this *servant leadership* was his washing the feet of the Apostles. The hierarchy of the Church is different from any other governance—such as a government or a corporation—for it is defined not by authoritarianism but rather by service performed out of love. The task of those who are "higher" is to serve those who are "lower," and not the other way around. We can see in this a reflection of God's own love, for although God is infinitely greater than any of his creatures, he demonstrates his greatness by lifting us up and offering us his own divine life of grace. This is why one of the Pope's titles is "Servant of the Servants of God."

The Papacy

The Pope is the apostolic successor of St. Peter and he shares Peter's authority to rule the Church, possessing the gift of infallibility in defining doctrines of faith and morals.

Christ instituted the Church as a collegial body with the Pope at her head.

> When Christ instituted the Twelve, "he constituted [them] in the form of a college or permanent assembly, at the head of which he placed Peter, chosen from among them."[2] Just as "by the Lord's institution, St. Peter and the rest of the apostles constitute a single apostolic college, so in like fashion the Roman Pontiff, Peter's successor, and the bishops, the successors of the apostles, are related with and united to one another."[3] (CCC 880)

> The Lord made Simon alone, whom he named Peter, the "rock" of his Church. He gave him the keys of his Church and instituted him shepherd of the whole flock.[4] "The office of binding and loosing which was given to Peter was also assigned to the college of apostles united to its head."[5] This pastoral office of Peter and the other apostles belongs to the Church's very foundation and is continued by the bishops under the primacy of the Pope. (CCC 881)

Coat of Arms of Pope Francis.
The symbols on the shield represent the Holy Family: IHS for Jesus, the star for the Virgin Mary, the spikenard flower for St. Joseph.

Focus Question 9:

What is the infallibility of the Pope?

Focus Question 10:

What is the Roman Curia, and why does it exist?

Focus Question 11:

What do bishops exercise?

Focus Question 12:

What is a "particular Church"?

VOCABULARY

BISHOP

A consecrated successor to the Apostles, usually given charge of the pastoral and catechetical care of a particular jurisdiction, or diocese; he is called to teach, sanctify, and govern the faithful of his own diocese, and also to work together in caring for the worldwide Church.

DIOCESE

The territory and the churches under a bishop's authority; a community of the Christian faithful in communion of faith and Sacraments with their bishop ordained in Apostolic Succession; also called a "particular church"; in the Eastern Catholic churches, it is called an *eparchy*.

ECUMENICAL COUNCIL

An ecumenical council is a meeting of all the bishops of the world under the authority of the Pope. The word "ecumenical" comes from the Greek word *oikoumene*, meaning "the whole inhabited world." The Council of Jerusalem, described in the Acts of the Apostles, is the scriptural prototype of a council of the whole Church. The most recent Ecumenical Council was the Second Vatican Council (1962-65).

To ensure that the faithful would be truthfully taught, Christ guaranteed that St. Peter and his successors, the Popes, would be free from error—infallible in their public teachings on matters of faith and morals. Papal *infallibility* is made possible by the work of the Holy Spirit in the Church. Hence, the papacy preserves the truth of God that liberates Church members from error.

The Roman Curia

The Roman Curia is the administrative or governing body of the Catholic Church. It assists the Pope in his role as pastor of the universal Church. While the Pope has primary authority over the Church, it is not possible for him to administer this authority in every detail. For this reason, the Popes have traditionally created various offices or ministries to assist them in this responsibility.

The Roman Curia currently consists of the Secretariat of State, nine Congregations, three Tribunals, and twelve Pontifical Councils.

Bishops

Bishops are successors of the Apostles who exercise the fullness of the priesthood of Christ. Only those who have been validly ordained as bishops are able to confer the Sacrament of Holy Orders, whether to the episcopacy, the priesthood, or the diaconate.

Generally, each bishop is entrusted with a "particular Church," that is, a specific diocese (or archdiocese), in which he acts as Christ's chosen representative and the legitimate pastor of all the faithful within that diocese. He is the visible source of unity within the diocese and is responsible for the celebration of the Sacraments—most especially the Eucharist—as well as the teaching and governing of the flock entrusted to his care.

Bishops also remain in fellowship with their brother bishops and are concerned with the universal needs of the Church. Together with the Pope as

The Martyrdom of St. Ignatius. St. Ignatius (ca. 35-108) was the third Bishop of Antioch and a student of John the Apostle. His letters are considered the most important documents linking the Twelve Apostles with the early Church.

Pope Benedict XVI Ordains a Priest for the Diocese of Rome.
Priests also confer all of the Sacraments except for Holy Orders, which is reserved to the bishops.

Focus Question 13:
How are bishops in a *collegial* relationship?

Focus Question 14:
What is an Ecumenical Council?

Focus Question 15:
What is the name of the community normally entrusted to a priest?

Focus Question 16:
What is a priest's most basic task?

VOCABULARY

DEACON
A man who is ordained to assist the mission of the Church; transitional deacons are men who are preparing for ordination to the priesthood; permanent deacons are mature men, married or unmarried, who are ordained deacons in a permanent capacity; from the Greek for "helper."

HOLY ORDERS
The Sacrament of the Catholic Church, instituted by Christ, by which men are ordained to the episcopacy, priesthood, or diaconate.

PARISH
A defined territorial district within a diocese, with its own church and congregation, which is placed in the care of a priest.

PRIEST
In the Old Testament, one of the tribe of Levi. In the New Testament, an abbreviation of the Greek *presbyteros* ("elder"). A member of the order of presbyters; this baptized and confirmed male is ordained to be a co-worker with his bishop, to preside at public liturgies in his stead, and otherwise to assist the bishop in priestly service to the People of God.

their head, they form a single "college" as successors of the Apostles, united in teaching the one true faith. This shared authority and fellowship is called *collegiality*.

One way the bishops exercise this collegiality is through an *ecumenical council*, as we saw in its rudimentary form in the Council of Jerusalem. An Ecumenical Council is a meeting of all the bishops of the world under the authority of the Pope. The word "ecumenical" comes from the Greek word *oikoumene*, meaning "the whole inhabited world."

Ecumenical Councils bring bishops together to discuss central issues of the Church. The bishops meet and debate the questions before them, and ultimately the decision of the whole Church is expressed through the successor of St. Peter, the Pope. The most recent of these councils was the Second Vatican Council (1962-65).

The Priesthood

A diocesan priest is ordained to assist his bishop upon whom he depends for the proper exercise of this priestly power. He is normally assigned to carry out certain tasks of the apostolic ministry, often within an individual parish community. Principal among these tasks is the celebration of the Mass, which the priest offers *in persona Christi capitis* ("in the Person of Christ the Head"). Priests also confer all of the Sacraments except for Holy Orders, which is reserved to the bishops; they can confer Confirmation by special delegation from their bishop.

Religious priests are those who are associated with a particular religious order or institute, such as the Dominicans, Franciscans, or Benedictines. They are ordained to serve the mission of their order and are not necessarily bound to a particular diocese. Many religious priests take vows of chastity, poverty, and obedience. While their obedience is to their religious superior, they must also be obedient to the local bishop while serving in a particular diocese.

Focus Question 17:

What is the role of a deacon?

Focus Question 18:

Describe the difference between a transitional deacon and a permanent deacon.

Focus Question 19:

Even though the Church has a great deal to teach us, why does she have nothing to teach that is her own?

Focus Question 20:

What is the Magisterium?

Focus Question 21:

What are the two areas in which the Church teaches?

Focus Question 22:

Will there be any new revelations in the future?

GUIDED EXERCISE

Free write for a few moments on how the teachings of the Church are both closed in content and open to the development of that content.

VOCABULARY

MAGISTERIUM

The name given to the ordinary and universal teaching authority of the Pope and the bishops in communion with him, who guide the members of the Church without error in matters of faith and morals through the interpretation of Sacred Scripture and Tradition.

This Magisterium guides the members of the Church without error in matters of faith and morals.

The Diaconate

Deacons are ordained to provide a ministry of service (in Greek, *diakonia*). They assist at Mass, preach homilies, baptize, and can preside at the rite of the Sacrament of Matrimony. They are part of the hierarchy, but do not belong to the ministerial priesthood.

There are two types of deacons. Men who are preparing for ordination to the priesthood are ordained as *transitional deacons* for a time before they receive their ordination as priests. Other men, including married men, may be called to serve for life as *permanent deacons*.

THE CHURCH AS TEACHER

Jesus Christ is the greatest teacher the world has ever seen. This is not only because he knew *how* to teach, but also because of the greatness of *what* he taught, an expression of he who is "the way, and the truth, and the life" (Jn 14: 16).

Christ commissioned his Apostles and their successors to teach others what he taught them. The Catholic Faith has a definite content, which includes both intellectual and moral truths. That is to say, it contains both truths about reality and about how we should live. To give just one glimpse of the amazing scope of Catholic teachings, the *Catechism of the Catholic Church* summarizes the Faith in 2,865 paragraphs.

Even though we speak of the "teachings of the Church," the Church simply teaches what Christ has left her in the Deposit of Faith. She does not add anything to Christ's Revelation, nor does she take anything away from it. Just as the moon generates no light of its own, but rather reflects only the light of the sun, the teachings of the Church only reflect the teachings of Christ, who called himself the "Light of the World" (Jn 8: 12). He also called his faithful the "light of the world" (Mt 5: 14), urging us to reflect his own presence to others.

While parents can legitimately teach their children the truths of the Faith and your teacher in a class like this one can guide your instruction, the Church has an official teaching "office" or authority called the *Magisterium* (in Latin, *magister* means "teacher"). The Magisterium is the teaching authority of the Pope and the bishops in communion with him.

> In order to preserve the Church in the purity of the faith handed on by the apostles, Christ who is the Truth willed to confer on her a share in his own infallibility. By a "supernatural sense of faith" the People of God, under the guidance of the Church's living Magisterium, "unfailingly adheres to this faith."[6] (CCC 889)

This Magisterium guides the members of the Church without error in matters of faith and morals. Examples of matters of faith are the nature of the Blessed Trinity, the nature of Jesus Christ, the Virgin Birth, and the Eucharist. Examples of matters of morals are answers to questions regarding the moral limits of warfare and self-defense, marriage and sexuality, and issues in economic and social justice. The Magisterium correctly interprets the natural moral law and Divine Revelation because it enjoys the guidance of the Holy Spirit in truth.

Because Jesus Christ is the full and final Revelation of God, nothing "new" is ever going to be revealed to us. At the same time, the Church grows in her understanding of the Deposit of Faith over the centuries, even in terms of the identity of Christ. The Magisterium reflected upon the nature of the

Focus Question 23:
What are the Eastern Catholic Churches?

UNITED IN FAITH: EASTERN CATHOLIC CHURCHES

 arlier in the text, we discussed the various meanings of the word "church." Here it would be helpful to clarify that the Catholic Church includes not only the Western, or Latin, Church, but also the twenty-one Eastern Catholic Churches that are in union with the Pope, the successor of St. Peter. These churches include the Maronite Catholic Church, the Greek Catholic Church, the Armenian Catholic Church, the Syro-Malabar Catholic Church, and others.

These Churches are called "Eastern" because they developed historically when the Church had five *patriarchates*—Rome, Antioch, Alexandria, Jerusalem, and Byzantium (or Constantinople)—each headed by a bishop, with the bishop of Rome, the Pope, having primacy. These churches were founded and developed from the communities formed by the first Apostles in various parts of the Eastern world. Tragically, a series of disputes regarding Church doctrine and authority resulted in various Eastern Churches breaking away from their union with the Roman pontiff, culminating in a definitive schism involving nearly all the Eastern Churches that occurred in AD 1054.

Over time, portions of the faithful and their bishops from the various Eastern Churches returned to unity with Rome. These are the Eastern Catholic Churches of today. (Those Eastern Churches that remain separated from Rome are called Eastern Orthodox Churches.) The Maronite Catholic Church has the distinction of being the only Eastern Catholic Church never to have separated from allegiance to Rome.

The Eastern Catholic Churches have their own set of church laws, i.e., canon law; their own local bishops, who also are successors of the Apostles; and their own dioceses (called *eparchies*). They celebrate the same Seven Sacraments, which they call *divine mysteries*, and the Mass, which they call the *divine liturgy*. They use a variety of liturgical rites that resemble the rites of the Roman Catholic Church but which developed independently throughout their histories. Because these Churches are in communion with Rome, members of the Roman Catholic faithful can attend Sunday Mass and receive the Eucharist in the Eastern Catholic Churches and vice versa. Their doctrine and spirituality are fully compatible with the Western Church but often stress different truths or aspects of the same Faith.

These Churches, together with the Western Church, make up the "one, holy, catholic and apostolic Church" that we profess in the Creed. While these individual Churches have their cultural and historical differences, they share the same beliefs and recognize the authority of the Pope. Because they are united in their beliefs, Sacraments, apostolic origins, and upon the "rock" of the successor of St. Peter, all the members of the faithful are rightly called "Catholic."

VOCABULARY

PATRIARCHATE

Any of the five regional centers of early Christianity, based in Rome, Antioch, Alexandria, Jerusalem, and Byzantium (or Constantinople), each headed by a bishop, with the bishop of Rome (or Pope) having primacy.

An iconostasis is a screen of icons used in the Eastern Churches. It separates the nave, where the people meet for worship, from the sanctuary and altar where the Eucharist is celebrated.

CLOSURE

Describe the similarities and differences between the Roman Catholic Church and the Eastern Catholic Churches.

ALTERNATIVE ASSESSMENT

Read the following selection from Luke's Gospel.

And he said to them, "The kings of the Gentiles exercise lordship over [their people]; and those in authority over them are called benefactors. But not so with you; rather let the greatest among you become as the youngest, and the leader as one who serves....I am among you as one who serves." (Lk 22: 25-27)

Then free write on the following question:

⚒ How does (1) the way that Christ instructed his Apostles to exercise their leadership in the Church reflect (2) the way God the Father rules over creation and (3) how Christ brought salvation into the world?

Christ Handing the Keys to St. Peter (detail) by Perugino.

The teachings of Christ are true for all time, even to the end of time.

Blessed Trinity for centuries as it discerned the truth about how Christ is both fully human and fully divine. Remember that something is called a mystery because it is inexhaustible and can never be fully understood; we can deepen our understanding with time and reflection without ever fully exhausting the depths of the mystery. So it is with the mystery of God.

The teachings of Christ are true for all time, even to the end of time. The world, however, continually changes and evolves: New ideas and philosophies arise, new inventions are generated, cultures go through transformations, and even the language we use to communicate develops over the course of time. These factors can vary widely among the various parts of the world.

The Church's doctrines, therefore, also must be articulated in new ways as new situations arise in history, culture, or science. We can see contemporary examples of this in the world of science. The Apostolic Church once had no teaching on the morality of *in vitro* fertilization or embryonic stem-cell research, since these questions arose only in the course of relatively recent developments in scientific research. The Church has had to speak to these moral questions based on the moral principles taught by Christ and mediated by the Church through the centuries. In the mid-to-late-1900s, the development of nuclear arms raised new questions pertaining to armed aggression; more recently, various groups arguing for euthanasia or assisted suicide and certain advances in medical life-support for terminally-ill patients have also surfaced moral questions which the Church has had to answer. The Church continually must consider the principles of moral law it has received from Christ and apply them to whatever issues develop in every generation.

DISCUSSION QUESTIONS

1. How does the Church help the Kingdom of God to grow on earth?

2. What is the Church's hierarchy?

3. Describe the difference between the common priesthood of the faithful and the ministerial priesthood.

4. What is "servant leadership"?

5. What is the infallibility of the Pope?

6. What are the roles of bishops, priests, and deacons?

7. What is the Magisterium?

8. Will there be any new revelations in the future?

9. What are the Eastern Catholic Churches?

ENDNOTES – CHAPTER 6

1. *Roman Catechism* I, 10, 20.
2. *LG* 19; cf. Lk 6: 13; Jn 21: 15-17.
3. *LG* 22; cf. CIC, 330.
4. Cf. Mt 16: 18-19; Jn 21: 15-17.
5. *LG* 22 §2.
6. *LG* 12; cf. *DV* 10.

Chapter 7
Church of the Word and the Sacraments

The Sacraments give us what we need in order to receive and remain in communion with God and one another.

CHAPTER 7
Church of the Word and the Sacraments

OPENING ACTIVITY

Incorporate Christ's feeding of the five thousand into the class's Opening Prayer (Jn 6: 1-13).

After this Jesus went to the other side of the Sea of Galilee, which is the Sea of Tiberias. And a multitude followed him, because they saw the signs which he did on those who were diseased. Jesus went up on the mountain, and there sat down with his disciples.

Now the Passover, the feast of the Jews, was at hand. Lifting up his eyes, then, and seeing that a multitude was coming to him, Jesus said to Philip, "How are we to buy bread, so that these people may eat?" This he said to test him, for he himself knew what he would do. Philip answered him, "Two hundred denarii would not buy enough bread for each of them to get a little." One of his disciples, Andrew, Simon Peter's brother, said to him, "There is a lad here who has five barley loaves and two fish; but what are they among so many?" Jesus said, "Make the people sit down." Now there was much grass in the place; so the men sat down, in number about five thousand. Jesus then took the loaves, and when he had given thanks, he distributed them to those who were seated; so also the fish, as much as they wanted. And when they had eaten their fill, he told his disciples, "Gather up the fragments left over, that nothing may be lost." So they gathered them up and filled twelve baskets with fragments from the five barley loaves, left by those who had eaten.

Free write for a minute on what strikes you most about this event.

Share your responses.

Review of Chapter 6:

✠ Christ established the Church with a hierarchy for the purpose of governing the faithful and communicating his truth and grace to the world.

✠ Members of the hierarchy—the Pope, bishops, priests, and deacons—are servants of the Church who are commissioned to teach and sanctify the faithful.

✠ The Magisterium, or teaching authority of the Church, under the guidance of the Holy Spirit, teaches on matters of faith and morals without error.

In this chapter, we will study how the ministry of the Church is entrusted by Christ with the Word of God and the Sacraments he instituted in order to confer grace to his faithful.

THE GREAT COMMISSION

Recall how Christ commissioned the Apostles to "make disciples of all nations, baptizing them in the name of the Father and of the Son and of the Holy Spirit, teaching them to observe all that I have commanded you" (Mt 28: 19-20).

This mandate is full of meaning:

✠ To become a disciple of Christ, a person must hear his invitation to salvation and respond to it. In other words, a person must receive the "good news," the Gospel preached by Christ, and make a willful choice to accept the great gift of redemption. To "make disciples of all nations," then, means that the Apostles are to preach the Gospel everywhere and exhort their listeners to respond in faith.

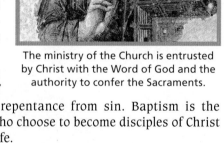

The ministry of the Church is entrusted by Christ with the Word of God and the authority to confer the Sacraments.

✠ To respond to the Gospel in faith, to enter the Kingdom of God, requires conversion and repentance from sin. Baptism is the Sacrament conferred on those who choose to become disciples of Christ and accept his offer of eternal life.

✠ To teach these disciples "all that I have commanded you" means the Apostles teach authoritatively in Christ's name. This teaching authority, as we have seen, extends to the successors of the Apostles, the Magisterium of the Church today.

The Church, then, has been entrusted with the authoritative preaching and teaching of God's own Word, both in Scripture and in Tradition, and with the authority to confer the Sacraments instituted by Christ.

St. Peter Preaching in the Presence of St. Mark by Fra Angelico.
The authentic interpretation of the Word of God, both in Scripture and in Tradition, is the task of the bishops of the Church united under the Pope, the successor of St. Peter.

ENTRUSTED WITH THE WORD

In preaching and teaching the Gospel to all nations, the Apostles primarily communicated the Word of God orally and in their lived example. In this way, they taught according to the word and example of Christ himself and according to the guidance of what the Holy Spirit had taught them. Their teachings and their continued expression through the Church, a living transmission inspired by the Holy Spirit, is called *Sacred Tradition* or just *Tradition*.

The Apostles and some who were associated with them also committed some of their acts and teaching to writing, also under the inspiration of the Holy Spirit. These are the Scriptures of the New Testament that have been handed down through the generations.

Together, Scripture and Tradition form one *Deposit of Faith*. This is the Faith which the Church continues to teach throughout the ages. As the *Catechism* points out:

> [T]he Church, to whom the transmission and interpretation of Revelation is entrusted, "does not derive her certainty about all revealed truths from the holy Scriptures alone. Both Scripture and Tradition must be accepted and honored with equal sentiments of devotion and reference."[1] (CCC 82)

The teaching authority of the Church, in turn, entrusts this sacred Deposit of Faith to all the faithful. The authentic interpretation of the Word of God, both in Scripture and in Tradition, is the task of the bishops of the Church united under the Pope, the successor of St. Peter.

Yet, the Magisterium is not to be understood as somehow "owning" this Word, as though the Church can interpret it however she pleases, but rather as at its service, seeking only to teach according to the mind of Christ. The faithful, therefore, properly receive and assent to her teachings in faith; for as Christ told his Apostles with regard to their preaching, "He who hears you, hears me" (Lk 10: 16; cf. CCC 84-87).

BASIC QUESTIONS

This chapter attempts to answer the following basic questions:

- What is a Sacrament?
- What is each of the Seven Sacraments?

KEY IDEAS

The key ideas of this chapter are:

- A Sacrament is an efficacious sign of grace, instituted by Christ and entrusted to the Church, by which divine life is dispensed.
- Baptism conquers Original Sin and makes us children of God.
- Confirmation completes Baptism, equipping the Christian for active participation in the life of the Church.
- The Eucharist is the true Body and Blood of Christ, which the faithful consume in Holy Communion.
- Penance is the Sacrament of God's forgiveness for post-baptismal sins.
- Anointing of the Sick is for those in danger of death.
- Holy Orders has three distinct orders—bishop (episcopate), priest (presbyterate), and deacon (diaconate).
- The Sacrament of Matrimony raises natural marriage to the dignity of a Sacrament.

Focus Question 1:
Summarize the meaning of the Great Commission.

Focus Question 2:
What is the Deposit of Faith?

Focus Question 3:
Who is entrusted with the authentic interpretation of Scripture and Tradition?

Focus Question 4:
What is a Sacrament?

Focus Question 5:
Why is Baptism called the "gateway" to the Sacraments?

Focus Question 6:
What is a useful way to group the Sacraments according to type?

VOCABULARY

GRACE

The free and unmerited favor of God given, first of all, through the Sacraments. Grace is a share in the divine life infused into the soul by the Holy Spirit to heal from sin and to sanctify.

Baptism is sometimes called the "gateway" to the Sacraments because it is the first to be received.

THE SEVEN SACRAMENTS

In instructing his Apostles to baptize those who respond positively to the Gospel message, Christ empowered his Apostles to confer this great Sacrament on new believers. We have mentioned the word "sacrament" already many times in this text. But what is a Sacrament?

A Sacrament is "an efficacious sign of grace, instituted by Christ and entrusted to the Church, by which divine life is dispensed to us" (CCC 1131). It is a visible sign that invisibly confers God's grace. The Sacraments of the Church are the channels of God's grace, which make it possible for us to become holy. They are seven in number: Baptism, Confirmation, the Eucharist, Penance, Anointing of the Sick, Holy Orders, and Matrimony.

A Sacrament is more than just a symbol. A symbol only represents something, but does not cause it to happen. A crown is a symbol of royalty, but simply putting on a crown does not make someone a king or queen. In contrast, the external, visible rite of the Sacrament is an *efficacious sign* because it actually accomplishes what it signifies.

Baptism is sometimes called the "gateway" to the Sacraments because it is the first to be received. By calling upon the Apostles in his final instructions to baptize—and, elsewhere, to forgive sins and celebrate the Eucharist—Christ gave the Apostles the authority and responsibility of conferring his grace to the faithful through his Sacraments.

There is a useful way of grouping the Sacraments according to type. The Sacraments of Baptism, Confirmation, and the Eucharist incorporate one

The external, visible rite of the Sacrament is an efficacious sign.

into the Christian life, so they are called *Sacraments of Initiation*. Penance and the Anointing of the Sick heal soul and body, so they are *Sacraments of Healing*. Holy Orders and Matrimony serve the family of the Church and the family of husband, wife, and children, so they are *Sacraments of Service*.

Here we will look briefly at each of the Seven Sacraments.

Baptism

In the Sacrament of Baptism, the efficacious sign is the pouring of water and recitation of the ritual words of Baptism. Water provides a symbol of washing and cleansing, and so this Sacrament washes away the stain of Original Sin and all actual sins from the person's soul.

St. John the Baptist performed a purely symbolic baptism, one that Christ himself received at the River Jordan. But even the Baptist acknowledged to his listeners that the Baptism that Christ would give would be something entirely different: "I baptize you with water for repentance, but he who is coming after me is mightier than I, whose sandals I am not worthy to carry; he will baptize you with the Holy Spirit and with fire" (Mt 3: 11).

Christ spoke of the Baptism he intended to institute when he said to the Pharisee Nicodemus, "Truly, truly, I say to you, unless one is born of water and the Spirit, he cannot enter the Kingdom of God" (Jn 3: 5). During his public ministry, Christ already had his Apostles baptizing new converts to the Faith (Jn 4: 2).

As we have seen, as he was about to ascend into Heaven, Christ commanded his Apostles to baptize "in the name of the Father, and of the Son, and of the Holy Spirit." Baptism figures prominently in the Acts of the Apostles and in the various Epistles, as we find frequent reference to Baptism being conferred upon individuals, entire households, or even thousands of new converts in a single day (cf. Acts 2: 41).

The Sacrament of Baptism:

- ✠ gives us a new birth in water and the Holy Spirit that fills us with sanctifying grace, or the grace of *justification*;

- ✠ removes all sin, both Original Sin and actual sins, i.e., those sins actually committed;

- ✠ unites us to the Death, Burial, and Resurrection of Christ;

- ✠ incorporates us into the Mystical Body of Christ, which is the Church;

- ✠ gives us new life and makes us adopted sons and daughters of God the Father;

- ✠ makes us a "new creature" and gives us a share in the divine nature of God;

- ✠ grants us the *theological virtues* of faith, hope, and love (or charity);

- ✠ calls us to seek perfect holiness through the exercise of the moral virtues;

- ✠ consecrates us to the worship of God; and

- ✠ calls us to serve God and neighbor as members of the common priesthood of the faithful.

Baptism can be received only once because it leaves an indelible *sacramental character* or *seal* that configures the recipient to Christ and his Church: One who is baptized now "belongs" to Christ. This seal marks us for redemption, like a passport for eternal life, which is ours if we remain faithful to our baptismal commitment.

Focus Question 7:
When did Christ institute the Sacrament of Baptism?

Focus Question 8:
What are three effects of Baptism?

Focus Question 9:
Why can Baptism not be repeated?

VOCABULARY

JUSTIFICATION
The gift of God's sanctifying grace by which we are made right in the eyes of God.

SACRAMENTAL CHARACTER (or SEAL)
An indelible mark conferred by the Sacraments of Baptism, Confirmation, and Holy Orders that configures the Christian to Christ and his Church, remains within him or her as a positive disposition for grace, promises and guarantees divine protection, and grants him or her a vocation to divine worship and to the service of the Church. Therefore, these Sacraments can be received validly only once in a lifetime.

THEOLOGICAL VIRTUES
The supernatural gifts of faith, hope, and love (or charity) given to us by the grace of Baptism.

The Baptism of Christ (detail) by Corot. St. John the Baptist performed a purely symbolic baptism, one that Christ himself received at the River Jordan.

Focus Question 10:

When did Christ confer the Sacrament of Confirmation upon the first members of the Church?

Focus Question 11:

What is the "laying on of hands" that followed Baptism in the early Church?

Focus Question 12:

What are the effects of the Sacrament of Confirmation?

VOCABULARY

SACRED CHRISM

Perfumed oil used for consecration in the Sacraments of Baptism, Confirmation, and Holy Orders; the oil is consecrated by the bishop and signifies the gift of the Holy Spirit.

Focus Question 13:

What is the connection between manna and the Eucharist?

Focus Question 14:

What kind of life does Christ promise the Eucharist will give us?

Focus Question 15:

When did Christ institute the Sacrament of the Eucharist?

Pentecost by Restout.
Confirmation is sometimes described as making one a "soldier of Christ."

Confirmation

During his public ministry, Christ had promised the Apostles he would send the Holy Spirit to them after he returned to the Father. As we read in Chapter 4, this promise was fulfilled at Pentecost, when the Spirit descended on the Apostles as in a mighty wind and "tongues as of fire, distributed and resting on each one of them." Filled with the Holy Spirit, the Apostles went outside and began to preach the Gospel.

The Acts of the Apostles recounts how when the Apostles baptized a convert, they also laid their hands on the new believer. "[W]hen Paul had laid his hands upon them, the Holy Spirit came on them; and they spoke with tongues and prophesied" (Acts 19: 5-6).

The Sacrament of Confirmation, along with the Sacraments of Baptism and the Eucharist, collectively are called the Sacraments of Initiation because together they fully initiate the believer into the Christian community. "[B]y the sacrament of Confirmation, [the baptized] are more perfectly bound to the Church and are enriched with a special strength of the Holy Spirit. Hence they are, as true witnesses of Christ, more strictly obliged to spread and defend the faith by word and deed."[2] This is why Confirmation is sometimes described as making one a "soldier of Christ."

The signs of the Sacrament of Confirmation, which "confirms" one's Baptism, are the laying on of hands and the anointing with *Sacred Chrism*, an act added in the early Church to better signify the gift of the Holy Spirit (cf. CCC 1289). The ordinary minister of Confirmation is a bishop, although a priest may receive permission to confer this Sacrament in some circumstances.

Eucharist

As we read in Chapter 3, Christ established the Sacrament of the Eucharist at his Last Supper, when he consecrated the bread and wine of the Passover celebration and changed it into his own Body and Blood, inviting those gathered to partake of this meal. This act completes the meaning of what Christ said earlier in the Gospel when he told the crowd:

[U]nless you eat the flesh of the Son of man and drink his blood, you have no life in you; he who eats my flesh and drinks my blood has eternal life, and I will raise him up at the last day. For my flesh is food indeed, and my blood is drink indeed. (Jn 6: 53-55)

In telling his Apostles to "do this in memory of me," Christ directed his Apostles, his first priests, to celebrate the Eucharist, which is the Mass. As we read earlier, in the Mass, the unique sacrifice of Christ on the Cross is perpetually re-presented (made present) on the altar.

> The sacrifice of Christ and the sacrifice of the Eucharist are *one single sacrifice*: "The victim is one and the same: the same now offers through the ministry of priests, who then offered himself on the cross; only the manner of offering is different." "And since in this divine sacrifice which is celebrated in the Mass, the same Christ who offered himself once in a bloody manner on the altar of the cross is contained and is offered in an unbloody manner...this sacrifice is truly propitiatory [makes peace between God and man]."[3] (CCC 1367)

Like the Passover meal, the Mass is also a sacrifice of praise and thanksgiving. The word *eucharist* means "thanksgiving."

Although the bread and wine do not change in appearance, they are transformed into the Body and Blood of Christ. The Church calls this change *transubstantiation* to indicate a change in substance but not in appearance. *Real Presence* is the term used to describe Christ's true and substantial presence under the appearance of bread and wine.

From the beginning days of the Church, the faithful "devoted themselves to the Apostles' teaching and fellowship, to the breaking of bread and the prayers" (Acts 2: 42), in other words, to what we today call the Mass. The Church soon established Sunday, the day of Christ's Resurrection, as the appropriate day each week to celebrate the Eucharist, which today and throughout time "remains the center of the Church's life" (CCC 1343).

The faithful benefit profoundly from participating in the Mass and receiving the Eucharist worthily, and they are encouraged to do so often. To be worthy, one must be in full communion with the Church and free from mortal sin.

The Last Supper (detail) by Bouts.
In telling his Apostles to "do this in memory of me," Christ directed his Apostles, his first priests, to celebrate the Eucharist, which is the Mass.

Focus Question 16:
When one receives the Eucharist, what is one receiving?

Focus Question 17:
What is the connection between the Eucharist and the Sacrifice of Christ on the Cross?

Focus Question 18:
What does *eucharist* mean?

Focus Question 19:
What is *transubstantiation*?

Focus Question 20:
What does the term "the breaking of the bread" mean in the New Testament?

Focus Question 21:
What are the two conditions for worthy reception of the Eucharist?

GUIDED EXERCISE

Do a think/pair/share on the following question:

- Based on what Christ said to people who felt repelled by his talk about eating his body and drinking his blood ("unless you eat the flesh of the Son of Man..."), how would you respond to people who say the Eucharist is only a symbolic meal?

VOCABULARY

REAL PRESENCE
Name given to the truth that Christ is fully, truly, and substantially present in the Eucharist under the appearance of bread and wine.

TRANSUBSTANTIATION
Scholastic term used by the Church to describe how the bread and wine are changed into the Eucharist; consecration of the bread and wine by a priest at Mass changes the substance of the bread and wine into the Body and Blood of Christ while leaving the appearances or forms of bread and wine.

THANKSGIVING
Prayer that expresses gratitude to God for his blessings and care; one of the four main types of prayer.

Focus Question 22:
When did Christ institute the Sacrament of Penance?

Focus Question 23:
What are mortal and venial sins?

VOCABULARY

ABSOLUTION

An essential element of the Sacrament of Penance in which the priest, by the power entrusted to the Church by Christ, pardons the sins of the penitent.

CONCUPISCENCE

Our tendency to sin and our vulnerability to sin; a lingering result of Original Sin.

CONTRITION

Sorrow of the soul and hatred for the sin committed, together with a resolution not to sin again. It is the most important act of the penitent and is necessary for the reception of the Sacrament of Penance. It is one of the four main types of prayer.

PENANCE

The Sacrament of God's forgiveness in which the penitent is reconciled with God and with the Church. The acts of the penitent—contrition, confession of sins, and satisfaction or reparation—together with the prayer of absolution by the priest, constitute the essential elements of the Sacrament of Penance. The Sacrament is also called Reconciliation or Confession. The word *penance* also refers to the particular prayers or acts the penitent is assigned by the priest as satisfaction for the sins confessed.

RESTITUTION

The act of compensation by a penitent, whenever possible, for the damage done to another person, or to his or her possessions or reputation as a result of sin (*see* SATISFACTION).

SATISFACTION

In the context of the Sacrament of Penance, an act whereby the sinner makes amends for sin, especially in reparation to God for offenses against him; the penance assigned by the priest during confession is the reparation for that sin.

"'Be merciful, even as your Father is merciful. Judge not, and you will not be judged; condemn not, and you will not be condemned; forgive, and you will be forgiven.'"
(Lk 6: 36-37)

Penance

Although Baptism washes away our sins, we nevertheless commit actual sins after Baptism. This is due to *concupiscence*, our tendency toward sin, a lingering result of Original Sin. For this reason, we need to receive frequently the grace of God for the forgiveness of our sins. This access is available through the Sacrament of Penance.

The principle purpose of Christ's mission of Redemption was to release humanity from its bondage to sin and make it possible for us to enjoy eternal life with God in Heaven. During his public ministry, Christ often forgave people's sins, something his opponents considered blasphemous because only God can forgive sins.

Recall from Chapter 4 that one of the first things Christ did after rising from the dead was to give the Apostles, his first priests and bishops, the authority to forgive sins (cf. Jn 20: 22-23). The Apostles exercised this authority and preached about the confession of sins among the first Christian communities. "If we confess our sins, [God] is faithful and just," said St. John, "and will forgive our sins and cleanse us from all unrighteousness" (1 Jn 1: 9). St. Paul makes the further clarification that "confession" is something you do "with your mouth," not just with your heart and mind (cf. Rom 10: 10).

Confession of sins is also taught in the *Didache*, a first century Christian document: "Thou shalt confess thy transgressions in the Church and shalt not come unto prayer with an evil conscience." It also speaks of the importance of confession before receiving Communion: "On the Lord's Day gather together, break bread and give thanks, first confessing your sins so that your sacrifice may be pure."

The Church distinguishes two degrees of sin. *Venial sins* are lesser offenses that harm our relationship with God. *Mortal sins*—sins of a grave matter that we commit with forethought and full consent of the will—break our communion with God and his Church, rendering us unable to receive the Eucharist in Holy Communion until those mortal sins are forgiven and our communion restored through the Sacrament of Penance. In this great Sacrament, the priest acts in the Person of Christ the Head; it is Christ himself who forgives through the ministry of the priest.

The Sacrament of Penance necessarily involves not just words, but also an interior conversion. We must truly repent by admitting our sins and turning away from sin; we must have true *contrition*, sorrow for what we have done, and resolve to avoid all future sin; we must confess these sins before God through his priest; we must receive *absolution* from the sins from the priest; and we must complete whatever act of penance, *satisfaction*, or *restitution* the priest requires of us.

Frequent use of the Sacrament of Penance strengthens us against sin and helps us live more closely in accordance with the will of God.

Anointing of the Sick

As we read in Chapter 3, Christ cured many people of their diseases and disabilities. Healing was a foreshadowing of the coming Kingdom of God, a proof that Christ was the promised Messiah (cf. Lk 7: 20-23).

Christ often used physical signs to heal, such as the laying on of hands, mud, washing, even his own spittle. Often he asked the person seeking healing to believe in him. On one occasion, a woman of great faith was cured merely by touching his garment.

During his public ministry, Christ also empowered the Apostles to heal the sick and cast out demons. "So they went out and preached that men should repent. And they cast out many demons, and anointed with oil many that were sick and healed them" (Mk 6: 13). After the Resurrection, the Acts of the Apostles relate how the Apostles were able to do great "works" of healing, in much the same way that Christ did, including the remarkable story of how St. Peter first cured a man who had been paralyzed for eight years and then raised a woman from the dead (cf. Acts 9: 32-42).

The Letter of St. James also bears witness to this Sacrament in the early Church and how the elders (priests) used oil in the healing ritual.

> Is any among you sick? Let him call for the elders of the church, and let them pray over him, anointing him with oil in the name of the Lord; and the prayer of faith will save the sick man, and the Lord will raise him up; and if he has committed sins, he will be forgiven. (Jas 5: 14-15)

The Church continues to exercise Christ's healing power today by the Sacrament of the Anointing of the Sick through the ministry of a priest, who confers the Sacrament by the laying on of hands and the anointing with the Oil of the Sick. The Sacrament can be administered for any illness or condition where there is a danger of death.

Anointing of the Sick gives the suffering person peace and courage to overcome the trials and difficulties of illness or infirmity. It empowers him or her to participate in the saving Passion of Christ. It forgives sins if the person is not able to make a confession. In some instances, the Sacrament also will help restore the patient to health, if it is God's will.

Physical healing is not always part of God's plan, however—after all, we all eventually must die. However, in every case, we need grace to suffer well and to prepare our souls for death. When St. Paul asked that a "thorn," which had tormented him for a long time, be taken away, Christ's reply was, "My grace is sufficient for you, for my power is made perfect in weakness" (2 Cor 12: 9). The Sacrament of the Anointing of the Sick supplies this grace.

Focus Question 24:
Did Christ use physical signs when he healed people?

Focus Question 25:
What is the physical sign used in the Anointing of the Sick?

Focus Question 26:
What are the usual effects of the Anointing of the Sick?

GUIDED EXERCISE

In the time of Christ and the Apostles, the main effect of the Anointing of the Sick seemed to be miraculous healing. Today, the main effect seems to be helping the afflicted person face death well.

Discuss why this might be an appropriate change.

For example, what would be the effect if Anointing of the Sick always produced a miraculous healing?

VOCABULARY

EXTREME UNCTION
A term formerly used for the Sacrament of the Anointing of the Sick; it is no longer used because it refers to the use of the Sacrament only in instances of imminent death, whereas the Church encourages the Sacrament for anyone in danger of death from disease, infirmity, or old age.

We need grace to suffer well and to prepare our souls for death.

Focus Question 27:

When did Christ institute the Sacrament of Holy Orders?

Focus Question 28:

What are the three degrees in the Sacrament of Holy Orders?

Focus Question 29:

What are some of the main responsibilities of priests and bishops?

Focus Question 30:

What are the three "marks" of Holy Orders?

VOCABULARY

ORDINAND

The man to be ordained in the Sacrament of Holy Orders.

ORDINATION

The rite by which the Sacrament of Holy Orders, which "ordains" a man to the episcopate, presbyterate, or diaconate, is celebrated.

Focus Question 31:

When did God create marriage?

Focus Question 32:

What effect has Original Sin had on relations between the sexes?

The Sacrament of Matrimony is a vocation of service.

Feed My Lambs (detail) by Tissot.
In calling the Twelve Apostles and making St. Peter their head, Christ created the Church with a hierarchy.

Holy Orders

As we read in previous chapters, in calling the Twelve Apostles and making St. Peter their head, Christ created the Church with a hierarchy. In the decades after the Ascension of Christ, as we read in the New Testament, the Church developed her hierarchy into the three degrees of episcopate, presbyterate, and diaconate—bishops, priests, and deacons.

Christ conferred upon the Apostles the power and obligation to baptize, to forgive sins, to anoint with oil, and to celebrate the Eucharist. Administering the Sacraments is central to this apostolic ministry. Holy Orders, thus, "is the sacrament through which the mission entrusted by Christ to his apostles continues to be exercised in the Church until the end of time" (CCC 1536).

The conferral of Holy Orders is called *ordination* after the ancient Roman term *ordo*, which referred to an established governing body. Because Christ was male and chose only males as his Apostles, Holy Orders is conferred only upon men.

The Sacrament of Holy Orders is conferred by a bishop. During the Rite of Ordination, the bishop lays his hands on the *ordinand* (the person receiving the Sacrament) and prays that God will pour out his Holy Spirit on him or her. Like Baptism, Holy Orders imprints an indelible sacramental character on the person who receives it (cf. CCC 1597). And Holy Orders is said to have three "marks": service to God and the faithful; fellowship with one's brother priests, deacons, and bishops; and the personal responsibility to be faithful to one's vocation.

Matrimony

As we read in Genesis, God created human beings male and female with a mission to "be fruitful and multiply, and fill the earth." The Sacred Author goes on to explain that the union of one man and one woman is God's plan: "Therefore a man leaves his father and mother and cleaves to his wife, and they become one flesh" (Gn 2:24).

God's plan for man and woman was disrupted but not destroyed by Original Sin. Instead of the equality and complementarity that man and woman were meant to enjoy, lust, domination, disrespect, and discord entered male-female relationships.

Christ restored marriage to its original meaning and elevated it to the dignity of a Sacrament. When some Pharisees asked him about the Mosaic provisions allowing divorce, Christ replied:

> Have you not read that he who made them from the beginning "made them male and female" and said, "For this reason a man shall leave his father and mother and be joined to his wife, and the two shall become one flesh?" So they are no longer two but one flesh. What therefore God has joined together, let not man put asunder. [In answer to a further question about divorce, Jesus said] I say to you, whoever divorces his wife...and marries another, commits adultery. (Mt 19: 1-6, 9)

St. Paul wrote of married love extensively in his Letter to the Ephesians. In fact, he says that the model that God used when he created marriage between a man and woman was the relationship between Christ and his Church (cf. Eph 5: 25-26, 31-32).

The Sacrament of Matrimony is a vocation of service. Husbands and wives assist each other in living the Faith, helping each other to grow in sanctity so as to someday enjoy eternal life. If blessed with children, they are called to raise them lovingly in the Catholic Faith.

The Sacrament of Matrimony is unique in that it is the man and woman themselves who are the ministers of the Sacrament. Matrimonial sacramental grace perfects the couple's love and strengthens their unity (cf. CCC 1641).

Focus Question 33:
Why is divorce impossible from Christ's point of view?

Focus Question 34:
On what did God model human marriage?

Focus Question 35:
What is the effect of Matrimonial grace?

Focus Question 36:
Who is the minister of the Sacrament of Matrimony in the Western Church?

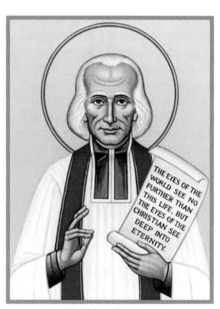
St. John Vianney.
Patron saint of parish priests.

ST. JOHN VIANNEY

 nown as the Curé (curate or priest) of Ars, St. John Vianney lived from 1786-1859.

Although he had a vocation to the priesthood, he also suffered from what we might today call a learning disability. He had an incredibly difficult time in his priestly studies, especially learning Latin. He even flunked his final seminary examinations and had to retake them. Following his ordination, he was assigned to Ars, an out-of-the-way village in rural France. Before long, people began coming to him for spiritual direction from other parishes, then from all over France, and finally from around the world.

Toward the end of his life, he would spend from sixteen to eighteen hours a day in the confessional giving spiritual direction. Bishops, priests, religious, young men and women, sinners, people in all difficulties, and the sick sought him out. By 1855, the number reached twenty thousand a year. His advice was characterized by common sense and supernatural insights. He could often tell someone their sins before that person had a chance to speak. Sometimes he would correct people who left sins out of their confessions. He also worked miracles: obtaining money and food for charity; displaying supernatural knowledge of the past and future; and healing the sick, especially children.[4]

By being God's instrument, this man who could hardly qualify to be a priest became the model and patron saint of parish priests. His feast day is August 4.

Focus Question 37:
How easy was it for St. John Vianney to become a priest?

Focus Question 38:
Where did St. John Vianney spend most of his time?

Focus Question 39:
How is St. John Vianney honored today?

FROM *YouCat*

How does the sacrament of Matrimony come about?

The SACRAMENT of Matrimony comes about through a promise made by a man and a woman before God and the Church, which is accepted and confirmed by God and consummated by the bodily union of the couple. Because God himself forms the bond of sacramental marriage, it is binding until the death of one of the partners.

The man and the woman mutually administer the sacrament of Matrimony. The PRIEST or the DEACON calls down God's BLESSING on the couple and, furthermore, witnesses that the marriage comes about under the right circumstances and that the promise is comprehensive and is made publicly. A marriage can come about only if there is *marital consent*, that is, if the man and the woman enter marriage of their own free will, without fear or coercion, and if they are not prevented from marrying by other natural or ecclesiastical ties (for example, an existing marriage, a vow of celibacy). (*YouCat* 261)

CLOSURE

Describe each of the Seven Sacraments in one sentence each.

ALTERNATIVE ASSESSMENT

Free write for five minutes on something in this lesson you found hard to understand, in order to understand it better.

The Church continues the ministry of Christ on earth.

CONCLUSION

In establishing his Church, Christ entrusted her leadership with the ministry of the Word of God and the Sacraments. The Church continues the ministry of Christ on earth by preaching the good news of salvation to the world, teaching all that Christ has taught, and administering the Sacraments to those who respond to Christ's invitation to enter into the People of God, his Church.

DISCUSSION QUESTIONS

1. What is a Sacrament?
2. When did Christ institute the Sacrament of Baptism?
3. What are three effects of Baptism?
4. What is the "laying on of hands" that followed Baptism in the early Church?
5. What are the effects of receiving Confirmation?
6. When one receives the Eucharist, what is one receiving?
7. What is the connection between the Eucharist and the Sacrifice of Christ on the Cross?
8. What is transubstantiation?
9. What are the two conditions for worthy reception of the Eucharist?
10. When did Christ institute the Sacrament of Penance?
11. What are mortal and venial sins?
12. What are the usual effects of the Anointing of the Sick?
13. When did Christ institute the Sacrament of Holy Orders?
14. What are the three orders in the Sacrament of Holy Orders?
15. When did God create marriage?
16. What is the effect of Matrimonial grace?

ENDNOTES – CHAPTER 7

1. *DV* 9.
2. *LG* 11; cf. *OC*, Introduction 2.
3. Council of Trent (1562), *Doctrina de ss. Missae sacrificio*, c. 2: DS 1743; cf. Heb 9:14, 27.
4. Adapted from S. Otten, "St. Jean-Baptiste-Marie Vianney," in *The Catholic Encyclopedia* (New York: Robert Appleton Company, 1910).

The Church
Sacrament of Salvation

Chapter 8
Names and Images of the Church

God has given us images of the Church to make imaginable realities difficult to comprehend.

CHAPTER 8
Names and Images of the Church

✠ Christ entrusted the pastors of his Church with the teaching of the Word of God and the conferring of the Sacraments.

✠ The Sacraments are visible signs that confer the grace they signify.

As we read in the last chapter, the Sacraments are signs and channels of God's grace. The Church, which Christ established as the primary means to dispense his grace to the faithful, is herself a sacrament to the world.

In this chapter, we will briefly examine the Church as the Sacrament of Salvation and as the Sacrament of Communion. We will also briefly look at several images of the Church as used in Scripture and Tradition and how they likewise apply to the Church.

OPENING ACTIVITY

Incorporate into the class's Opening Prayer St. Paul's discourse on the Church as the Body of Christ (1 Cor 12: 4-31).

Afterwards ask the students to identify some roles St. Paul mentions that are not very evident in the Church today and some roles they can think of that St. Paul does not list.

BASIC QUESTION

This chapter attempts to answer the following basic questions:

✠ Why is the Church called the Sacrament of Salvation and the Sacrament of Communion?

✠ What are the meanings of the images of the Church as the Mystical Body of Christ, as the Bride of Christ, as the Family of God, and as the People of God?

THE CHURCH AS SACRAMENT

Just as each of the Seven Sacraments is a visible sign by which God confers his grace, so, too, is the Church a visible sign of God's grace. She is the Sacrament of Salvation because she is both the sign and the means of God's salvation for humanity. She is also the Sacrament of Communion because she gathers all of humanity into communion with God and with one another. Here is how the *Catechism* puts it:

> "The Church, in Christ, is like a sacrament—a sign and instrument, that is, of communion with God and of unity among all men."[1] The Church's first purpose is to be the sacrament of the *inner union of men with God*. Because men's communion with one another is rooted in that union with God, the Church is also the sacrament of the *unity of the human race*. In her, this unity is already begun, since she gathers men "from every nation, from all tribes and peoples and tongues";[2] at the same time, the Church is the "sign and instrument" of the full realization of the unity yet to come. (CCC 775)

The New Testament word communion—*communio* in Latin (*koinonia* in Greek)—expresses the essential core of the Church's mystery.[3] In communion there is a *vertical dimension*: man's communion with God who is "above" us. It also includes a *horizontal dimension*: our communion with the other members of Christ's faithful in a relationship of radical equality.[4]

Focus Question 1:

In what way is the Church itself a "sacrament"?

Focus Question 2:

Why do we call the Church the Sacrament of Salvation?

Focus Question 3:

Why is the Church a Sacrament of Communion?

What does this mean? Recall that the Church is both a visible reality and an invisible reality. For the Church to be a sign it must be visible, and the Church is a visible human institution. The Church's communion is sacramental, then, because it is a visible sign of an invisible reality. The *visible dimension* is seen in people united around the teaching of the Apostles, the Sacraments, and the hierarchical order of Pope and bishops. The *invisible dimension* is our intimate communion with the Holy Trinity and the other members of Christ's Church on earth, in Heaven, and in Purgatory.

GUIDED EXERCISE

Work with a partner to choose one of the images of the Church presented here (flock, sheepfold, vine, vineyard, building) and identify both the visible and invisible elements.

One can point to the Pope, the bishops, priests, deacons, members of religious orders, and a vast number of lay people who are members. We can

All the Church's visible means and activities exist to accomplish what is essentially invisible to us now: communion with God and with one another.

see church buildings and all the other properties that the Church operates directly or indirectly, such as schools, hospitals, and orphanages. The Church has a visible government and her own laws. The Church has a visible liturgy and a vast literature, which includes the Sacred Scriptures. And she has a two-thousand-year history that can be studied.

All these exist as instruments to carry out God's intention to share his Divine Life with all mankind: "At the end of time...all the just, from Adam and 'from Abel, the just one, to the last of the elect,' will be gathered together with the Father in the universal Church" (*LG* 2). All the Church's visible means and activities exist to accomplish what is essentially invisible to us now: communion with God and with one another.

The Church also is the Sacrament of Communion because she is God's instrument to bring men into communion with God and with each other through the grace of the Sacraments.

Each individual enters into the Church's communion by faith and by Baptism.[5] Through Baptism, the faithful are incorporated into a Body—the Church—which the Risen Lord builds up and sustains through the Eucharist. The Eucharist, the root and center of the community, is the source of communion among the members of the Church, uniting each one of them with Christ himself:

> **Because there is one bread, we who are many are one body, for we all partake of the one bread. (1 Cor 10: 17)**

> When we share in the Body and Blood of Christ we become what we receive.[6]

The Eucharist is not simply some "thing" that makes communion happen. The Eucharist is literally Jesus Christ himself. God himself is the source and instrument of communion with him and his people.

Focus Question 4:
What does the Eucharist "do" for communion?

Focus Question 5:
What images of the Church relate to the role of Christ as the Good Shepherd?

VOCABULARY

MYSTERY

An inexhaustible truth, something that can be known with certainty through faith but can never be fully understood by human reason.

TEMPLE OF THE HOLY SPIRIT

A title of the Church used by St. Paul; it highlights the relationship between the Church and the Old Testament Temple in Jerusalem.

Sts. Peter and Paul Present God's Temple, Byzantine Icon.
Christ is the foundation, the cornerstone, and Christians are living stones that make up his building, his holy Temple.

OTHER IMAGES OF THE CHURCH

Scripture and Tradition give us various other images of the Church that help describe her role and purpose. For example, two closely related images of the Church are a *flock* of sheep and a *sheepfold*. A sheepfold is an enclosure where the sheep are protected from predators. The person who protects and brings the sheep to their pasture is their shepherd or "pastor." Christians are like a flock of sheep and the sheepfold is like the Church. Christ is the Good Shepherd who laid down his life for us, his sheep. Christ protects and feeds us through his human shepherds, our pastors.

Three other closely related images are of the Church as a *cultivated field*, as a *vineyard*, and as the branches of a *vine*. Apart from its vine, a branch can do nothing. The Church is like a choice vineyard, cultivated by the vinedresser, Christ, who prunes us to make us bear good fruit. Christ is also a grapevine. We are his branches. If we are cut off from Christ, we wither and die.

The Church is also a *temple* where God dwells or a *house* built on solid ground. Christ is the foundation, the cornerstone, and Christians are living stones that make up his building, his holy Temple.

We will now look more deeply at four of the primary images of the Church as employed in Scripture and Tradition:

✠ the Mystical Body of Christ

✠ the Bride of Christ

✠ the Family of God

✠ the People of God.

The Holy Spirit acts in the Mystical Body of Christ the way the soul acts in the human body.

THE CHURCH AS THE MYSTICAL BODY OF CHRIST

As we read earlier, St. Paul used the image of the Church as the Body of Christ to describe the intimate relationship between the Church and Christ. Recall how when Saul was on his way to Damascus to persecute Christians, the Lord asked him, "Saul, Saul, why are you persecuting me?" (Acts 9: 4). Christ speaks of the Church and him as one.

This image indicates that the Church is not simply a group of people gathered around Christ, but a people united with him and in him. This reality is made explicit in our reception of Christ's Body and Blood in Holy Communion. As the *Catechism* puts it, "From the beginning, Jesus associated his disciples with his own life...[a]nd he proclaimed a mysterious and real communion between his own body and ours: 'He who eats my body and drinks my blood abides in me, and I in him'"[7] (CCC 787). Through the Sacrament of the Eucharist, the faithful are united together in Christ's Mystical Body; that is, brought into communion with one another through communion with Christ.

What does this term "mystical body" mean? In a mysterious but real way we are also united to him as the parts of a body are related to the body's head or mind. This is why St. Paul refers to Christ as the head of the Mystical Body.

> [Christ] is before all things, and in him all things hold together. He is the head of the body, the church. (Col 1: 17-18)

A physical head directs its body. This is an apt image of Christ's role in the Church. As the Second Vatican Council document *Lumen Gentium* puts it, "By the greatness of His power He rules the things in Heaven and the things on earth, and with His all-surpassing perfection and way of acting He fills the whole body [of the Church] with the riches of His glory" (*LG* 7).

The faithful have diverse roles in the Church, just as in the natural body the different parts have different functions (1 Cor 12 ff.). St. Paul points out some of the roles different members may play in the Church, for example, "first apostles, second prophets, third teachers, then workers of miracles, then healers, helpers, administrators, speakers in various kinds of tongues." One role every member is invited to play to an unlimited extent is to love (cf. 1 Cor 13).

The Holy Spirit acts in the Mystical Body of Christ the way the soul acts in the human body, by giving it life, unifying it, and moving it. The life of Christ is communicated to the faithful by means of the Sacraments.[8] Baptism, Confirmation, and the Eucharist are the three Sacraments of Initiation, which incorporate the faithful into the Body of Christ.

Thus, the image of the Church as the Mystical Body of Christ uses the relationship between the parts of a human body to its head to reveal the communion of Christ and the Church. It highlights the mutual importance of the members of the Church to one another and their subordination under their head, Jesus Christ.

THE CHURCH AS THE BRIDE OF CHRIST

From the time of the Apostles onward, as noted earlier, Christians have used the words "she" and "her" when referring to the Church. This is because of the Church's relationship to Jesus Christ, which is described in terms of marriage: the Church is the Bride of Christ. Just as we use feminine pronouns to describe brides, so, too, do we use these pronouns to describe the Bride that Jesus Christ has taken for himself.

Focus Question 6:
How does Christ identify himself with the Church in St. Paul's experience?

Focus Question 7:
How does Christ identify himself with his Church in the Eucharist?

Focus Question 8:
What is a *mystical body*?

Focus Question 9:
What is an example of an "organ" of the Body of Christ?

Focus Question 10:
What is the role of the Holy Spirit in the Body of Christ?

VOCABULARY

BODY OF CHRIST
A name of the Church used frequently by St. Paul; it highlights the unity of Christ and the Church.

FROM *YouCat*

What does it mean to say that the Church is the "Body of Christ"?

Above all through the SACRAMENTS of Baptism and Holy EUCHARIST, an inseparable union comes about between Jesus Christ and Christians. The union is so strong that it joins him and us like the head and members of a human body and makes us one. (*YouCat* 126)

Focus Question 11:
Why don't we refer to the Church as "he" or "it"?

Focus Question 12:

What does Christ do for his Bride, the Church?

Focus Question 13:

How do husbands properly imitate Christ?

GUIDED EXERCISE

Have a class discussion on the following questions:

- In what ways is it correct to say that Christ loves each one of us?

VOCABULARY

BRIDE OF CHRIST

A name of the Church derived from the writings of St. Paul; it highlights the purity and holiness that Christ has bestowed upon the Church.

FROM *YouCat*

What does it mean to say that the Church is the "Bride of Christ"?

Jesus Christ loves the CHURCH as a bridegroom loves his bride. He binds himself to her forever and gives his life for her.

Anyone who has ever been in love has some idea of what love is. Jesus knows it and calls himself a bridegroom who lovingly and longingly courts his bride and desires to celebrate the feast of love with her. We are his Bride, the CHURCH. In the OLD TESTAMENT God's love for his people is compared to the love between husband and wife. If Jesus seeks the love of each one of us, how often is he then *unhappily in love*—that is to say, with all those who want nothing to do with his love and do not reciprocate it?! (*YouCat* 127)

Christ referred to himself as a bridegroom (cf. Mt 9: 15) and St. John the Baptist also called Christ a bridegroom (cf. Jn 3: 29). In the Book of Revelation, the New Jerusalem, a figure of the Church, is described as a bride splendidly adorned for her husband and is called the Bride of the Lamb, or Christ (cf. Rev 21: 2, 9-10).

In his Letter to the Ephesians, St. Paul draws an analogy that moves from the Church as the Body of Christ to the Church as the Bride of Christ: "Christ is the head of the church, his body, and is himself its Savior" (Eph 5: 23). Moreover, "the church is subject to Christ" in everything (Eph 5: 24). Christ has truly loved the Church: "Christ loved the church and gave himself up for her, that he might sanctify her, having cleansed her by the washing of water with the word, that he might present the Church to himself in splendor, without spot or wrinkle or any such thing, that she might be holy and without blemish" (Eph 5: 25-27).

Out of his great love, Christ laid down his life for his beloved bride. Furthermore, he makes her perfectly beautiful. He does this through Baptism, the "washing of water," which makes her splendid, without spot or wrinkle.

St. Paul's advice to husbands to love their wives the way Christ loved the Church helps us see the image of the Church-as-bride more clearly. "Husbands should love their wives as their own bodies. He who loves his wife loves himself. For no man ever hates his own flesh, but nourishes and cherishes it, as Christ does the church, because we are members of his body" (Eph 5: 27-30). St. Paul, quoting Genesis, says that Christ feels about his Church the way a bridegroom feels about his bride: "For this reason a man shall leave his father and mother and be joined to his wife, and the two shall become one flesh. This mystery is a profound one, and I am saying that it refers to Christ and the church" (Eph 5: 31-32).

When Adam first saw Eve, the bride that God had taken from his side, he exclaimed, "This at last is bone of my bones and flesh of my flesh" (Gn 2: 23). For Adam, then, Eve is both his bride and a part of himself. In interpreting this Old Testament passage in light of the teaching of Christ, St. Paul recognizes that it is specifically as Christ's Bride that the Church is made "one flesh" with him and is therefore truly his Body. Christ loves the Church as he loves himself. He nourishes and cherishes his Bride.

Thus, the image of the Church as the Bride of Christ uses the relationship between a bridegroom and bride to reveal the communion of Christ and his Church. It highlights Christ's initiative in saving and sanctifying humanity to make us worthy of his love.

THE CHURCH AS THE FAMILY OF GOD

Joseph Cardinal Ratzinger, before he became Pope Benedict XVI, wrote that Christ's favorite image of the Church is as the family of God.

> God is the father of the family, Jesus the master of the house, and it therefore stands to reason that he addresses the members of this people as children, even though they are adults, and that to gain true understanding of themselves, those who belong to this people must first lay down their grown-up autonomy and acknowledge themselves as children before God.[9]

Christ is the eternal Son, sent to regather in himself those whom the Father has called to be his beloved sons and daughters (cf. Eph 1: 5). For this reason, the *Catechism* tells us "the Church is nothing other than 'the family of God'" (CCC 1655). "Becoming a disciple of Christ means accepting the invitation

Let the Children Come to Me (detail) by Vogel.
Christ has revealed that God is an eternal and perfect Father.

Focus Question 14:
How does Christ identify as members of his family those who do God's will?

Focus Question 15:
What name did Christ give us for God the Father?

Focus Question 16:
How is our idea of a family different from ancient cultures?

Focus Question 17:
How is Christ's idea of family revolutionary?

VOCABULARY

ABBA
A name Christ used for God the Father and invited us to use in our prayer as well. It is similar to "Daddy," indicating a close, familiar, and loving relationship.

FAMILY OF GOD
A name of the Church derived from the teaching of Christ; it highlights the intimate communion that the Father offers to man in the person of Jesus Christ, in whom we are made sons and daughters of God.

GUIDED EXERCISE
Conduct a think/pair/share using the following question:

✠ In what ways can family or tribal ties be healthy and unhealthy?

First *think* about your own response; then *discuss it* with a partner; finally *share* your response with the class.

We are children of God with Jesus Christ our brother.

to belong to *God's family*, to live in conformity with His way of life: 'For whoever does the will of my Father in heaven is my brother, and sister, and mother' (Mt 12: 49)" (CCC 2233).

The Fatherhood of God is not simply a metaphor. Christ has revealed that God is an eternal and perfect Father—our *Abba*, meaning "Father" or, still closer, "Daddy"—beside whom even the best of earthly fathers pales in comparison.

In most ancient cultures and still in many cultures today, the large, extended family defined an individual's world. Rather than comprising only parents, grandparents, children, and grandchildren, a person's family included *all* the descendants of the patriarch of the tribe—usually a man who had lived centuries before. Each tribe was a distinct family whose members shared the same faith and called one another "brothers" and "sisters," children of a common father. In fact, most ancient Semitic languages had no word for "cousin," since "brother" or "sister" served the purpose.

In ancient Israel, the people were split into twelve tribes, each descended from one of the twelve sons of Jacob (also named Israel). Christ himself belonged to such a family, the nation of Israel and the Tribe of Judah. His large extended family was so closely knit that the twelve-year-old Jesus could disappear for an entire day without Mary and Joseph worrying about him, assuming instead that he was somewhere safe in the family's large caravan returning home from the Passover festival in Jerusalem (cf. Lk 2: 41-51).

Yet, Christ's idea of family—based on God's fatherhood—seemed to run contrary to the old tribal notion. Christ spoke of God as not merely the "God of our fathers," or the God of the Jewish people, but as the universal Father. God's family transcends all national, tribal, and familial divisions. It is free of class distinctions, all people being brothers and sisters in Christ. "For in Christ Jesus, you are all sons of God through faith....There is neither Jew nor Greek, there is neither slave nor free, there is neither male nor female; for you are all one in Christ Jesus" (Gal 3: 26, 28). In the ancient world, this certainly was a revolutionary concept.

The Son of God became a man in order to draw men and women together and to unify them within *his* family. Christ described our adoption into the Church as being "born anew" (Jn 3: 3). He spoke of our bond with God as a "new covenant" (Lk 22: 20). He spoke of our ultimate destiny as a "marriage feast"

VOCABULARY

PEOPLE OF GOD

Those born into the Church through faith in Christ and Baptism. The term is taken from the Old Testament, in which God chose Israel to be his people. Christ instituted the new and eternal covenant by which a new priestly, prophetic, and royal People of God, the Church, participates in the mission and service of Christ.

FROM *YouCat*

What is unique about the People of God?

The founder of this people is God the Father. Its leader is Jesus Christ. Its source of strength is the Holy Spirit. The entryway to the People of God is Baptism. Its dignity is the freedom of the children of God. Its law is love. If this people remains faithful to God and seeks first the kingdom of God, it changes the world.

In the midst of all the peoples on earth, there is one people that is like no other. It is subject to no one but God alone. It is supposed to be like salt, which adds flavor; like yeast, which permeates everything; like light, which drives away the darkness. Anyone who belongs to the People of God must count on coming into conflict with people who deny God's existence and disregard his commandments. In the freedom of the children of God, however, we have nothing to fear, not even death. (*YouCat* 125)

Pope Benedict XVI embraced by the Family of God.
Christ is the eternal Son, sent to regather in himself those whom the Father has called to be his beloved sons and daughters

(Rev 19: 9). Birth, covenant, and marriage all share one thing in common: They incorporate an individual into a family—in this case, a supernatural family, the Family of God, the Catholic Church.

Thus, the image of the Church as the Family of God uses the relationships in a human family to highlight the fraternal communion between Christ and Christians. It highlights that God is our common Father, the Church our Mother, and we are children of God with Jesus Christ our brother.

THE CHURCH AS THE PEOPLE OF GOD

One of the images of the Church that the Second Vatican Council highlighted was the People of God. In his plan of salvation, God has willed "to make men holy and save them, not as individuals without any bond or link between them, but rather to make them into a people who might acknowledge him and serve him in holiness." This is why he "chose the Israelite race to be his own people and established a covenant with it....All these things, however, happened as a preparation for and figure of that new and perfect covenant which was to be ratified in Christ"[10] (CCC 781).

The Church, therefore, was prefigured in the people of Israel. "As Israel according to the flesh, which wandered in the desert, was already called the Church of God, so too, the new Israel, which advances in this present age in search of a future and permanent city, is called also the Church of Christ."[11] The Church on earth is called the Pilgrim Church because her members are searching for the New Jerusalem, or Heaven.

The image of the Church as the People of God is closely related to the *qahal*, the assembly of Israel at Mount Sinai. God made his covenant with Moses and the Israelites at Mount Sinai, promising that if they kept the covenant, they would be his Chosen People, a kingdom of priests and a holy nation (cf. Ex 19: 6).

God's decision to form for himself a people—as opposed to a random assortment of individuals—reflects the God-given social nature of man. The human person always lives and functions in relation to others. We are drawn to live in communities. All that we have, we have received from someone

SHEEP AND SHEPHERD

Herding sheep was such a common experience in biblical times that it provided an easy metaphor for expressing one's meaning. Christ often used stories and analogies of shepherds and sheep to teach his listeners about his identity and his relationship with humanity. The Sacred Writers of Scripture did the same.

Here are a few of these references:

✠ The Gospels of Sts. Matthew and Mark both refer to Christ having compassion on the crowds who came to hear him preach because they seemed "like sheep without a shepherd" (Mt 9: 26; Mk 6: 34). The phrase implies people who were lost and did not know their way home, needing someone to lead them.

✠ In the Parable of the Lost Sheep, Christ is the shepherd who leaves the ninety-nine sheep who are safe in order to go look for the one sheep who has strayed. Finding the lost one, he brings it back home and rejoices. This is the image of the forgiveness of Christ who seeks out sinners and returns them to his fold, the Church.

✠ Christ predicted how the Apostles would abandon him when he told them after the Last Supper, "You will all fall away because of me this night; for it is written, I will strike the shepherd, and the sheep of the flock will be scattered'" (Mt 26: 31). Here he quotes from the prophet Zechariah (cf. Zec 13: 7). Apart from the shepherd, the sheep lose their way.

✠ In the tenth chapter of the Gospel of St. John, Christ offers a beautiful statement about his loving relationship with his faithful, comparing it to a shepherd with his sheep. The sheep know the voice of the shepherd and follow him. He is the Good Shepherd who cares for his sheep; he knows his sheep, and his sheep know him. He lays down his life for his sheep so that they may have eternal life.

✠ In his Parable of the Sheep and the Goats, Christ as the "Son of man" comes in glory to separate the sheep from the goats. The sheep are the "righteous" who live virtuous lives and show love and compassion to others and, thus, are invited to enter eternal life; the goats are those who fail in this regard and are condemned to eternal punishment.

✠ The Book of Revelation offers a final image of the Church in Heaven, in perfect beatitude, in the presence of Christ:

> **For the Lamb in the midst of the throne will be their shepherd, and he will guide them to springs of living water; and God will wipe away every tear from their eyes. (Rev 7: 17)**

Focus Question 21:
Describe some of the images of the shepherd and the sheep as they apply to Christ and his Church.

The Good Shepherd by Champaigne. He lays down his life for his sheep so that they may have eternal life.

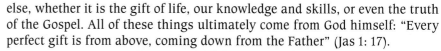

CLOSURE

Summarize in one paragraph one of the major images of the Church presented in this chapter.

ALTERNATIVE ASSESSMENT

Choose one of the activities or exercises from this chapter and rewrite your response based on everything you have learned.

else, whether it is the gift of life, our knowledge and skills, or even the truth of the Gospel. All of these things ultimately come from God himself: "Every perfect gift is from above, coming down from the Father" (Jas 1: 17).

Israel was the first People of God, chosen and commissioned by God to bring all the nations into the communion with him that he had desired from the beginning. Although Israel failed in this mission, we know that God did not abandon his desire to unite mankind to himself, as Jeremiah prophesized:

> Behold, the days are coming, says the LORD, when I will make a new covenant with the house of Israel and the house of Judah....I will put my law within them, and I will write it upon their hearts; and I will be their God, and they shall be my people. (Jer 31: 31-33)

Thus, the image of the Church as the People of God uses the assembly of the Chosen People on Mount Sinai who collectively said "yes" to the Mosaic Covenant in order to reveal the communion between God and his Church. It highlights the ordinarily communal nature of God's plan of salvation.

CONCLUSION

Because the Church is a mystery that cannot be fully explained or understood, images are useful in describing certain of her characteristics. All at once, the Church is the font of grace established by Christ for the world, the sign of communion between God and humanity, the Mystical Body of Christ, the Family of God, and any number of other names and images used by Scripture and Tradition to express her essence and function.

DISCUSSION QUESTIONS

1. Why do we call the Church the Sacrament of Salvation?

2. Why is the Church a Sacrament of Communion?

3. What does the Eucharist "do" for communion?

4. What is the meaning of the image of the Church as the Mystical Body of Christ?

5. What is the meaning of the image of the Church as the Bride of Christ?

6. What is the meaning of the image of the Church as the Family of God?

7. What is the meaning of the image of the Church as the People of God?

8. Describe some of the images of the shepherd and the sheep as they apply to Christ and his Church.

The Holy Family by Barocci.
God's family transcends all national, tribal, and familial divisions.

ENDNOTES – CHAPTER 8

1. LG 1.
2. Rev 7: 9.
3. John Paul II, Address to the Bishops of the United States of America, September 16, 1987, n. 1: "Insegnamenti di Giovanni Paolo II" X, 3 (1987), p. 553.
4. Ratzinger, Joseph, Letter to the Bishops of the Catholic Church on some Aspects of the Church Understood as Communion, 3.
5. Cf. Eph 4: 4-5; Mk 16: 16.
6. St. Leo the Great, Sermo 63, 7.
7. Jn 6: 56.
8. LG 7.
9. Ratzinger, Joseph. Called to Communion (Ignatius Press: San Francisco, 1996), pp. 23-24.
10. LG 9; cf. Acts 10: 35; 1 Cor 11: 25.
11. LG 9.

The Church
Sacrament of Salvation

Chapter 9
The Four Marks of the Church:
The Church Is One

If there can only be one Church, which one is it?

OPENING ACTIVITY

Do an online search to look at various ancient seals (try "British Museum ancient seals").

Seals have been found in cylindrical shapes, in signet rings, and as stamps.

They are skillfully carved and produce beautiful impressions. Can you surmise from your search what seals were used for?

BASIC QUESTIONS

This chapter attempts to answer the following basic questions:

⌖ What does it mean that the Church is *one*?

⌖ How has the unity of the Church been wounded?

⌖ What is ecumenism?

KEY IDEAS

The key ideas of this chapter are:

⌖ There is only one Church united by Christ himself.

⌖ The unity of the Church has been wounded by apostasy, schism, and heresy.

⌖ Ecumenism is the task of working toward Christian unity or reunification.

Focus Question 1:

What was the purpose of "marking" or "sealing" something in the ancient world?

Focus Question 2:

What are the four "marks" of the Catholic Church?

CHAPTER 9
The Four Marks of the Church: The Church Is One

Review of Chapter 8:

✠ The Church is the Sacrament of Salvation because it is through the Church that the grace of redemption is communicated to humanity.

✠ The Church is the Sacrament of Communion because her mission is to bring all of humanity into communion with God and with one another.

✠ The Church also is described in Scripture and Tradition by a variety of illustrative images, including the Mystical Body of Christ, the Bride of Christ, the Family of God, and the People of God.

In the ancient world, a seal acted as a person's signature or identification mark. These seals were cylinders, stamps, or signet rings with images. They were rolled or pressed into clay or wax to make an impression. If a document had your seal on it, it meant it was yours or you were agreeing to it.

From the earliest times, Christians have identified four essential characteristics or *marks* of the Church. These four marks, which we recall each time we recite the Nicene Creed, are *One*, *Holy*, *Catholic*, and *Apostolic*. The idea is that God has impressed these marks on his Church. If you see these marks you can know it is the Church of Christ.

Although these four marks are of the Church's very essence, she does not possess them on her own. All that the Church has, she receives from God. Through the gift of the Holy Spirit, Christ sustains the Church and continues to make her one, holy, catholic, and apostolic. As we will see, it is to the Catholic Church alone that Christ gives these characteristics in their fullness.

THE CHURCH IS ONE

Holy, catholic, and apostolic are marks which will be examined in the next chapter. They cannot be understood without the first, that the Church is one.

What do we mean when we say, "The Church is one"? We mean two inter-related things: There is only one Church of Christ and Christ is her source of unity.

By calling the Church one, we are first acknowledging her uniqueness and singularity. Just as we profess faith in one God and not in multiple gods, so, too, we believe that Christ has instituted one Church and not multiple churches.

It is evident from the Gospel that Christ desired "one flock, one shepherd" (Jn 10: 16; cf. Mt 12: 25). Christ himself said that he is the only way to salvation: "I am the way, and the truth, and the life; no one comes to the Father, but by me" (Jn 14: 6).

In establishing the Church on earth, Christ gives all mankind the opportunity to be united to him, the one Savior of the world, by becoming part of his one Mystical Body.

Pentecost (detail) by Vivarini.
The Church's unity comes from her divine source, God, who in his Trinity is perfect unity, one God in three Persons.

Second, by saying that the Church is one, we are affirming the unity and solidarity that exists within the Church. The members of the Church are united among themselves in fellowship, helping one another to achieve salvation.

However, the solidarity uniting the members of the Church goes beyond that of a mere social organization. Whether it is a political party, a school club, a bowling league, or a neighborhood association, every civic organization exists by people being united around common goals, interests, or opinions. In the Church, although her members might indeed be united around common goals, interests, or opinions, the Church's unity does not originate in these things. Rather, the Church's unity comes from her divine source, God, who in his Trinity is perfect unity, one God in three Persons.

Unity in the Mystical Body

The image of the Church as the Mystical Body of Christ is perhaps the best one for expressing the unity that the Church receives from God. As we read in the last chapter, in the Mystical Body of Christ, the many diverse members of the Church are united to Christ, our head, to form the whole Christ, united and animated by the Holy Spirit, the "soul" of the Mystical Body. Being parts of the body, the members are united with each other.

The unity of the Mystical Body of Christ is visible in a number of ways:

✠ **Unity of faith.** In the Creed, the Church professes the one Faith that has been passed down intact from the Apostles.

✠ **Unity of worship.** The Pilgrim Church celebrates in common the same Seven Sacraments that were instituted by Christ during his time on earth. The Eucharistic sacrifice of the Mass, while always offered in a particular community, is never a celebration of that community alone. The community is the image and true presence of the one, holy, catholic, and apostolic Church. Wherever the Eucharist is celebrated, the totality of the mystery of the Church becomes present.

✠ **Unity of leadership.** Through the Sacrament of Holy Orders, the Church's Apostolic Succession ensures uninterrupted continuity with the teaching and leadership of St. Peter and the Apostles (cf. CCC 815).

Focus Question 3:
What do we mean when we say the Church is "one"?

Focus Question 4:
What gives the Church her unity or solidarity?

FROM *YouCat*

Why can there be only <u>one</u> *Church?*

Just as there is only one Christ, there can be only one Body of Christ, only one Bride of Christ, and therefore only one CHURCH of Jesus Christ. He is the Head, the Church is the Body. Together they form the "whole Christ" (St. Augustine). Just as the body has many members yet is one, so too the one Church consists of and is made up of many particular churches (dioceses). Together they form the whole Christ.

Jesus built his Church on the foundation of the APOSTLES. This foundation supports her to this day. The faith of the apostles was handed down from generation to generation under the leadership of the Pope, the Petrine ministry, "which presides in charity" (St. Ignatius of Antioch). The SACRAMENTS, too, which Jesus entrusted to the apostolic college, still work with their original power. (*YouCat* 129)

Focus Question 5:
What are the three ways the Church shows unity?

WOUNDS TO UNITY

Focus Question 6:

How was the division within the Church over whether Gentile converts had to live by the Mosaic Law resolved?

Focus Question 7:

According to Christ, if someone rejects the Church, whom else is he rejecting?

Focus Question 8:

What are the three kinds of wounds the Church can suffer in regard to the Faith?

GUIDED EXERCISE

As a class, brainstorm as many possible reasons you can for why religiously inclined Christians would reject the Faith, adopt false teachings, or separate themselves from the Church.

Focus Question 9:

Why were there apostates in the early Church?

Focus Question 10:

Can apostasy be forgiven?

Focus Question 11:

What are the two main schisms in Church history?

Focus Question 12:

What is the distinction between schismatics and separated brethren?

Schism is a breach of the unity of the visible Church.

Since the beginning, divisions and disagreements have arisen among Christians that have threatened and even seriously wounded the visible unity of the Pilgrim Church.

We read earlier about the disagreement in the Apostolic Church over whether Gentiles should undergo circumcision in order to become Christians. The resolution of this dispute at the Council of Jerusalem is a good example of how the authority given by Christ to St. Peter and his successors maintains and strengthens the Church's visible unity.

There have been times, however, when some Christians rejected the teaching and leadership of the Church's shepherds—the Pope and the bishops in union with him. In doing so, they rejected the teachings of Christ himself and wounded the unity of the whole Mystical Body. As Christ said to his Apostles, "He who hears you hears me, and he who rejects you rejects me, and he who rejects me rejects him who sent me" (Lk 10: 16).

These wounds take three forms:

✠ **Apostasy**, the total rejection of the Christian Faith by someone already baptized.

✠ **Heresy**, the deliberate and persistent post-baptismal denial of a truth of the Faith taught by the Church.

✠ **Schism**, the post-baptismal refusal of unity with the Pope, or the refusal of communion with the members of the Church.

All of these are very grave sins that result from the choices and actions of individuals. Schism is especially tragic for it often involves entire communities of people who become separated from Christ and his Church.

Apostasy

During much of the first three centuries of the Christian era, it was illegal to be a Christian and, oftentimes, the mere fact of being Christian made a person subject to capital punishment. Many of the martyrs could have escaped death if they had simply renounced Christianity. Their glory lies in that they did not.

Those few who succumbed to this temptation became apostates. A serious question arose in the early Church about what to do with people who were baptized, formally rejected the Faith under threat of death, and then wished to return to it. While some said such persons could never be forgiven, the Catholic position was that they could. However, since the rejection of the Faith was a public act, one needed to make a public confession and do a public penance.

Schisms

There have been two great schisms in the history of the Church. The first, with the Eastern Orthodox Churches, took place in the eleventh century. The second was with the various ecclesial communities that were founded during the Protestant Reformation in the sixteenth century.

Catholics today must be careful to distinguish between those who initially separated themselves from the Church (called *schismatics*) and those members of later generations who were born into these schismatic communities (often referred to as *separated brethren*). These separated brethren cannot be considered guilty of the sin of separation—it is often

The Council of Nicæa, AD 325, was called by Emperor Constantine to unite the Christian empire which was divided over Arianism.

through no fault of their own that they remain unaware of the truth of the Catholic Faith. Rather, provided they are baptized, they are to be recognized as fellow Christians and brothers and sisters in Christ.

The Catholic Church acknowledges elements of sanctification and truth within the separated communities of Protestantism and to a much greater degree in the Churches of Eastern Orthodoxy. Included among these elements are the Sacred Scriptures, some or all of the Seven Sacraments, the theological virtues of faith, hope, and love (charity), and the Gifts of the Holy Spirit. However, all these elements, which come from Christ and lead back to him, belong by right to the Catholic Church, the one Church founded by Christ, which possesses them in their fullness. The presence of these elements in these separated churches may provide an avenue for their eventual return to Catholic unity.

Heresies in the Early Church

Catholic doctrine derives from the revealed truths contained in the Deposit of Faith that Christ entrusted to his Church and which is found in Sacred Scripture and Sacred Tradition. However, from the earliest days of Christianity, some tried to corrupt these teachings.

Heresy is the denial or alteration of some part or parts of the Deposit of Faith. The word heresy comes from a Greek word that means "choice" and carries the connotation of "picking and choosing." The first heresies that afflicted the early Church were especially dangerous, since they struck at the heart of Christianity—the figure of Christ.

Gnosticism and Arianism were two of the major heresies the Church had to overcome in her first six centuries.

Gnosticism

The word *Gnosticism* is derived from the Greek word *gnosis* ("knowledge") and refers to a set of beliefs that salvation may be achieved by some people through secret knowledge. By the second century, Gnosticism had incorporated elements of the Old and New Testaments. Gnosticism taught

Focus Question 13:
Are separated brethren Christians?

Focus Question 14:
Are there good elements in Protestantism and Eastern Orthodoxy from the Catholic perspective?

VOCABULARY

APOSTASY
The total repudiation of the Christian Faith by someone already baptized. This is forbidden by the First Commandment and goes against the theological virtue of faith.

EASTERN ORTHODOXY
The group of Eastern Churches that broke from communion with the Catholic Church. Most are national churches, such as the Russian Orthodox Church and the Armenian Orthodox Church.

SCHISM
A breach of the unity of the visible Church; the refusal to submit to the Pope or be united with the Church.

SCHISMATIC
An individual who is part of an organized group that breaks away from the unity of the Catholic Church and thus creates a schism.

SEPARATED BRETHREN
Persons who were born into schismatic communities, including the Protestant and Eastern Orthodox churches, and thus cannot be considered guilty of the sin of separation because it is often through no fault of their own that they remain unaware of the truth of the Catholic Faith; rather, provided they are baptized, they are to be recognized as fellow Christians and brothers and sisters in Christ.

Focus Question 15:
What is heresy?

Focus Question 16:
What is the heresy of *Gnosticism*?

Focus Question 17:
How did Gnosticism regard material reality?

Focus Question 18:
Why are the ideas of secret knowledge and salvation for the few completely contrary to the true Faith?

VOCABULARY

HERESY

The obstinate denial by a baptized person of a truth of the Faith taught by Christ, which must be believed with divine faith.

GNOSTICISM

An ancient heresy that taught, among other things, that salvation came from obtaining secret experiential knowledge and that the material world was evil, a corruption of spirit. Christ was the Redeemer, but he was neither true God nor true man; he was an apparition, a lesser divine being who inhabited a human body; he neither had a body nor died on the Cross.

Focus Question 19:
What was the heresy of Arianism?

Focus Question 20:
Why was Arianism especially dangerous given the times?

Today's "new age" movement is a modern form of gnosticism.

that there were two gods: the creator god who propagated evil (the God of the Old Testament) and the unknowable divine being (the God of the New Testament).

The *logos* (Christ) had been sent to give secret knowledge to a select few so that they could return to the unknowable divine being. This was only possible if the individuals understood the secret knowledge of the redeemer's teaching and practiced the appropriate Gnostic rituals.

Gnosticism rejected the Church's teaching regarding both Christ's human and divine natures. According to Gnostic thought, Christ did not have a human nature, because it would be material and therefore evil. Likewise, Christ could not have inhabited a human body nor die on the Cross. Instead, his body was an apparition.

The early Church vigorously opposed these Gnostic teachings, emphasizing the goodness of the created world, the existence and supremacy of the one true God, the clear meaning of the Old and New Testament Scriptures, and the reality of Christ's human and divine natures, along with his redemptive Passion, Death, and Resurrection. Gnosticism, with its secret knowledge for a select few, violated the universal nature of the Christian Faith. Christ died to save everyone and commanded his Apostles to preach the Gospel to all nations.

Today's "new age" movement is a modern form of gnosticism. These practices teach that hidden powers are released through amulets, crystals, and secret incantations; that knowledge can be gained through fortune-telling, horoscopes, zodiac signs, and tarot cards; and that salvation ultimately comes from within a person, thus eliminating the need for a Redeemer.

Arianism

Arius (ca. 250-336) was a priest from Alexandria in modern-day Egypt who claimed that Jesus Christ was neither God nor equal to the Father.

Arius's belief in a transcendent Supreme God could not conceive that anything coming from God could be equal to God. He taught that Christ was a supreme creation of God, but not his eternally begotten Son, Second Person of the Blessed Trinity. This denial of Christ's divinity was at the root of the Arian heresy, which invariably led to a rejection of virtually all of the Church's central tenets, especially her doctrines on the Blessed Trinity and the Redemption.

Arianism was responsible for ushering in the greatest doctrinal crisis that the Church would experience until the sixteenth century. This heresy ravaged the Church in the east and was adopted by many of the Visogothic tribes that dominated central and northern Europe. These tribes became a serious threat to the existence of orthodox Christianity when they ravaged the tottering Western Roman Empire.

The Church responded to this threat by reaffirming the traditional belief in the divinity of Jesus Christ as articulated in the Nicene and Athanasian Creeds, which proclaimed that Christ is consubstantial with the Father. Through clear and consistent teaching, along with the catechetical and missionary work and sacrifices of many saintly men and women, this heresy was ultimately eliminated in the sixth and seventh centuries.

Periodically, however, there has resurged a tendency to stress Christ's humanity at the expense of his divinity. Some today allow that Christ was a wise teacher, but they deny his divinity, his Redemptive Death on the Cross, and his Resurrection.

Groups such as the Jehovah's Witnesses and the Church of Jesus Christ of Latter Day Saints (Mormons) view Christ as the "son of God," but not equal to or consubstantial with the Father, making them incompatible with the teachings of the Catholic Church in regard to the divinity of Jesus Christ.

The Protestant Reformation

The Protestant Reformation was an interrelated series of heresies, which led to schisms that took place from 1517 to 1648. At the time, the Catholic Church was in need of reform. Indeed, several Popes and saints of the time had attempted to curb abuses that were occurring within the Church.

At the same time, a new social class was emerging in Europe. Princes found themselves reaping the benefits of the prosperity of the Renaissance, and wealth was now available in greater quantities to far more people. These princes and other emerging power-players in the burgeoning commercial class were dissatisfied with the old social order in which the Church played a major role as a landowner and moral judge.

In 1517, a monk named Martin Luther began publishing criticisms against the sale of *indulgences*, which are a means for the faithful to obtain remission from the temporal punishment due to sins whose guilt has already been forgiven. Luther was right to criticize the sale of indulgences, but he erred when he began arguing against the validity of indulgences themselves. About the same time, a Swiss priest by the name of Huldrych Zwingli started a similar campaign in Switzerland. Both Luther and Zwingli began their criticisms hoping to correct abuses within the Church. However, their theological reasoning led them to dismiss the very authority of the Church, and they soon began to attack the teaching, worship, and structure of the Church herself.

Within the next several decades, many other "reformers" arose throughout Europe. Two of the most famous were John Calvin and King Henry VIII. Soon, full-blown schisms broke out in Germany, Switzerland, England, Denmark, Sweden, and Scotland.

It is important to remember that even before the time of the Reformation, there was a growing tension between these rising nation-states and the Church as rulers wished to consolidate control of the local churches under

Luther Nailing His 95 Theses to the Door of Wittenberg Church (detail) by Vogel. The visible unity of the Church on earth was deeply wounded by these schismatic movements, but this period also saw the beginnings of the true reform that the Church had needed.

Focus Question 21:
What is the Protestant Reformation?

Focus Question 22:
How was Protestantism related to contemporary politics?

FROM *YouCat*

Are non-Catholic Christians our sisters and brothers also?

All baptized persons belong to the CHURCH of Jesus Christ. That is why also those Christians who find themselves separated from the full communion of the Catholic Church are rightly called Christians and are therefore our sisters and brothers.

Instances of separation from the one Church of Christ came about through falsifications of Christ's teaching, human failings, and a lack of willingness to be reconciled—usually on the part of representatives on both sides. Christians today are in no way guilty for the historical divisions of the Church. The Holy Spirit also works for the salvation of mankind in the CHURCHES AND ECCLESIAL COMMUNITIES that are separated from the Catholic Church. All of the gifts present there, for example, Sacred Scripture, SACRAMENTS, faith, hope, love, and other charisms, come originally from Christ. Where the Spirit of Christ lives, there is an inner dynamic leading toward "reunion," because what belongs together wants to grow together. (*YouCat* 130)

Focus Question 23:

How many sects has Protestantism evolved into?

Focus Question 24:

What was the Catholic response to the Reformation?

VOCABULARY

INDULGENCE

The remission before God of the temporal punishment due to sin whose guilt has already been forgiven, available to the faithful under certain conditions prescribed by the Church. A partial indulgence removes part of this punishment, while a plenary indulgence removes all the punishment.

PROTESTANTISM

The name given to any of the Christian denominations that broke from the Catholic Church during the 16th-century Reformation, or to the splinter churches that broke from these schismatic communities; today these include the Lutheran, Anglican (Episcopal), Methodist, Presbyterian, and Baptist churches, to name a few. More generally, the term refers to any Christian ecclesial community, excluding the Orthodox Churches, not in union with the Catholic Church.

REFORMATION

An interrelated series of schisms from the Catholic Church that took place from 1517 to 1648. These include the breaking away of Martin Luther and other reformers in the 16th century as well as the schism of King Henry VIII that resulted in the founding of the Church of England, or Anglican Church.

Focus Question 25:

What is ecumenism?

their own power. Protestantism offered an opportunity for these leaders to seize control of the lands and power formally held by local churches and religious orders and to extend temporal control over matters of justice and moral legislation.

Once independent of the central authority of the Catholic Church, these new Christian communities soon found that they disagreed with one another as well. The movements they started remained separated from one another, and often these communities are still limited to their country of origin. In many ways, the Christian communities that emerged from this period have continued the pattern of splintering that they inherited from their founders, for today there are more than 30,000 different Protestant denominations throughout the world.

The visible unity of the Church on earth was deeply wounded by these schismatic movements, but this period also saw the beginnings of the true reform that the Church had needed. God gave the world saints like Ignatius of Loyola, Francis Xavier, John of the Cross, Teresa of Avila, and Francis de Sales to correct the course of the Pilgrim Church. The emergence of the Catholic Reformation (also called the Counter-Reformation) brought with it new religious fervor on the part of Catholics throughout Europe, new clarification of Church doctrine at the Council of Trent, and new religious orders of men and women—such as the Jesuits and the Discalced Carmelites—dedicated to living in imitation of Christ.

TOWARD GREATER CHRISTIAN UNITY

The task of working toward Christian unity or reunification is called *ecumenism* (literally, *uniting the whole*). As members of the Church, we are called to engage in ecumenism.

In the writings of the Second Vatican Council—and particularly in the *Decree on Ecumenism*—we are able to identify four principles for engaging in ecumenical work.

First, each of us is called to greater conversion of heart. Divisions are brought about because of sin, but the cultivation of virtue and holiness gives us unity of life and moves each of us toward greater Christian unity with others.

Pope Paul VI met with Patriarch of Constantinople Athenagoras I in Jerusalem, January 1964. They issued a joint statement withdrawing mutual excommunications that had formalized the Catholic-Orthodox schism in 1054.

POPE ST. LEO THE GREAT: "PETER HAS SPOKEN"

Pope St. Leo the Great lived in the fifth century and his papacy lasted from AD 440 to 461. By the time of his birth in Italy, the once-great Roman Empire had become divided between east and west, with the Western Empire—centered in Rome—rapidly approaching complete collapse. In addition to the heresies he would have to combat as Pope, one of Leo's biggest challenges would be to ensure the continued survival and growth of the Church amidst the chaos that had resulted from the Western Empire's disintegration.

As Pope, Leo's primary goal was to preserve the Church's unity and adherence to the teaching of Christ. The heresies of Pelagianism, Nestorianism, Monophysitism, and Manichaeism were raging throughout the Church, and Leo understood that it was his pastoral responsibility to defend the faithful from these dangerous errors. He convoked the Council of Chalcedon in 451 and issued a letter—often referred to as the "Tome of Leo"—which clarified the Church's teaching on the disputed issues. When those present heard the words of Pope Leo's letter, they readily assented to his teaching and exclaimed, "Peter has spoken through Leo."

But Pope Leo's accomplishments were not limited to Church doctrine. In perhaps the most memorable event of his papacy, Leo was called upon to intercede on behalf of the people of Rome with Attila the Hun, who had rampaged through northern and central Italy and was now threatening the Eternal City itself. Leo went to meet the notorious barbarian outside the walls of the city, and although we do not know what was said during their encounter, his efforts to prevent the Huns' invasion proved successful: Attila and his men left Rome without a fight.

Because of his pastoral and political achievements, after his death Pope Leo was hailed as "the Great," the first of only three Popes to have received such acclamation. He was declared a saint, and in 1754 Pope Benedict XIV conferred upon him the further honor of being named a Doctor of the Church. His feast day is November 10.

Pope St. Leo the Great.
The first of only three Popes to be named "the Great."

GUIDED EXERCISE

Using the four ways to support ecumenism presented in this chapter, discuss how they could be applied to Catholic teens living today. How could each one of us live each one of these ways right now?

VOCABULARY

ECUMENISM

The efforts to reunite all Christians on earth and to cooperate among Christian faith traditions in achieving common goals.

Second, a deeper understanding between Catholics and our separated brethren is also encouraged, both in terms of theological dialogue and personal knowledge of one another. As has been the case in the past, simple misunderstandings between Catholics and non-Catholics have given rise to suspicion and greater division. Therefore, efforts should be made to understand the positions of our separated brethren and to look for areas of agreement.

Third, although we are to seek common ground with our separated brethren, it is essential that the truth of the Catholic Faith always be represented accurately and in its entirety. The Catholic Church is the pillar and foundation of truth, and the infallible teaching authority given to her by Christ is essential for preserving the visible unity of the Pilgrim Church. "Nothing is

Focus Question 26:
What are the four ways we are called upon to support ecumenism?

FROM *YouCat*

What must we do for the unity of Christians?

In word and deed we must obey Christ, who expressly wills "that they may all be one" (Jn 17: 21).

Christian unity is the business of all Christians, regardless of how young or old they are. Unity was one of Jesus' most important concerns. He prayed to the Father, "that they may all be one…so that the world may believe that you have sent me" (Jn 17: 21). Divisions are like wounds on the Body of Christ; they hurt and fester. Divisions lead to enmities and weaken the faith and credibility of Christians. Overcoming the scandal of separation requires the conversion of all concerned but also knowledge of one's own faith convictions, dialogues with others, and especially prayer in common, and collaboration among Christians in serving mankind. Those in authority in the Church must not let the theological dialogue be interrupted. (*YouCat* 131)

CLOSURE

Summarize in one paragraph what "one" means as the first mark of the Catholic Church.

ALTERNATIVE ASSESSMENT

Conduct a class discussion on why denying the divinity of Christ invariably leads to the rejection of the doctrines of the Trinity and the Redemption.

Christ and the Samaritan Woman by Siemiradzki.
We cannot create genuine unity by watering down the truth.

so foreign to the spirit of ecumenism as a false conciliatory approach which harms the purity of Catholic doctrine and obscures its assured genuine meaning."[1] In other words, we cannot create genuine unity by watering down the truth.

Finally, the Church affirms the responsibility of all Christians to pray for the unity that Christ wills for the Church on earth. At times, we may be able to pray in common with our separated brethren.

> Christ always gives his Church the gift of unity, but the Church must always pray and work to maintain, reinforce, and perfect the unity that Christ wills for her. This is why Jesus himself prayed at the hour of his Passion, and does not cease praying to his Father, for the unity of his disciples: "That they may all be one. As you, Father, are in me and I am in you, may they also be one in us…so that the world may know that you have sent me."[2] (CCC 820)

DISCUSSION QUESTIONS

1. What do we mean when we say the Church is "one"?
2. What are the three kinds of wounds the Church can suffer in regard to the Faith?
3. What are the two main schisms in Church history?
4. What is the distinction between schismatics and separated brethren?
5. What is heresy?
6. What is the Protestant Reformation?
7. What was the Catholic response to the Reformation?
8. What is ecumenism?

ENDNOTES – CHAPTER 9

1. Decree on Ecumenism (*Unitatis Redintegratio*), 11.
2. Jn 17: 21; cf. Heb 7: 25.

Chapter 10
The Four Marks of the Church:
The Church Is Holy, Catholic, and Apostolic

The Church is Christ's resplendent Bride. Everyone has been invited to the wedding.

OPENING ACTIVITY

Begin the class with St. Justin Martyr's description of what Christians do on "the day of the sun" (see text below).

Then discuss how these actions directly correspond to the Sunday Mass we know.

This is an illustration of the apostolicity of the Church, how it is founded on and preserves the faith and worship of the Apostles.

BASIC QUESTIONS

This chapter attempts to answer the following basic questions:

✠ How is the Church holy?

✠ How is the Church catholic?

✠ How is the Church apostolic?

KEY IDEAS

The key ideas of this Chapter are:

✠ The Church is holy because she is united to God who his holy.

✠ The Church is catholic because of her universal nature.

✠ The Church is apostolic because she is founded on and maintains her connection with the Twelve Apostles.

CHAPTER 10
The Four Marks of the Church: The Church Is Holy, Catholic, and Apostolic

Review of Chapter 9:

✠ The Church is "One, Holy, Catholic, and Apostolic." These are the four characteristics or "marks" of the Church.

✠ The Church is one because it is unique: Christ founded one Church, and all members of the Church are united in his one body.

✠ The Church has been afflicted by various schisms and divisions, but remains in essence one. All Christians are called to work toward greater unity with one another.

In Chapter 9 we examined the first of the four marks that Christ gave his Church to identify her as his own. There is but one Church unified in Christ.

In addition to being *One*, the Church is also *Holy*, *Catholic*, and *Apostolic*. The Church is holy because her founder is holy. As Christ's salvation is universal, so is the Church "catholic" or universal: She exists for all peoples in all times and places. And the Church is apostolic because she was founded by Christ upon the Apostles.

We will explore each of these attributes in this chapter so we can see how they are present in the Church.

THE SECOND MARK: THE CHURCH IS HOLY

To understand how the Church is holy, we will need to account both for the Church's intrinsic holiness and for the presence of sin in her members on earth. The Church is always holy but her individual members may not be.

Sanctity in the Church

What does "holy" mean? *Holy* is a Germanic-based English word that means the same thing as the Latin-based English word *sacred*. Sacred shares its root with *saint* (a person in Heaven), *sanctify* (to make holy), *sacrament* (a sign which gives God's grace), *sacrifice* (to destroy as an offering to God), and sacrilege (to treat something dedicated to God in an inappropriate manner).

One meaning of holy is "related to God" or "set aside for God." For example, the grounds of a monastery are "holy" because the place is dedicated to God. In a Catholic church, the tabernacle, the altar, and the building itself are all sacred because they are there for religious purposes. To steal a chalice from a *sacristy* (a room where "holy" things used in liturgical rites are kept) so you can use it to drink from is not just an act of theft but also a sacrilege because it is a sacred vessel. The Pope is called the Holy Father because his "office" is to serve God by ruling his Church. We call the written portion of Divine Revelation the Holy Bible or Sacred Scripture because its primary author is the Holy Spirit and its primary purpose is leading people to God.

The Holy Trinity by Pereda.
God is holy—sacred—because he is completely good.

Focus Question 1:
What are the two basic meanings of holy or sacred?

Focus Question 2:
Why is the Church holy?

Focus Question 3:
What is supposed to happen to sinners in the Church?

FROM *YouCat*

Why is the Church holy?

The Church is holy, not because all her members are supposedly holy, but rather because God is holy and is at work in her. All the members of the Church are sanctified by Baptism.

Whenever we allow ourselves to be touched by the Triune God, we grow in love and become *holy* and whole. The saints are lovers—not because they are able to love so well, but because God has touched them. They pass on the love they have received from God to other people in their own, often original way. Once God takes them home, they also sanctify the Church, because they "spend their heaven" supporting us on our path to HOLINESS. (*YouCat* 132)

But there is more to holiness. Holy refers to God's perfect moral goodness. God is holy—sacred—because he is completely good. The opposite of holy is unholy, sinful, or impure—in other words, morally bad. While God is all-holy, human beings can be holy or sinful, depending on their moral goodness.

Why is the Church holy? The Church is holy because her head, Christ, is holy. The Church is holy because the Holy Spirit, who fill her members, is holy. The Church is holy because her means of serving humanity are all holy: Divine Revelation, grace, and the Sacraments. Also holy are all her members in Heaven. Canonized saints are saints formally recognized by the Church because they led visibly holy lives while on earth.

Sinners in the Church

But the Church on earth is made up of sinners. How can the Church be holy if we sinners are members of it? The Pilgrim Church possesses a real but imperfect holiness (cf. CCC 825). The Church's holiness is not defiled by the presence of sinners; rather, her holiness is so complete that it is intended to transform them. The Catholic Church is where sinners are enabled to become saints.

> "The Church is...holy, though having sinners in her midst, because she herself has no other life but the life of grace. If they live her life, her members are sanctified; if they move away from her life, they fall into sins and disorders that prevent the radiation of her sanctity. This is why she suffers and does penance for those offenses, of which she has the power to free her children through the blood of Christ and the gift of the Holy Spirit."[1] (CCC 827)

Recall the image of the Church as the Bride of Christ. Christ "loved the Church as his Bride, giving himself up for her so as to sanctify her; he joined her to himself as his body and endowed her with the gift of the Holy Spirit for the glory of God"[2] (CCC 823). Christ the bridegroom saves and sanctifies his bride, making her unspotted so she will be worthy of him. Through the means the Church offers to human beings, sinners can become holy.

St. Athanasius (detail) by Coello.
Canonized saints led visibly holy lives while on earth.

Focus Question 4:

Why do members of the Church do penance?

Focus Question 5:

What is impeccability?

Focus Question 6:

What is the problem with sin when it comes to the missionary efforts of the Church?

Focus Question 7:

Why should we ask forgiveness and forgive?

GUIDED EXERCISE

Conduct a think/pair/share on the following question:

✤ What does the image of Christ as the bridegroom and the Church as his bride tell us about holiness and sin in the Church?

Focus Question 8:

What does the word "catholic" mean?

Focus Question 9:

What are the two ways the Church is said to be catholic?

FROM *YouCat*

Why is the Church called catholic?

"Catholic" (Greek *kat' holon***) means related to the whole. The Church is catholic because Christ called her to profess the** *whole* **faith, to preserve** *all* **the sacraments, to administer them and proclaim the Good News to** *all***; and he sent her to** *all* **nations.**

(*YouCat* 133)

Pope Bl. John Paul II leaves a letter at the Western Wall, Jerusalem, March 26, 2000. "God of our fathers, You chose Abraham and his descendants to bring your Name to the Nations: we are deeply saddened by the behaviour of those who in the course of history have caused these children of yours to suffer, and asking your forgiveness we wish to commit ourselves to genuine brotherhood with the people of the Covenant."

Unfortunately, the sins of individual members of the Church can obscure her holiness in the eyes of the world. Even the Pope, though infallible in teaching faith and morals, is not given the gift of personal *impeccability* (inability to sin). The Church, therefore, calls her members to purification, penance, and renewal, so that the perfect holiness she has received from Christ might be seen in the faithful, so they can draw others to Christ. The goodness of Christians attracts people to the Church while their sins can be a stumbling block.

In 2000, Pope Bl. John Paul II publicly asked forgiveness for the sins committed by members of the Church throughout history. At the same time, he asked the members of the Church to forgive the sins committed against them. In this regard, he said, "The Church today feels and has always felt obliged to *purify her memory* of those sad events from every feeling of rancor or revenge."[3] A first step toward holiness is to acknowledge one's sins and to ask forgiveness for them. Another big step is to forgive those who have hurt one.

THE THIRD MARK: THE CHURCH IS CATHOLIC

Today, the word *catholic* is typically used with a capital "c" as a denominational term, much like "Baptist" or "Lutheran," referring to a specific, limited group of Christians. This is the opposite of what the word *catholic* really means: It comes from the Greek word *katholikos*, meaning "universal" or "pertaining to the whole."

The Church is said to be *catholic* in two ways. First, the Church is catholic because she is whole and complete. Christ has united himself to her entirely and has given her the fullness of his holiness. This is closely related to the oneness of the Church. Second, the Church is catholic because she has received universal authority from Christ to fulfill her universal mission. As Christ told the Apostles after his Resurrection, "All authority in heaven and on earth has been given to me. Go therefore and make disciples of all nations" (Mt 28: 18-19).

From the day of Pentecost, Christ's Holy Spirit has empowered the Apostles and their successors to proclaim the saving truth of the Gospel to the entire human race. All men and women, young and old, in every age, are invited to become a part of Christ's Mystical Body, which is the universal or "catholic" Church. No one nation or ethnicity can claim the Church as its alone because, like Christ, the universal Church transcends these human boundaries. As St. Paul put it, "For there is no distinction between Jew and Greek; the same Lord is Lord of all and bestows his riches upon all who call upon him" (Rom 10: 12).

In this sense, the catholicity of the Church transcends time and space. The Church is for all human beings throughout time. The Church is for people living in the twenty-first century. It was for people living in the tenth century. And if the world has not ended by then, it will be for people in the thirty-first century. The Church also extends in space. The Church is not just for Italians or Europeans but also for all people in the entire world. If human beings ever live on other planets, it will be for them, too. This is the meaning of the Church as catholic.

The universality of the Church can also be seen in her "particularity." The New Testament refers to the many local communities of Christians, for example, in Rome, Corinth, Galatia, etc. Insofar as these communities preserved Christian unity in their teaching, worship, and leadership, each was the Church of Christ. As the *Catechism* puts it, "'The Church of Christ is really present in all legitimately organized local groups of the faithful, which, in so far as they are united to their pastors, are also quite appropriately called Churches in the New Testament'"[4] (CCC 832).

That means that the universal Church is not simply the sum total of these local churches; each local Church—diocese, parish, etc.—possesses the presence of Christ in its fullness.

The catholicity of the Church leaves room for great diversity. Because the universal Church exists locally in a multitude of nations and cultures, her external expressions of faith and worship often take on a diversity of appearances, according to the culture in which the Church has taken root. This diversity reflects both the Church's universality and her unity of mission. According to the *Catechism*, "The rich variety of ecclesiastical disciplines, liturgical rites, and theological and spiritual heritages proper to the local churches 'unified in a common effort, shows all the more resplendently the catholicity of the undivided Church.'"[5] (CCC 835)

> The liturgical traditions or rites presently in use in the Church are the Latin (principally the Roman rite, but also the rites of certain local churches, such as the Ambrosian rite, or those of certain religious orders) and the Byzantine, Alexandrian or Coptic, Syriac, Armenian, Maronite and Chaldean rites. In "faithful obedience to tradition, the sacred Council declares that Holy Mother Church holds all lawfully recognized rites to be of equal right and dignity, and that she wishes to preserve them in the future and to foster them in every way."[6] (CCC 1203)

A final dimension of the Church's catholicity is that her membership includes three "groups" of Christians. The first is us, all the faithful living today, also called the Pilgrim Church or the *Church militant*. The other two groups are found within the "faithful departed," those who have died. The souls in the state of Purgatory are being purified, so they will be fit for Heaven. The souls in Purgatory are also called the *Church suffering*. Then there are the souls in Heaven enjoying eternal bliss with the Blessed Trinity and all the saved throughout the ages, also called the *Church triumphant*.

Focus Question 10:

For what group of people does the Church exist?

Focus Question 11:

What are particular churches?

Focus Question 12:

How is diversity within catholicity present in the various rites of the Church?

Focus Question 13:

What are the two "places" in which the Church is found, besides on earth?

FROM YouCat

Who belongs to the Catholic Church?

Anyone who, in union with the POPE and the bishops, is united to Jesus Christ through profession of the Catholic faith and reception of the SACRAMENTS is in full communion with the Catholic Church. [836–838]

God willed *one* CHURCH for *all*. Unfortunately we Christians have been unfaithful to this wish of Christ. Nevertheless, even today we are still deeply united with one another by our faith and common Baptism. (*YouCat* 134)

St. Kateri Tekakwitha (1656-1680).
St. Tekakwitha is the first Native American (Algonquin-Mohawk)
to be canonized by the Church.

Focus Question 14:
Why is the Church apostolic?

Focus Question 15:
What is the threefold sense of the Church's apostolicity?

GUIDED EXERCISE

Free write for a few minutes on how Apostolic Succession is related to the apostolicity of the Church.

FROM *YouCat*

Why is the Church called apostolic?

The CHURCH is called apostolic because she was founded by the apostles, holds fast to their Tradition, and is governed by their successors.

Jesus called the APOSTLES to be his closest collaborators. They were his eyewitnesses. After his Resurrection, he appeared to them repeatedly. He bestowed on them the Holy Spirit and sent them as his authoritative messengers to all the world. They assured unity in the early Church. They conferred their mission and authority upon their successors, the bishops, through the laying on of hands. This process is called APOSTOLIC SUCCESSION. (*YouCat* 137)

The Church was built on and remains on the foundation of the Apostles.

The Last Supper (detail) by Duccio.
The Church is called apostolic because she is founded on the Apostles.
Christ chose these twelve men to be the foundation of his Church.

THE FOURTH MARK:
THE CHURCH IS APOSTOLIC

The fourth mark of the Church is that she is *apostolic*. This mark relates primarily to Christ's selection of the Twelve Apostles as the foundation of his Church. Christ chose these twelve men to be witnesses to his Resurrection, sent out as his ambassadors to the entire world. Like the twelve ministers who assisted Solomon, the son of David, in ruling the kingdom of Israel, the Twelve Apostles were given the task of assisting Christ, the new son of David, in ruling his Kingdom. They were appointed symbolic rulers of the Twelve Tribes of Israel, and were entrusted with Christ's own authority to teach, sanctify, and govern his Church.

The Apostles passed on their office to successors, just as they enrolled a successor to Judas who killed himself after betraying Christ.

> "In order that the mission entrusted to them might be continued after their death, [the apostles] consigned, by will and testament, as it were, to their immediate collaborators the duty of completing and consolidating the work they had begun, urging them to tend to the whole flock, in which the Holy Spirit had appointed them to shepherd the Church of God. They accordingly designated such men and then made the ruling that likewise on their death other proven men should take over their ministry."[7] (CCC 861)

In other words, the Apostles appointed bishops—"their immediate collaborators"—to work with them and to carry on their apostolate after they died. Likewise those bishops were to provide for "other proven men" to carry on after their time.

The Church is called apostolic because she is founded on the Apostles in a threefold sense:[8]

✠ Apostolic Foundation. The Church was built on and remains on the foundation of the Apostles.

✠ Apostolic Faith. The Church guards and transmits the teachings of the Apostles. She does this with the help of the Holy Spirit who dwells in her.

✠ Apostolic Succession. The Church continues being taught, sanctified, and directed by the Apostles in the persons of their successors in the

EARLY ACCOUNT OF THE MASS

S t. Justin Martyr (ca. AD 100–ca. 165) was one of the most famous martyrs to die under the persecution of the Roman Emperor Marcus Aurelius.

Born of pagan parents in Shechem in Samaria in Palestine, Justin studied philosophy from his early youth, and converted to Christianity when he was thirty. Tradition has it that Justin was walking along the sea one day when he met a mysterious old man. The old man convinced him that true knowledge of God could not come only from philosophy, but must be supplemented by reading the revealed word of the prophets.

After his conversion, Justin continued studying philosophy and became an excellent apologist for the Faith. Justin worked tirelessly during the Roman persecutions to defend the Church against those pagans who falsely accused her of many evil things.

In his *First Apology*, which he addressed to Emperor Antoninus Pius and his two adopted sons, Marcus Aurelius and Lucius Verus, Justin provides important descriptions of the celebration of Baptism and the Eucharist.

Below, we see an account of the Eucharist celebration as it existed in the early Church, showing that our belief and worship today are essentially the same as in the second century:

> On the day we call the day of the sun, all who dwell in the city or country gather in the same place.
>
> The memoirs of the apostles and the writings of the prophets are read, as much as time permits.
>
> When the reader has finished, he who presides over those gathered admonishes and challenges them to imitate these beautiful things.
>
> Then we all rise together and offer prayers for ourselves… and for all others, wherever they may be, so that we may be found righteous by our life and actions, and faithful to the commandments, so as to obtain eternal salvation.
>
> When the prayers are concluded we exchange the kiss.
>
> Then someone brings bread and a cup of water and wine mixed together to him who presides over the brethren.
>
> He takes them and offers praise and glory to the Father of the universe, through the name of the Son and of the Holy Spirit and for a considerable time he gives thanks [in Greek, *eucharistian*] that we have been judged worthy of these gifts.
>
> When he has concluded the prayers and thanksgivings, all present give voice to an acclamation by saying: 'Amen.'
>
> When he who presides has given thanks and the people have responded, those whom we call deacons give those present the "eucharisted" bread, wine, and water and take them to those who are absent.[10] (CCC 1345)

Here we can see Sunday worship which includes the Liturgy of the Word, the homily, the petitions, the offertory, the sign of peace, the Eucharistic Prayer and Consecration said by the "presider," which concludes with the Great Amen, and the distribution of Communion.

Justin Martyr's *Second Apology* was addressed to the Roman Senate just after Marcus Aurelius became emperor in AD 161. Shortly thereafter he and six others were denounced as Christians. When they refused to commit apostasy by sacrificing to the gods, they were beheaded. His feast day is June 1.

Focus Question 16:
How did St. Justin Martyr regard philosophy?

Focus Question 17:
What is an example of how we worship just like the early Church?

Focus Question 18:
How could St. Justin Martyr have saved his life?

St. Justin Martyr.
Justin worked tirelessly during the Roman persecutions to defend the Church against pagans who falsely accused her of many evil things.

The Church guards and transmits the teachings of the Apostles with the help of the Holy Spirit who dwells in her.

GUIDED EXERCISE

Free write for five minutes on which of the *four* marks of the Church seems the greatest or most important to you and why.

CLOSURE

Summarize in one paragraph what the marks of holy, catholic, and apostolic mean.

ALTERNATIVE ASSESSMENT

Discuss how the following statement encapsulates the second, third, and fourth marks of the Church:

The Church is Christ's resplendent Bride. Everyone has been invited to the wedding.

pastoral ministry. These successors are the college of bishops, presided over by St. Peter's successor, the Pope.

During the installation of a bishop, the ritual of laying on of hands reflects this direct linkage with the Apostles. Each bishop has been touched by his predecessor in an unbroken line all the way back to the Apostles.

> The Church teaches that "the bishops have by divine institution taken the place of the apostles as pastors of the Church, in such wise that whoever listens to them is listening to Christ and whoever despises them despises Christ and him who sent Christ."[9] (CCC 862)

Aided by the Holy Spirit, the Pope and those bishops in communion with him are responsible for preserving and proclaiming the teachings of Christ that have been passed down from the Apostles in Scripture and in Sacred Tradition.

CONCLUSION

These four marks—One, Holy, Catholic, and Apostolic—belong to the Catholic Church alone. No other church can validly make this claim. The divisions within Christianity resulting from the Great Schism with the Eastern Orthodox Churches, the Protestant Reformation, and the continuous splintering of Protestantism are wounds to the unity of the Church founded by Christ. All Christians of good will must pray and work to heal the disunity of the Church in keeping with Christ's own prayer "that they may all be one; even as thou, Father, art in me, and I in thee, that they also may be in us, so that the world may believe that thou hast sent me" (Jn 17: 21).

In the next three chapters we turn to the great work of the Church, her work of assisting each one of us to become holy.

DISCUSSION QUESTIONS

1. What are the two basic meanings of holy or sacred?
2. Why is the Church "holy"?
3. What is the problem with sin when it comes to the missionary efforts of the Church?
4. What does the word "catholic" mean?
5. What are the two ways the Church is said to be catholic?
6. What are the two "places" in which the Church is found, besides on earth?
7. Why is the Church "apostolic"?
8. What is the threefold sense of the Church's apostolicity?

The Repentant Peter by El Greco. The successors to the Apostles are the college of bishops, presided over by St. Peter's successor, the Pope.

ENDNOTES – CHAPTER 10

1. Paul VI, *CPG* § 19.
2. *LG* 39; cf. Eph 5: 25-26.
3. John Paul II, Homily of the Holy Father, March 12, 2000, n. 3-4
4. *LG* 26.
5. *LG* 23.
6. *SC* 4.
7. *LG* 20; cf. Acts 20: 28; St. Clement of Rome, *Ad Cor.* 42, 44: PG 1, 291-300.
8. Cf. CCC 857.
9. *LG* 20 § 2.
10. St. Justin, *Apol.* 1, 65-67: PG 6, 428-429; the text before the asterisk (*) is from chap. 67.

The Church
Sacrament of Salvation

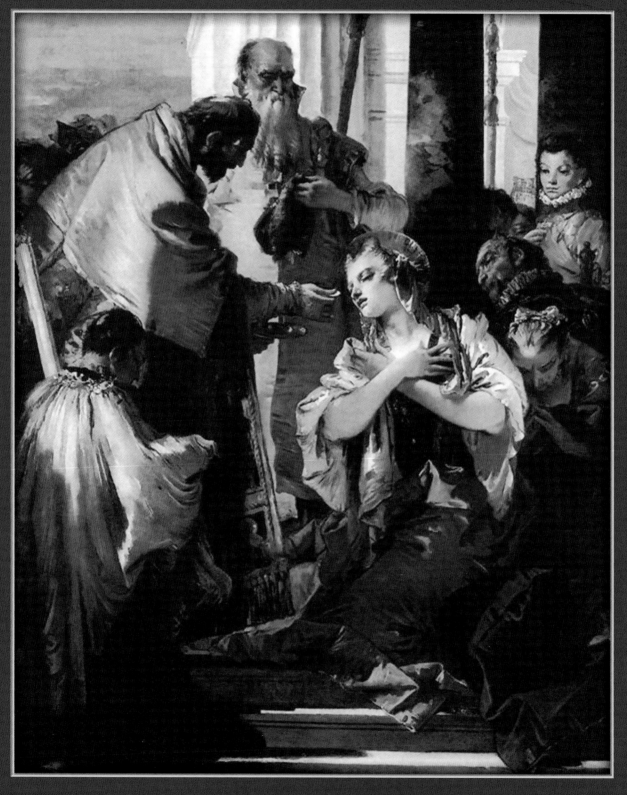

Chapter 11
The Church in the Life of the Faithful: The Universal Call to Holiness

Whoever you are, you are called to the fullness of Christian life and to perfect charity.

OPENING ACTIVITY

Free write for a few minutes on what you think the opening quote in the text of this chapter means (CCC 949). For example, what is meant by "faith," as in the "faith of the faithful" and the "faith of the Church"? Or, how is faith a treasure? What is meant by "enriched by being shared"?

Share your responses.

BASIC QUESTIONS

This chapter attempts to answer the following basic questions:

✠ What is the common priesthood of the faithful?

✠ What is the vocation of the laity?

✠ What is the universal call to holiness and how can the laity accomplish it?

KEY IDEAS

The key ideas of this chapter are:

✠ Every baptized Christian shares in the universal priesthood of Christ and is able to offer sacrifices for the benefit of self and others.

✠ The vocation of the laity is to engage in temporal affairs, ordering them according to the plan of God.

✠ Every person is called by God to become holy, which lay people can accomplish by sanctifying their everyday life in the secular world.

Focus Question 1:
What is divine filiation?

Focus Question 2:
Who has the responsibility to help build the Church?

Focus Question 3:
What are charisms?

CHAPTER 11
The Church in the Life of the Faithful: The Universal Call to Holiness

Review of Chapter 10:

✠ The Church is holy despite the sins of her members because her head is Christ, and Christ is holy.

✠ The Church is catholic because she is universal: Her mission is to gather all of humanity, and she is the universal means of salvation.

✠ The Church is apostolic because she is rooted in the apostolic mission. Her bishops are successors of the Apostles, and she continues to teach the Faith handed down by the Apostles who received it from Christ.

What are the lay faithful of the Church to do with the Faith? As we read earlier, by Baptism we are all called to seek holiness, even perfect holiness. This chapter will explore the question: How do we live with that goal in mind?

COOPERATING WITH GRACE

The faith of the faithful is the faith of the Church, received from the apostles. Faith is a treasure of life which is enriched by being shared. (CCC 949)

We have already learned a lot about the prehistory, origin, and early years of the Church. Christ founded the Church—his Mystical Body. He entrusted a weighty leadership responsibility to his Apostles and their successors. And he gave his Church the Sacrament of Baptism, which makes all of the faithful true members of God's family and adopted sons and daughters of the Father.

"See what love the Father has given us," St. John wrote, "that we should be called children of God; and so we are" (1 Jn 3: 1). A very important part of the life of each Christian is to discover what it means to be a child of God and to live the implications of this truth. This teaching is called *divine filiation*, the condition of being a son or daughter of God.

Even though Christ gave his Church a hierarchical structure in which some rule over others in a spirit of service, he also gave members a radical equality: "'In virtue of their rebirth in Christ there exists among all the Christian faithful a true equality with regard to dignity and the activity whereby all cooperate in the building up of the Body of Christ in accord with each one's own condition and function'"[1] (CCC 872). In other words, each of the faithful is equal in his or her importance (dignity) and work (activity).

Because each person is uniquely created in the image and likeness of God, every member of the Church is given charisms—special graces and gifts from the Holy Spirit—that enable the People of God to build up the Body of Christ. These charisms are given to each individual in keeping with the circumstances of his or her particular state of life. In the next three chapters we will look at how the Church helps the faithful pursue and achieve holiness so as to live in communion with God.

Individuals become holy by cooperating with God's grace. The more heroically they cooperate, the holier they become. Why is heroic cooperation necessary? It is not easy to live as a Christian in the world. Concupiscence, our inclination to sin that is a result of Original Sin, often distorts our intellect and weakens our will. If we ignore the Faith or practice it halfheartedly, we will tend to follow the most convenient and easiest paths in life, and these routes tend to lead to sin.

However, if we embrace our Faith and conscientiously devote ourselves to seeking personal holiness in service to God and neighbor, we will find ourselves strengthened against temptation and drawn ever closer to Christ. This is the struggle that requires heroism, but God is always at our side helping us with his grace *if we want to be helped*. Paradoxically, the closer we get to Christ through his grace and our efforts, the easier things become.

The lifelong challenge and goal that faces every Christian is to know, love, and serve God in this life in order to live happily forever with him and all his friends in the next.

LIVING OUR COMMON PRIESTHOOD

O ne of the images of the word Church we have examined is People of God, the communion of all the faithful in Christ. This beckons back to the Old Testament and the Israelites as God's Chosen People. Like Israel, we are a pilgrim people, believers seeking redemption, holiness, and ultimately God. As the First Letter of Peter puts it, this new people is established as "a chosen race, a royal priesthood, a holy nation…who in times past were not a people, but now are the People of God" (1 Pt 2: 9-10).[2] As we noted earlier in the text, by Baptism all share in the one common priesthood of the faithful, which is a sharing in the priestly ministry of Christ.

By stating that "all share" in this priesthood by Baptism, we mean just that: men, women, and children all are "priests" in this sense. But how does one who is not a member of the ministerial priesthood participate in the common priesthood of Christ?

The Fall of Jericho (detail) by Fouquet.
After the Israelites were liberated from Egypt, God established an order of priests to lead the people in worship and to take care of the Ark of the Covenant. Like Israel, we are a pilgrim people, believers seeking redemption, holiness, and ultimately God.

GUIDED EXERCISE

Do a focused reading of the paragraph beginning, "Why is heroic cooperation necessary?" using the following question:

✺ Why do we need heroism to correspond to God's grace?

First read the question; then read the passage, keeping the question in mind; then reread the question; then attempt to answer the question in writing.

VOCABULARY

CHARISM
A special grace from the Holy Spirit that enables the People of God to build up the Body of Christ.

DIVINE FILIATION
God's adoption of the baptized as his children.

GRACE
The free and unmerited favor of God that is given, first of all, through the Sacraments. Grace is a share in the divine life infused into the soul by the Holy Spirit to heal from sin and to sanctify.

Focus Question 4:
What does it mean when we call the members of the Church "a royal priesthood"?

Each person is uniquely created in the image and likeness of God.

Focus Question 5:

What is the common priesthood of the faithful?

Focus Question 6:

How does one participate in the common priesthood of Christ?

Focus Question 7:

What can we offer according to our share in the common priesthood of the faithful?

VOCABULARY

COMMON PRIESTHOOD

The priesthood of all the faithful; by virtue of our Baptism and Confirmation, the laity and those in the ministerial priesthood (bishops, priests, deacons) share in the one priesthood of Christ and share in his mission of salvation.

HOLY ORDERS

The Sacrament by which the mission entrusted by Christ to his Apostles continues to be exercised in the Church through the laying on of hands in ordination. The Sacrament has three distinct orders—bishop (episcopate), priest (presbyterate), and deacon (diaconate)—and confers an indelible character on the soul.

MINISTERIAL PRIESTHOOD

The priesthood of those who have received Holy Orders, which is at the service of all the faithful.

Focus Question 8:

Who are the laity?

Focus Question 9:

What is the vocation of the laity?

Focus Question 10:

How is the vocation of the laity related to God's covenant with Adam?

Pope Bl. John Paul II greets the People of God in Assisi, Italy.
Every priest offers sacrifices for himself and for others in order to lead all to salvation.

Every priest offers sacrifices for himself and for others in order to lead all to salvation. Christ sacrificed himself for the life of the world. We who are baptized, as members of the common priesthood, are called to do likewise, offering ourselves to God.

What do we have to offer God in sacrifice? The answer is everything but our sins. We have our possessions, our work, our prayer, our sufferings, our pleasures and joys, our relationships with others, our very selves, our very lives, our every thought, word, and deed. We can even humbly offer our weaknesses.

THE VOCATION OF THE LAITY

As mentioned earlier, the term "laity" means all the faithful who are not in Holy Orders or in a religious state approved by the Church. Bishops, priests, and deacons have a vocation for sacred ministry. The vocation of men and women in religious life is to live the evangelical counsels of poverty, chastity, and obedience in the spirit of the Beatitudes.

This does not mean that lay people do not have a vocation. Their vocation is *secular* in nature. The laity "seek the Kingdom of God by engaging in temporal affairs and ordering them according to the plan of God" (*LG* 31). The vocation of the laity is really the same vocation God gave to Adam and Eve: to "fill the earth and subdue it" (Gn 1: 28). "Fill the earth" refers to marriage and the family. "Subdue it" means transforming the world in the manner God wants us to.

In describing the vocation of the laity, the Fathers of the Second Vatican Council wrote:

> [The laity] live in the world, that is, in each and in all of the secular professions and occupations. They live in the ordinary circumstances of family and social life, from which the very web of their existence is woven. They are called there by God that by exercising their proper function and led by the spirit of the Gospel they may work for the sanctification of the world from within as a leaven. In this way they

may make Christ known to others, especially by the testimony of a life resplendent in faith, hope and charity. Therefore, since they are tightly bound up in all types of temporal affairs it is their special task to order and to throw light upon these affairs in such a way that they may come into being and then continually increase according to Christ to the praise of the Creator and the Redeemer.[3]

Thus, the laity are called to engage in everyday family and professional activities, evangelizing and sanctifying the world "from within." The laity includes the old and young, the married and un-married. All who live and work in the midst of the world are on the "front lines" of the Church's evangelical mission.[4] Christ commands all the faithful to be salt and light to the world: "Let your light so shine before men, that they may see your good works and give glory to your Father who is in heaven" (Mt 5: 16). The arena of the laity is the world. The laity can love the world and, with God's help, transform it.

UNIVERSAL CALL TO HOLINESS

One of the fundamental truths of the faith that the Second Vatican Council reemphasized was the *universal call to holiness*. We read earlier how all the baptized are called to seek holiness. This means that every person, whatever his or her state in life, has a vocation to be holy. "[A]ll are called to sanctity and have received an equal privilege of faith through the justice of God."[5] The Council invited the laity into a greater sense of their own vocation and their own role in continuing the mission of Christ.

The universal call to holiness is firmly rooted in Sacred Scripture and Tradition. During his ministry, Christ constantly called people to greater holiness through prayer, repentance, self-denial, charitable works, detachment from the things of this world, the Beatitudes, and the keeping of the Commandments, particularly the great commandment of love, even so far as loving one's enemies. As he told the crowds in his Sermon on the Mount, "Be perfect, as your heavenly Father is perfect" (Mt 5: 48). "All Christians in any state or walk of life are called to the fullness of Christian life and to the perfection of charity."[6]

Jesus Preaching on the Mount by Doré.
Every person, whatever his or her state in life, has a vocation to be holy.

Focus Question 11:
How should lay people regard and act toward the world they live in?

GUIDED EXERCISE

Perform a "paragraph shrink" in the passage from *Lumen Gentium* which begins, "live in the world, that is, in each and in all of the secular professions and occupations."

In a paragraph shrink, you identify the main idea and the two to four most important subordinate or supporting ideas, and then rewrite the paragraph in one or two sentences.

VOCABULARY

LAITY

All the faithful, except those in Holy Orders and those in the state of religious life approved by the Church. These faithful are by Baptism made one body with Christ and are constituted among the People of God, and are in their own way made sharers in the priestly, prophetical, and kingly functions of Christ. They carry out for their own part the mission of the whole Christian people in the Church and in the world.

VOCATION

The particular plan or calling that God has for each individual in this life and hereafter. All people have a vocation to love and serve God and are called to the perfection of holiness. The vocation of the laity consists in seeking the Kingdom of God by engaging in temporal affairs and by directing them according to God's will. Priestly and religious vocations are dedicated to the service of the Church.

Focus Question 12:
What is the universal call to holiness?

Focus Question 13:
How does the universal call to holiness affect lay people?

FROM *YouCat*

How is the universal priesthood of all the faithful different from the ordained priesthood?

Through Baptism Christ has made us into a kingdom of "priests to his God and Father" (Rev 1:6). Through the universal priesthood, every Christian is called to work in the world in God's name and to bring BLESSINGS and grace to it. In the Upper Room during the Last Supper and when he commissioned the APOSTLES, however, Christ equipped some with a sacred authority to serve the faithful; these ordained priests represent Christ as pastors (shepherds) of his people and as head of his Body, the Church.

Using the same word, "PRIEST," for two related things that nevertheless "differ essentially and not only in degree" (Second Vatican Council, *LG* 10, 2) often leads to misunderstandings. On the one hand, we should observe with joy that all the baptized are "priests" because we live in Christ and share in everything he is and does. Why, then, do we not call down a permanent blessing on this world? On the other hand, we must rediscover God's gift to his Church, the ordained priests, who represent the Lord himself among us. (*YouCat* 259)

Focus Question 14:

Where does a layperson seek holiness?

"Young people especially should give serious thought to the question of what place God might want them to have in the Church." (*YouCat* 139)

Catholic high school students help prepare meals at a nutrition center.
Sanctify Ordinary Life: Any work of service or charity can answer the call to holiness.

How do the laity seek holiness in the secular world? By seeking holiness in every circumstance and event in their lives. For example, the laity can offer their worship, prayers, study, work, apostolic undertakings, recreation, and family life to God.

> "[A]ll their works, prayers, and apostolic undertakings, family and married life, daily work, relaxation of mind and body, if they are accomplished in the Spirit—indeed even the hardships of life, if patiently borne—all these become spiritual sacrifices acceptable to God through Jesus Christ. In the celebration of the Eucharist these may most fittingly be offered to the Father along with the body of the Lord. And so, worshiping everywhere by their holy actions, the laity consecrate the world itself to God, everywhere offering worship by the holiness of their lives."[7] (CCC 901)

Here are some practical ways in which a layperson can live his or her call to holiness:

✠ Conscious, active, and regular *participation in the liturgy* of the Church, especially the Holy Mass, and *frequent reception of the Sacraments*, especially the Eucharist and Penance. The Mass is where we hear the Word of God, offer our lives as a sacrifice, and receive back Christ in the Eucharist. The Sacrament of Penance is the way we start over after sinning.

✠ *Praying* every day. In prayer, we have a heart-felt conversation with God our Father and Christ our brother. In prayer, we give thanks for the good things we enjoy, say we are sorry for whatever bad we or others have done, adore God for his goodness and greatness, and ask for the things we and others need and want.

✠ *Practicing sacrifice and self-denial.* One can never overcome concupiscence and live a noble life if one has no self-control and gives in to every impulse. The virtue of fortitude helps one do what is right, despite fear or pain. The virtue of temperance helps one not to be a slave to pleasure.

✖ *Sanctifying ordinary life*—family life, human relationships, professional work, and all of one's activities. One makes these realities holy by offering them to God and then by participating in them the best one can.

✖ Participating in the *apostolic activities* of the Church. As mentioned earlier, we all are called to be apostles.

We will further expand on how to live the universal call to holiness in the next chapter.

THE CHURCH AS SANCTIFIER

The Church is there to help us find holiness and, finding it, become holy ourselves. One of the major roles the Church plays in the life of the faithful is to sanctify her members through her Sacraments and through her teachings. As sanctifier, the Church does two things for us: She takes away our sins and fills us with God's grace.

The Church's primary way of sanctifying is through the Sacraments. In each of the Seven Sacraments, Christ confers grace. We have already mentioned Baptism. Confirmation strengthens us to live as mature Christians. The Eucharist gives us Christ himself as spiritual food. Penance forgives our post-baptismal sins. Anointing of the Sick helps us face illness and death. Holy Orders gives men the power of acting in the person of Christ as a bishop, priest, or deacon. Matrimony makes marriage a means for spouses to grow in holiness.

The Church's discipline, or "rules," is also an aid to our sanctification. For example, the Church requires all her members to attend Mass every Sunday. This is a way the Church helps the faithful as "branches" to stay united to Christ the "vine." Fasting and abstinence, such as from meat on Fridays during Lent, help us turn away from sin and convert our wills more effectively to Christ.

All salvation comes from Christ the Head through the Church his Body. This is the basis of the doctrine that "outside the Church there is no salvation." Thus, all the means available to be saved come to humanity through the Church.

The Church helps the faithful as "branches" to stay united to Christ the "vine."

GUIDED EXERCISE

Based on the five ways presented that a layperson can sanctify ordinary life, free write on the following questions:

✖ Which way seems easiest for you and why?

✖ Which way seems hardest for you and why?

✖ Which way seems most important to you and why?

✖ Which way seems least important (but not unimportant) and why?

FROM *YouCat*

What is the lay vocation?

The LAITY are sent to engage in society so that the kingdom of God can grow among men.

A layperson is not a second-class Christian, for he shares in the priestly ministry of Christ (the universal priesthood). He sees to it that the people in his walk of life (in school, family and work) come to know the Gospel and learn to love Christ. Through his faith he leaves a mark on society, business, and politics. He supports the life of the Church, for instance, by becoming a lector or an extraordinary minister, by volunteering as a group leader, or by serving on church committees and councils (for example, the parish council or the board of directors of an institution). Young people especially should give serious thought to the question of what place God might want them to have in the Church. (*YouCat* 139)

Focus Question 15:
How is the Church an instrument of sanctification?

Focus Question 16:
What is the meaning of the statement, "Outside the Church there is no salvation"?

Focus Question 17:

How can people who are not officially members be saved by the Church?

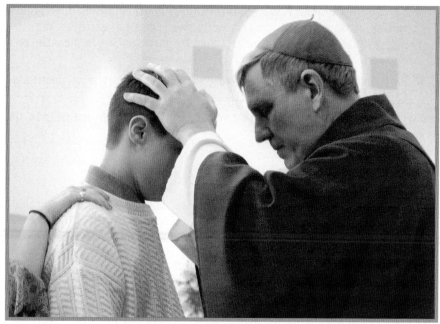

The laity need the grace of the Sacraments and the guidance of the Church to grow and mature along the path to holiness.

Salvation Outside the Church?

But what about those who, through no fault of their own, do not know Christ and his Church? Can they be saved?

The Church teaches that those who "'seek God with a sincere heart, and, moved by grace, try in their actions to do his will as they know it through the dictates of their conscience...may achieve eternal salvation'"[8] (CCC 847).

Obedient to her mission, the Church strives to evangelize the entire world. When encountering other cultures and religions, the Church tries to see whatever goodness and truth people already possess as a preparation for the Gospel. Through the process called *inculturation*, the Church seeks to preserve whatever is good in those cultures.

She also tries to correct things in a culture which can be sanctified in light of the Gospel. For example, in Germanic cultures, the Church turned the pagan practice of worshiping evergreen trees into the custom of the Christmas tree, a symbol of eternal life, and so, of Christ.

Finally, when the Church encounters something in a culture which is entirely bad, it rejects it. An example of this is abortion, in ancient pagan cultures as well as contemporary culture. There is nothing good in abortion that can be sanctified in any way.

CONCLUSION

Lay people share in the common priesthood of Christ, enjoy the universal call to holiness, and can become holy by sanctifying all of the events and circumstance of their lives in the secular world. This is God's will for them, but it is something they cannot accomplish on their own. They need the grace of the Sacraments and the guidance of the Church to grow and mature along the path to holiness.

In Chapter 12, we will explore more fully how the lay faithful can grow in holiness and virtue as they live out their Christian vocation.

St. Dominic and the Albigenses
by Berruguete.
When the Church encounters something in a culture which is entirely bad, it rejects it.

ST. GIANNA BERETTA MOLLA

Greater love has no man than this, that a man lay down his life for his friends. (Jn 15: 13)

t. Gianna Beretta Molla was a wife, mother, and medical doctor who lived in the mid-twentieth century. She was born in Italy in 1922 in a large, devout Catholic family—the tenth of thirteen children—a family that would also produce two priests and one nun.

Gianna considered entering religious life, but ultimately decided to pursue medicine instead. Although she remained focused on her medical studies, she also devoted much of her free time to charity as a volunteer. She graduated from medical school in 1949 and immediately went to work among the poor and the elderly, opening a clinic near her hometown in 1950. She received an additional degree in children's medicine in 1952 in order to give special attention to the mothers with young children who came to her for help.

This was when Gianna met her future husband, Pietro Molla, an engineer who lived across the street from her clinic. They were married at their local parish in late 1955 in a ceremony presided over by her older brother, Fr. Guiseppe. Little more than a year later, Gianna gave birth to her first child, Pierluigi. Gianna and Pietro welcomed him with great joy, and over the next three years, they celebrated the births of two more children, Mariolina and Laura.

In the fall of 1961, after two miscarriages, Gianna again became pregnant. During the course of this pregnancy, however, Gianna's doctors discovered that she had developed a tumor that was threatening both her life and the life of her unborn child. The doctors recommended that she abort her child and undergo surgery to remove the tumor. But for Gianna, this was unacceptable. In addition, she said, "If you must decide between me and the child, do not hesitate. Choose the child—I insist on it. Save the baby."

On Good Friday in 1962, after nine months of pregnancy, Gianna checked into the hospital, giving birth the following day to a baby girl, Gianna Emanuela. Although the doctors struggled to save the lives of both mother and child, in the end, the complications of the delivery proved too much for the elder Gianna. She died exactly one week after the birth of her infant daughter, having indeed been called by Christ to lay down her life for the life of another.

At her canonization in 2004—at which Gianna's husband and children were present—Gianna Molla was praised by Pope Bl. John Paul II for this heroic act of self-giving. Christ, "having loved his own…[,] loved them to the end" (Jn 13: 1). Gianna loved her own child even to the point of dying for her. Her feast day is April 28.

Focus Question 18:
How did St. Gianna behave like Christ?

VOCABULARY

MATRIMONY
The Sacrament by which a man and a woman are joined in Christian marriage, a lifelong and exclusive bond recognized by the Church. It is one of the Seven Sacraments of the Catholic Church.

St. Gianna Beretta Molla.
She was called by Christ to lay down her life for another.

Seek holiness in every circumstance and event in your life.

CLOSURE

Summarize in one paragraph the laity's vocation to become holy in the middle of the world.

ALTERNATIVE ASSESSMENT

Free write for a few minutes, relating the following quote from the Second Vatican Council to the content of this chapter:

All Christians in any state or walk of life are called to the fullness of Christian life and to the perfection of charity. (*LG* 31)

Christ Carrying the Cross by Lotto.
What do we have to offer God in sacrifice? The answer is everything but our sins.

DISCUSSION QUESTIONS

1. What is divine filiation?

2. What does it mean when we call the members of the Church "a royal priesthood"?

3. How does one live out participation in the common priesthood of Christ?

4. Who are the laity?

5. What is the vocation of the laity?

6. What is the universal call to holiness?

7. Where does a layperson seek holiness?

8. How is the Church an instrument of sanctification?

9. What is the meaning of the statement "Outside the Church there is no salvation"?

10. How can people who are not officially members be saved by the Church?

"Faith is a treasure of life which is enriched by being shared." (CCC 949)

ENDNOTES – CHAPTER 11

1. CIC, can. 208; cf. *LG* 32.
2. *LG* 9.
3. *LG* 31.
4. Cf. CCC 899.
5. *LG* 32.
6. *LG* 31.
7. Cf. *LG* 33.
8. *LG* 16; cf. DS 3866-3872.

The Church
Sacrament of Salvation

Chapter 12

The Church in the Life of the Faithful: Holiness in Daily Life

With God's grace we can choose morally good acts on our path to holiness.

OPENING ACTIVITY

Draw a graphic like this on the board and then brainstorm acts which are morally good and easy to accomplish, morally good but hard to accomplish, morally evil and easy to do, and evil but difficult to carry out. Try to find at least one of each type.

MORAL VALUE OF AN ACT		
	Morally Good	Morally Evil
Easy		
Hard		

(LEVEL OF DIFFICULTY)

BASIC QUESTION

This chapter attempts to answer the following basic question:

✣ How do prayer, sacrifice, virtue, apostolate, family life, work and school, and good citizenship relate to holiness of life for a layperson?

KEY IDEAS

The key ideas of this chapter are:

✣ In regard to holiness of life for a lay person,

- prayer creates a connection with God, the source of grace;

- sacrifice helps one grow in self-control;

- virtue makes good actions easier;

- apostolate is God's will for every Christian;

- family life, work, and citizenship are the realities which lay persons sanctify.

CHAPTER 12
The Church in the Life of the Faithful: Holiness in Daily Life

Review from Chapter 11:

✣ We become holy by our cooperation with the gift of grace.

✣ As members of the faithful, we exercise our common priesthood by offering our lives and sacrifices to God for ourselves and for others.

✣ The vocation of lay persons is secular; we seek to live our ordinary lives in holiness and virtue.

✣ We answer our call to holiness and sanctify our lives through participation in the liturgy and Sacraments, prayer, self-denial, and apostolate.

In Chapter 11, we examined the universal call to holiness, and, in an earlier chapter, we looked at the Sacraments, seven fountains of grace which make holiness possible. This chapter will approach the subject in a practical manner by outlining more specifically how the laity, especially young people, can pursue holiness in their everyday lives. We begin with prayer, sacrifice, virtue, and apostolate, before focusing on holiness as it applies to family life, work and school, and good citizenship.

To be holy means to cultivate interior virtue, to live and act in a morally good way. When we seek to be holy, we open ourselves up to the grace of God, and it is this grace that helps us to know and do what is morally good and right, that which is God's will for us. Doing the right and virtuous thing is sometimes attractive to us, but not always; sometimes it is difficult to do good and avoid evil. Yet, to seek and grow in holiness is ultimately related to our ultimate happiness, for we can only be truly happy in God.

We can live out our call to holiness through prayer, sacrifice, exercise of the virtues, active apostolate, and in the conduct of our ordinary lives.

Agony in the Garden (detail) by Bellini.
Sometimes it is difficult to do good and avoid evil. Prayer creates a connection with God, the source of grace to live and act in a morally good way.

PRAYER

Prayer is the raising of one's mind and heart to God or the requesting of good things from God.[1]

God wants us to pray always.[2] We pray both to get to know God and to receive good things from him. Jesus Christ gave us the Our Father or Lord's Prayer, which St. Thomas Aquinas calls the perfect prayer and Tertullian says is a summary of the whole Gospel.

Christ was himself a man of intense prayer. In the Gospels, we see Christ using the formal or traditional prayers of Judaism.[3] He also prayed spontaneously, raising heartfelt prayers of thanks to his Father in Heaven.[4] He sometimes prayed alone in silence,[5] but he also prayed with groups of friends.[6] Christ prayerfully read the Scriptures,[7] and he prayed the Psalms.[8] He celebrated holy days, made pilgrimages, and attended the Jewish liturgy.[9] Christ also practiced fasting,[10] as did his Apostles,[11] which Christianity has traditionally called the "prayer of the senses." Following Christ, the Church presents to us many ways to pray.

The acronym **PACT** can help us remember four main forms of prayer.[12] They are *petition, adoration, contrition,* and *thanksgiving.*

- **Petition** means to ask God for the good things we and other people want and need.
- **Adoration** is praise of God for his goodness and greatness.
- **Contrition** is expressing sorrow for our and other people's sins and offenses.
- **Thanksgiving** is gratitude for all the good things we have received.

Our prayer can be:

- liturgical, for example, the prayers of the Mass or the Liturgy of the Hours;
- formal, using memorized prayers like the Our Father or the Hail Mary; and
- spontaneous, speaking to God straight from the heart.

Additionally, our prayer can be:

- vocal, whether mental (unspoken), spoken aloud, or sung;
- meditative, that is, engaging one's reason, imagination, emotions, and desires, while considering God or some truth of the faith; and
- contemplative, by quietly listening for God to speak to us.

Practically speaking, we can pray:

- alone or with others;
- kneeling or sitting in church, in the privacy of home, on the streets, or in nature, or even while working, driving, or performing everyday activities;
- using the Holy Bible;
- using popular devotions to the Blessed Virgin Mary or one of the saints, such as the Rosary or a novena;
- at specific times of the day, such as morning or night prayers, grace before meals, or the *Angelus* in the morning, noon, and evening;
- when making a pilgrimage or going away on a retreat; and
- accompanied by a sacrifice, such as while fasting or when one simply does not feel like praying.

Focus Question 1:
What state in life or vocation will this chapter focus on?

Focus Question 2:
What is holiness?

VOCABULARY

STATE OF LIFE

A general category of structured Christian living, used primarily in reference to the clerical, consecrated, and married states.

VOCATION

The particular plan or calling that God has for each individual in this life and hereafter. All people have a vocation to love and serve God and are called to the perfection of holiness. The vocation of the laity consists in seeking the Kingdom of God by engaging in temporal affairs and by directing them according to God's will. Priestly and religious vocations are dedicated to the service of the Church.

Focus Question 3:
What is prayer?

Focus Question 4:
How often should we pray?

Focus Question 5:
To what does the acronym PACT refer?

GUIDED EXERCISE

Based on the many ways listed under "Our prayer can be," choose one of them and free write on how you already do (or could) incorporate that form of prayer into your life.

VOCABULARY

NOVENA

A devotional series of prayers, usually done over a period of nine days, seeking intercession for a particular request or need.

Focus Question 6:
What is mortification?

Focus Question 7:
Why is mortification or voluntary sacrifice necessary for building self-control?

Focus Question 8:
What are some reasons to do difficult things?

Focus Question 9:
How did the early Christians show love through self-denial?

VOCABULARY

MORTIFICATION
The practice of self-denial as a way to discipline our bodies and their appetites so as to strengthen the soul and focus more on interior life.

Focus Question 10:
What are virtues?

Focus Question 11:
What are the theological virtues?

Focus Question 12:
What are the four cardinal virtues?

FROM THE *CATECHISM*

Human virtues are firm attitudes, stable dispositions, habitual perfections of intellect and will that govern our actions, order our passions, and guide our conduct according to reason and faith. They make possible ease, self-mastery, and joy in leading a morally good life. The virtuous man is he who freely practices the good. (CCC 1804)

PRACTICING SELF-DENIAL

In prayer we get to know God so we can be like him. Another way to seek holiness is through self-discipline and self-denial, also called *mortification*, literally *dying to the flesh*. Its purpose is to help us avoid sin and strengthen the will. Just as a dieter builds self-control by turning down a dessert, we can build spiritual self-control by controlling our own appetites. St. Paul compared growth in the spiritual life to the training of an athlete:

> Do you not know that in a race all the runners compete, but only one receives the prize? So run that you may obtain it. Every athlete exercises self-control in all things. They do it to receive a perishable wreath, but we an imperishable. Well, I do not run aimlessly, I do not box as one beating the air; but I pommel my body and subdue it, lest after preaching to others I myself should be disqualified. (1 Cor 9: 24-27)

Sometimes mortification is required to avoid sin. Examples are averting one's eyes from an immodestly dressed person or biting one's tongue when tempted to gossip. Sometimes mortification is necessary if we want to be mature persons, for example, bearing a headache or a small inconvenience without complaining. Mortification is also inevitable. If you want to get better at anything that is hard, you have to deny yourself the easy way out of just giving up. The same is true in our spiritual lives. Mortification can also be voluntary, for example, eating less of something you like and more of something you do not, as an act of self-denial.

Self-denial is even more valuable if it is connected to acts of charity. As St. Leo the Great taught, "Let what we deny ourselves by fast be the refreshment of the poor." In other words, when Christians fasted in the early Church, they didn't just *not eat*, they gave the food they would have eaten to the hungry.

Even though we are creatures designed for happiness, life is fraught with difficulties. In other words, suffering and hardships cannot be avoided. Through mortification, the Church gives us a way to make suffering valuable. We can "offer up" these difficulties to God. They then become spiritual sacrifices in which we unite our suffering to the sufferings of Christ and help redeem the world (cf. Col 1: 24).

VIRTUES

Holy actions are impossible without virtues, that is, good habits. Virtues enable us to carry out good acts regularly and relatively easily. Virtuous persons are also called persons of character.

We have spoken about the three theological virtues which God infuses into us at Baptism. Faith lets us believe what God discloses in Divine Revelation. Hope helps us never lose confidence in God's promises. Love or charity makes it possible for us to love God and others the way God loves us, even with a sacrificial love.

We also need *natural virtues*, good habits that anyone can acquire by training. The four main natural virtues—called cardinal virtues—are justice, prudence, fortitude, and temperance. Justice is giving other people the respect we owe them and carrying out all our responsibilities. Prudence is sound decision-making or having the wisdom to know what to do in any situation. Fortitude is doing the right thing even if we are afraid or facing pain. Temperance is being able to set aside pleasure, when necessary, to do what one ought. There are many other important virtues, like generosity, chastity, courtesy, orderliness, honesty, and so on.

Scenes from the Life of St. Francis: How St. Francis Preached to the Birds and then Blessed Montefalco and the Population by Gozzoli.
"Preach the Gospel always; and if necessary, use words."

Virtues are indispensable whether one just wants to be a decent person or if one aspires to be a saint. In fact, when the Church considers a person for canonization as a saint, the first step is to determine whether the candidate has lived all the virtues to a heroic degree.

WITNESSES FOR CHRIST

Before ascending into Heaven, Christ commanded his Apostles to "make disciples of all nations" (Mt 28: 19-20). This command applies to every Christian. Some terms for this work are being an apostle, a missionary, or a witness, or participating in the *apostolic mission* or an *apostolate* of the Church.

We have already indicated two of the most important means of participating in the Church's missionary work: prayer and sacrifice. When you pray for others and offer up difficulties for their benefit, you are already being a missionary.

A third and very important way is by example, the goodness of your life. Anyone who lives the faith authentically will be a good influence on others. This person's actions reflect God's values, touch other people, and cause irresistible questions to arise in their hearts.[13] This approach of silent witness coincides with St. Francis of Assisi's advice: "Preach the Gospel always; and if necessary, use words." Christ said, "Let your light so shine before men, that they may see your good works and give glory to your Father who is in heaven" (Mt 5: 16).

Finally comes actual witness. As St. Peter said, "Always be prepared to make a defense to any one who calls you to account for the hope that is in you" (1 Pt 3: 15). It is necessary to know the Faith so you are able to explain and defend it. That is the purpose of a class like this one.

GUIDED EXERCISE

Have a class discussion on the virtue of studiousness. For example, formulate a definition of studiousness, identify the obstacles to being studious, and brainstorm ways to overcome those obstacles.

Then discuss the following question:

- Is it possible to become holy by being studious? If not, why? If so, how?

VOCABULARY

CHASTITY
The moral virtue that provides for the successful integration of sexuality within the person leading to the inner unity of the bodily and spiritual being; in order words, a commitment to the moral use of one's sexuality in keeping with one's state of life. For unmarried men and women, including those in Holy Orders and the religious life, this means complete abstinence from all sexual activity; for married Christians, it means complete fidelity to one's spouse and respect for both the unitive and procreative purposes of married love.

Focus Question 13:
What are the four ways a Catholic can be an apostle?

Focus Question 14:

To what three basic vocations does God call people?

Focus Question 15:

What vows do religious persons make?

Focus Question 16:

What is the vocation of the laity?

Focus Question 17:

What are the two requirements for living one's basic Christian vocation?

Focus Question 18:

How do sacramentally married couples get the grace they need to be good spouses and parents?

Focus Question 19:

What is the basic duty of children toward parents?

VOCABULARY

APOSTOLATE

The work of the laity toward building up the Church through personal and corporate initiatives and efforts that evangelize, educate, or serve the needs of others.

CONSECRATED LIFE

A permanent state of life recognized by the Church, entered freely in response to the call of Christ to perfection, and characterized by the profession of the evangelical counsels of poverty, chastity, and obedience.

OBEDIENCE

As one of the evangelical counsels, it refers to a vow to respect one's religious superiors, an element of consecrated life.

POVERTY

As one of the evangelical counsels, a commitment to detachment from worldly goods and simplicity of life as a way of seeking justice and solidarity with the world's poor.

Childhood of Christ by Honthorst.
Youth is a time for discovering God's specific call or vocation.

FOLLOWING CHRIST IN OUR EVERYDAY LIFE

The Pilgrim Church is a visible society, structured and given order by Christ for the purpose of extending the Kingdom of God over the entire world. As we have seen, within the Body of Christ are many members or "organs," all of which have a contribution to make.

The universal call of all the Christian faithful is to live in imitation of Christ, pursuing holiness of life and the perfection of charity. Youth is a time for discovering God's specific call or vocation.

Some men are called by Christ to serve the Church through Holy Orders. Other men and women are called to witness the Gospel through the religious or consecrated life in which they live the vows of poverty, chastity, and obedience. Others are called to serve God as lay faithful, both married and unmarried, witnessing to Christ in their family life, in their daily activities, and in the public square. No matter what our state in life is—Holy Orders, lay, or religious life—each is called to serve God and neighbor.

In Our Family Life

By God's design, each person comes into the world through a family. God entrusts parents with the education of their children both in life and in faith. This task is so important that Christ has raised the natural institution of matrimony to a Sacrament. Through this Sacrament, Christian spouses receive grace that enables them to live their vocation as husband and father or wife and mother.

The Fourth Commandment is "Honor your father and mother." Children living at home should show love, gratitude, respect, and obedience to their parents. Grown children have a duty to look after their sick or aging parents and provide both material and moral support to them. Some teens already do this for a disabled parent or grandparent. Children also have duties to their siblings, which change according to their age, but never go away.

At Work and in School

Work is part of God's basic design for humanity. After God created Adam, "The LORD God took the man and put him in the garden of Eden to till it and keep it" (Gn 2: 15).

> *Human work* proceeds directly from persons created in the image of God and called to prolong the work of creation by subduing the earth, both with and for one another.[14] Hence work is a duty: "If any one will not work, let him not eat."[15] Work honors the Creator's gifts and the talents received from him. It can also be redemptive. By enduring the hardship of work[16] in union with Jesus, the carpenter of Nazareth and the one crucified on Calvary, man collaborates in a certain fashion with the Son of God in his redemptive work. He shows himself to be a disciple of Christ by carrying the cross, daily, in the work he is called to accomplish.[17] Work can be a means of sanctification and a way of animating earthly realities with the Spirit of Christ. (CCC 2427)

Because we are called to be witnesses to the Faith wherever we happen to be, our workplace or school provides a powerful opportunity to reflect the virtues of Christ. By performing our duties well and maintaining a cheerful and positive attitude, we can sanctify our work, ourselves, and those with whom we come in contact.

When we deal with others fairly and ethically, showing courtesy and kindness, we model proper Christian virtues. This may lead to friendships and acquaintances in the workplace that provide opportunities to witness to our faith more directly.

Attracted to our example and good spirit, our colleagues, classmates, and friends may want to learn more about us and the source of our virtue and happiness. Such moments can be entry points to witness our faith, our Church, and our commitment to Christ. Continued interest may invite a deeper discussion on the issues of faith, whether it be with other Catholics, our separated brethren, or persons of non-Christian religions. The only way others may ever hear of God or his Church may be through you.

Focus Question 20:
How does work relate to holiness?

Focus Question 21:
What is the professional work of a young person?

Focus Question 22:
Why do we have the duty of doing apostolate with others?

GUIDED EXERCISE

CCC 2427 is packed with valuable information. "Unpack" it by doing a "paragraph shrink."

Work with a partner to first identify the most important idea, then the two to four most important subordinate or supporting ideas, then rewrite the article in one or two sentences.

Christ Giving the Keys to Peter by Bentele.
The only way others may ever hear of God or his Church may be through you.

Our workplace or school provides a powerful opportunity to reflect the virtues of Christ.

Focus Question 23:

Whose job is the positive transformation of culture and politics?

Focus Question 24:

What is the common good?

Focus Question 25:

How do the laity normally promote the common good?

Focus Question 26:

To what extent should the laity be involved in public life?

FROM *YouCat*

Are Christians obliged to become involved in politics and society?

It is a special duty of the Christian LAITY to become involved in politics, society, and commerce in the spirit of the Gospel: in charity, truth, and justice. CATHOLIC SOCIAL TEACHING offers them clear guidance in this endeavor.

Partisan political activity is, however, incompatible with the ministry of bishops, PRIESTS, and religious, who must be of service to everyone. (*YouCat* 440)

It is an obligation of every individual to participate in achieving the common good.

The faithful must call for a continued conversion of the members of society, condemning injustice where it is found, and always promoting a defense of human dignity and improvements to the conditions of human life.

In Society

The laity is also called to be involved in culture and politics. They are responsible for shaping the "public square" according to the will of God.

The Magisterium rightly addresses issues of public policy insofar as they involve questions of morality and the common good. But it is up to the laity to transform the world according to the will of God: "It is the duty of citizens to work with civil authority for building up society in a spirit of truth, justice, solidarity, and freedom."[18]

The *common good* is "the sum total of social conditions which allow people, either as groups or individuals, to reach their fulfillment more fully and more easily."[19] "The common good consists of three essential elements: [1] respect for and promotion of the fundamental rights of the person; [2] prosperity, or the development of the spiritual and temporal goods of society; [and 3] the peace and security of the group and of its members."[20]

The common good, however, is not the sole responsibility of the government. Rather, it is an obligation of every individual to participate in achieving the common good, an ethical obligation "inherent in the dignity of the human person."[21] The faithful begin by being conscientious in their personal responsibilities, including the education of their families and their daily work.

To the extent possible, the faithful should participate in the public life of society. Such participation can include informed voting, campaigning for just causes and worthy candidates, or even running for public office. In whatever capacity, the faithful must call for a continued conversion of the members of society, condemning injustice where it is found, and always promoting a defense of human dignity and improvements to the conditions of human life.[22] An important dimension of our participation in public life is generous service, that is, voluntary acts of charity to those in need.

ST. THOMAS MORE

t. Thomas More (1478-1535) was one of the most important men of the English Renaissance and a true "renaissance man." He was also a giant of the Catholic Faith. He was Lord Chancellor of England, making him the second most important person in the country, under the king. More was also a lawyer, theologian, philosopher, author, diplomat, counselor, teacher, Sheriff of London, Member of Parliament, and friend of the eminent men of his age. His public speaking abilities and witty conversation were unmatched. He was a devoted husband and father, with one daughter and three sons. Atypical of his day, he gave his daughter an education that matched any young man's of the time. As a layman, he balanced family life, the education of his children, his work as a lawyer, and his literary and historical studies.

In his youth, St. Thomas had considered the priesthood—even living in a monastery for four years—but discerned that his vocation was to the lay state, which he lived as a Third Order (Secular) Franciscan and Benedictine Oblate. Known for his integrity, his splendid court garments hid an uncomfortable hair shirt, called a cilice, which he wore to mortify himself. His smile often hid his hunger due to regular fasting. He prayed and attended Mass daily.

More decided to resign his post as Chancellor because he opposed King Henry VIII's divorce and adulterous remarriage, a decision that slowly impoverished his family. To justify himself, King Henry pressured every important person in England to sign both the Act of Succession, which stated that Henry's children with Anne Boleyn were rightful heirs to the throne, and the Act of Supremacy, which acknowledged that Henry, not the Pope, was the head of the Church in England. More declined to sign either and was imprisoned in the Tower of London.

While awaiting his trial, he continued to keep his good humor. In his cell he wrote a prayer in which he exclaimed:

> Grant me, my Lord, a desire to be with you, not so as to avoid the calamities of this world, nor even to avoid the pains of purgatory nor those of hell, not to gain the joys of Heaven, not out of consideration for my own profit, but simply through true love for Thee.

After a hasty trial, he was sentenced to death by beheading. In a letter to his daughter Margaret (Meg) about his unworthiness to be a martyr, he wrote:

> Although I know well, Margaret, that because of my past wickedness I deserve to be abandoned by God, I cannot but trust in his merciful goodness...I will not mistrust him, Meg, though I shall feel myself weakening and on the verge of being overcome with fear...I trust he shall place his holy hand on me and in the stormy seas hold me up from drowning...Nothing can come but what God wills. And I am very sure that whatever that be, however bad it may seem, it shall indeed be the best.

On the scaffold before the executioner's blade fell, St. Thomas More said to the crowd: "I die the king's good servant, but God's first."

Focus Question 27:
What was St. Thomas More's state in life?

Focus Question 28:
How did St. Thomas integrate the Faith into his life?

Focus Question 29:
How far was St. Thomas More willing to go to stay true to the Faith?

St. Thomas Moore.
"I die the king's good servant, but God's first."

CLOSURE

Summarize in one paragraph what holiness is and how a student can grow in holiness.

ALTERNATIVE ASSESSMENT

Free write on how right intention, prayer, self-sacrifice, virtue, and apostolate help one become holy.

St. Leo the Great taught, "Let what we deny ourselves by fast be the refreshment of the poor." Christ calls us not only to provide materially for the poor but also to love them as Christ loves us.

DISCUSSION QUESTIONS

1. What is prayer?
2. What does the acronym PACT refer to?
3. What is mortification?
4. What are virtues?
5. To what three basic vocations does God call people?
6. How do sacramentally married couples get the grace they need to be good spouses and parents?
7. How does work relate to holiness?
8. Why do we have the duty of doing apostolate with others?
9. How does the laity normally promote the common good?
10. To what extent should the laity be involved in public life?

ENDNOTES – CHAPTER 12

1. St. John Damascene, cited in CCC 2590.
2. Lk 18: 1; 21: 36; 1 Thes 5: 17.
3. Cf. Mk 12: 29.
4. Cf. Jn 11: 41-42.
5. Cf. Lk 3: 21-22, 5: 16, 6: 12, Lk 11: 1.
6. Cf. Lk 9: 18.
7. Lk 4: 16-20.
8. Mk 15: 34.
9. Cf. Jn 7: 10-14.
10. Mt 4: 2.
11. Cf. Acts 13: 2, 14: 23.
12. A "pact" is an agreement. Christ has promised to answer our prayers, so he has made a kind of "pact" with us.
13. Cf. *Evangelii Nuntiandi*, 21.
14. Cf. Gn 1: 28; *GS* 34; *CA* 31.
15. 2 Thes 3: 10; Cf. 1 Thes 4: 11.
16. Cf. Gn 3: 14-19.
17. Cf. *LE* 27.
18. CCC 2255.
19. *GS* 26.
20. CCC 1925.
21. CCC 1913.
22. CCC 1916.

It is necessary to know the Faith so you are able to explain and defend it.

Chapter 13
The Church as the
Communion of Saints

In the end, we are either with or without God.

OPENING ACTIVITY

Incorporate into the class's Opening Prayer the Parable of the Sheep and the Goats (Mt 25: 31-36).

BASIC QUESTIONS

This chapter attempts to answer the following basic questions:

✠ What is the Communion of Saints?

✠ What are the Last Things?

KEY IDEAS

The key ideas of this chapter are:

✠ The Communion of Saints is the real unity which exists among all members of the Church on earth, in Purgatory, and in Heaven by virtue of her head, Jesus Christ.

✠ The Last Things are death, the Particular Judgment, Hell, Purgatory, or Heaven; and the General Judgment, which includes the resurrection of the body.

Focus Question 1:

What are the three states or conditions in which the Church currently exists?

Focus Question 2:

What is the Communion of Saints?

Focus Question 3:

What are the final two possible fates that face us after death?

CHAPTER 13
The Church as the Communion of Saints

Review of Chapter 12:

✠ Fostering a good prayer life is essential to living the call to holiness.

✠ Sacrifice and self-denial help us build virtue and avoid sin.

✠ The virtues help us make good moral decisions and strengthen us against temptation.

✠ Our primary apostolate, or Christian witness, to the world is by our lived example.

✠ We are called to lead lives of holiness wherever we are, in every circumstance, whether in the family, in the workplace, at school, or in society.

Earlier in this text, we discussed how the Church is a communion, or a Sacrament of Communion. This chapter will begin by looking at the Church as the *Communion of Saints*. This real but invisible fellowship of all the saved currently exists in three conditions. Then we will examine the final fate of all souls through the doctrines organized according to the *Last Things*.

THE CHURCH AS A COMMUNION OF SAINTS

We might tend to limit our idea of the Church as only the visible Church on earth. In reality, the one Church currently is, as noted in Chapter 10, made up of members in three different states or conditions.

✠ The **Church militant** is comprised of Christ's faithful here on earth.

✠ The **Church suffering** is comprised of the souls in Purgatory who have died in communion with God but have not yet been fully purified.

✠ The **Church triumphant** is comprised of the glorified members in Heaven, enjoying the beatific vision forever.

Yet, the Church is one. Christ unites each member of the Church to himself and all to one another. This is what the Communion of Saints means.

> These different parts of the Church form one and the same Church and one single body, because they have the same head, Jesus Christ; the same spirit, which gives them life and unity; and the same aim— eternal happiness—which some already enjoy and others await.[1]

Who Are the Saints?

Even though later in this chapter we will consider Heaven, Hell, and Purgatory under the "Last Things," there are ultimately only two final destinations for human beings: One is to be with God in Heaven, and the other is to be without God in Hell. Each of us will be one of the saved or one of the damned. The saints are those who are saved, and they are saved because they have cooperated with God's grace.

Virgin and Child with Saints by Boccaccino.
Saints represented in this painting are St. Catherine of Alexandria, St. Catherine of Tyre, St. Peter, and St. John the Baptist.

FROM *YouCat*

What does the "communion of saints" mean?

The "communion of saints" is made up of all men who have placed their hope in Christ and belong to him through Baptism, whether they have already died or are still alive. Because in Christ we are one Body; we live in a communion that encompasses heaven and earth.

The Church is larger and more alive than we think. Among her members are the living and the deceased (whether they are still undergoing a process of purification or are already in the glory of God), individuals known and unknown, great saints and inconspicuous persons. We can help one another even beyond the grave. We can call on our patrons and favorite saints, but also our departed relatives and friends whom we believe are already with God. Conversely, by our intercessory prayer, we can come to the aid of our dear departed who are still undergoing purification. Whatever the individual does or suffers in and for Christ benefits all. Conversely, this unfortunately means also that every sin harms the communion. (*YouCat* 146)

"Saint" can also refer to the members of the Church on earth who are in a state of grace. St. Paul refers to his fellow members of the Pilgrim Church as saints, although no one's salvation is assured while on earth. This is why we pray for the grace of final perseverance, i.e., remaining united to God until the very end of our lives. It is also why in the Hail Mary we pray for Our Lady's intercession, "now and at the hour of our death." We have freedom, which means we can always choose to reject God.

Even though they are not yet in Heaven, the souls in Purgatory are assured to be there when their purification is complete. Out of charity, the Church militant prays for all the souls in Purgatory on the Feast of All Souls on November 2.

All the souls in Heaven are saints. The Church militant celebrates the lives of these happy souls on the Feast of All Saints, November 1. Recall that we do not "worship" them but venerate, honor or show respect for them, and ask for their intercession.

The most specialized meaning of the word saint is a person whom the Church has "canonized" or officially recognized as certainly being in Heaven. As the *Catechism* reminds us:

> By *canonizing* some of the faithful, i.e., by solemnly proclaiming that they practiced heroic virtue and lived in fidelity to God's grace, the Church recognizes the power of the Spirit of holiness within her and sustains the hope of believers by proposing the saints to them as models and intercessors.[2] "The saints have always been the source and origin of renewal in the most difficult moments in the Church's history."[3] Indeed, "holiness is the hidden source and infallible measure of her apostolic activity and missionary zeal."[4] (CCC 828)

The canonized saints are "useful" for the Church militant because they are models of how to live on earth as followers of Christ and because they can intercede for us to God to help us get the things we need.

Focus Question 4:
What are the four meanings of the word "saint"?

Focus Question 5:
Why do we pray for the grace of final perseverance?

Focus Question 6:
Why are the canonized saints "useful" for the Church militant?

GUIDED EXERCISE

CCC 828 encapsulates a wealth of "facts" about canonized saints.

Work with a partner to make a bullet-point list of individual facts about canonized saints presented in this *Catechism* paragraph.

Focus Question 7:

Why are the saints models of
Christian living?

Focus Question 8:

What is intercessory prayer?

Focus Question 9:

Why is intercessory prayer natural?

Focus Question 10:

Why does it make sense to ask the saints
to intercede for us?

VOCABULARY

INTERCESSORY PRAYERS

Any prayers on behalf of another person.
We intercede for others when we pray
for them; the saints in Heaven intercede
for us when they pray for us. We can
pray to the saints and to the Blessed
Virgin Mary asking their intercession
before God on our behalf.

SAINT

A member of the Church—the Mystical
Body of Christ, the Communion of
Saints—on earth, in Purgatory, or
in Heaven. The Church may officially
declare a member of the Church in
Heaven to be a saint by canonization,
adding him to the calendar and
promoting his public veneration.

St. Vincent de Paul Helping the Plague-Ridden (detail) by Ansiaux.
St. Vincent de Paul (1581-1660) founded the Daughters of Charity in 1633 to care
for the poor and provide hospital care for them.

Models of Living

The first and always useful way human beings learn is through imitation.
You might not be consciously aware of it, but chances are that you walk like,
talk like, have the same posture as, and make the same facial expression
as your family. You picked these things up by unconsciously imitating your
parents and siblings.

The saints in Heaven can be our models. They have already passed through
their period of trial and pilgrimage on earth and have reached the perfection
of Heaven. With the exception of the Blessed Virgin Mary, who was conceived
without Original Sin, all the saints were sinners just like us. They had to
work to overcome temptation with the help of God's grace; when they sinned,
they relied on God's mercy. Some suffered martyrdom; others practiced heroic
virtues in faithfulness to the Gospel, especially the virtue of charity. We who
strive to be saints-in-the-making can model ourselves on the saints who are
already in Heaven.

Intercessors

We can and should rely on the saints as *intercessors* to help us. In forming
his people as a community, God chose to work through intermediaries.
For example, Jesus Christ revealed to the Apostles what his Father wanted
known. The Apostles then revealed to the people of their time what had been
revealed to them.

When a mother prays for her sick child, she is interceding for that child with
God. If the child is gravely ill, she will ask her relatives, friends, and even
her other children to also pray for him or her. She would be asking others to
intercede with God for the child as well.

From the beginning, the members of the Church militant have prayed not
just for each other but in fact for everyone on earth, including secular rulers.
Whenever we pray for someone else, we are interceding for them before
God. Christians have prayed for each other, both living and dead, from the
very beginning.

*The saints in Heaven
can be our models.*

THE LAST THINGS

We have said there are ultimately only two possible fates for human beings. In the end, each of us will either be in the Church in Heaven or separated from it in Hell. The doctrines of the Faith dealing with final realities are grouped together under the "Last Things." These final events and conditions are death, the Particular Judgment, Hell, Purgatory or Heaven, and the General Judgment, which includes the resurrection of the body.

Death

The Second Vatican Council fathers wrote that a human being rightly dreads the thought "of perpetual extinction" and "abhors and repudiates the utter ruin and total disappearance of his own person" (*GS* 18). This is what death seems to be and why we do not want to think about it, though some souls have "death wishes" because they are sick in soul.

What is death? The Church teaches that death is the separation of the immaterial soul from the material body. The body is composed of incredibly well-organized material parts—perhaps 50 trillion cells with possibly 20 trillion molecules per cell. At death, the body begins to decompose.

But the soul, which has the properties of reason and free will, is nonmaterial and simple—meaning it has no parts. Therefore, once God creates a person's soul at the moment of his or her conception, it can endure forever because there is nothing to break down in it. The soul is not only immaterial; it is also immortal.

At death, the possibility of merit, demerit, or conversion ceases. "Death puts an end to human life as the time open to either accepting or rejecting the divine grace manifested in Christ."[5] The soul immediately "goes" to Heaven, Hell, or Purgatory as deserved.

The Particular Judgment

The Particular Judgment refers to each person's individual encounter with Christ at the moment of death. God makes each person see his entire life and whether he is in a state of union with God or in hideous sin.

> Each man receives his eternal retribution in his immortal soul at the very moment of his death, in a particular judgment that refers his life to Christ: either entrance into the blessedness of heaven—through a purification[6] or immediately[7]—or immediate and everlasting damnation.[8] (CCC 1022)

St. John of the Cross wrote that, "At the evening of life, we shall be judged on our love"[9] (CCC 1022). This is a doctrine both comforting and chilling. God is love, which makes us confident. Yet, we have failed to love others many times, as the Parable of the Sheep and the Goats reminds us. This is why one of the basic forms of prayer is contrition: sorrow expressed for our own sins and those of others, and lack of love.

Purgatory

Purgatory is where the souls of the saved (i.e., those who have died in a state of grace) but are imperfectly purified, are "purged" and purified so as to achieve the holiness needed to enter Heaven.

Strictly speaking, Purgatory is not a physical place. Disembodied souls are nonmaterial and so do not need a "place" to be. Instead, Purgatory is a state of existence.

Focus Question 11:
What are the Last Things?

Focus Question 12:
Why don't people like to think about death?

Focus Question 13:
What is death?

Focus Question 14:
What does the moment of death mean in terms of salvation?

Focus Question 15:
What is the Particular Judgment?

Focus Question 16:
What are the three possible results of the Particular Judgment?

Focus Question 17:
Why is prayer of contrition important?

Focus Question 18:
Why is Purgatory appropriate for some souls?

Focus Question 19:
Why is Purgatory a condition, not a place?

FROM *YouCat*

What is purgatory?

Purgatory, often imagined as a place, is actually a condition. Someone who dies in God's grace (and therefore at peace with God and men) but who still needs purification before he can see God face to face is in purgatory.

When Peter had betrayed Jesus, the Lord turned around and looked at Peter: "And Peter went out and wept bitterly"—a feeling *like being in purgatory*. Just such a purgatory probably awaits most of us at the moment of our death: the Lord looks at us full of love—and we experience burning shame and painful remorse over our wicked or "merely" unloving behavior. Only after this purifying pain will we be capable of meeting his loving gaze in untroubled heavenly joy. (*YouCat* 159)

Focus Question 20:

Why are the souls in Purgatory joyful?

Focus Question 21:

Why are the souls in Purgatory in a state of suffering?

Focus Question 22:

What is our duty toward the souls in Purgatory?

FROM *YouCat*

Can we help the departed who are in the condition of purgatory?

Yes, since all those who are baptized into Christ form one communion and are united with one another, the living can also help the souls of the faithful departed in purgatory.

When a man is dead, he can do nothing more for himself. The time of active probation is past. But we can do something for the faithful departed in purgatory. Our love extends into the afterlife. Through our fasting, prayers, and good works, but especially through the celebration of Holy EUCHARIST, we can obtain grace for the departed. (*YouCat* 160)

Focus Question 23:

What is Hell?

Focus Question 24:

What places a person in the condition of Hell?

In Purgatory, the Holy Souls are joyful because they are saved. They are completely sure of seeing God and enjoying eternal happiness. Yet, this truth is also the source of their sufferings. Now that they finally see that God is the only thing that can really make them happy, they must wait for a complete and perfect communion with him that can only be achieved completely and perfectly in Heaven. On top of this, their separation is completely their own fault. In addition, these persons can do nothing for themselves now. When they were alive, they could have prayed, received the Sacraments, done penance, shown love to others, and so on. Now they can only wait.

As part of the communion of the saints, we can help the souls in Purgatory by praying, offering sacrifices, obtaining indulgences, and offering Masses for them.

Hell

Hell is eternal self-exclusion from communion with God and with the blessed in Heaven. The souls in Hell died unrepentant of mortal sin or refused the love and mercy of God at the end. Christ spoke often of Hell as "fire" and "darkness" where there will be "weeping and gnashing of teeth" as condemned souls are tormented by "the worm that dies not." The souls in Hell continually thirst for God while hating him.

Some people think God would never condemn someone to Hell. In a sense, this is true. Souls are in Hell because that is what they chose. Hell is a consequence of the freedom God gives us to love him and our fellow man. We cannot be united to God unless we freely choose to love him. We cannot

A Soul Tormented in Hell, 15th Century Illustration.
The souls in Hell continually thirst for God while hating him.
We cannot be united to God unless we freely choose to love him.

In Purgatory, the Holy Souls are joyful because they are saved.

love God if we sin grievously against him, our neighbor, or our own selves. "He who does not love remains in death. Anyone who hates his brother is a murderer, and you know that no murderer has eternal life abiding in him" (1 Jn 3:14-15). To die in mortal sin, without repentance, and without seeking refuge in the compassionate love of God, implies remaining separated from God forever because of our free choice.

Of what does the punishment of Hell consist? "The chief punishment of hell is eternal separation from God, in whom alone man can possess the life and happiness for which he was created and for which he longs" (CCC 1035).

Heaven

Heaven is the state of everlasting life in which we see God, become like him, and enjoy eternal happiness.

> This perfect life with the Most Holy Trinity—this communion of life and love with the Trinity, with the Virgin Mary, the angels and all the blessed—is called "heaven." Heaven is the ultimate end and fulfillment of the deepest human longings, the state of supreme, definitive happiness. (CCC 1024)

> This mystery of blessed communion with God and all who are in Christ is beyond all understanding and description. Scripture speaks of it in images: life, light, peace, wedding feast, wine of the kingdom, the Father's house, the heavenly Jerusalem, paradise. (CCC 1027)

Paradise by Menabuoi.
"...this communion of life and love with the Trinity, with the Virgin Mary, the angels and all the blessed..." (CCC 1027)

Focus Question 25:
Why would someone be in Hell?

Focus Question 26:
What is the chief punishment of Hell?

GUIDED EXERCISE

In his book *Fundamentals of the Faith*, philosophy professor Peter Kreeft wrote the following:

Hell follows from two other doctrines: Heaven and free will. If there is a Heaven, there can be a not-heaven. And if there is free will, we can act on it and abuse it.

Free write for a few minutes on whether you think this statement sheds light on the existence of Hell.

Then share your responses.

FROM *YouCat*

What is Hell?

Our faith calls "hell" the condition of final separation from God. Anyone who sees love clearly in the face of God and, nevertheless, does not want it decides freely to have this condition instead.

Jesus, who knows what hell is like, speaks about it as the "outer darkness" (Mt 8: 12). Expressed in our terms, it is cold rather than hot. It is horrible to contemplate a condition of complete rigidity and hopeless isolation from everything that could bring aid, relief, joy, and consolation into one's life. (*YouCat* 53)

Focus Question 27:
What is Heaven?

Based in the bullet-pointed list of some of the sources of the happiness of Heaven, free write for a few minutes on which one personally means the most to you and why.

Focus Question 28:

Can we fully grasp how good Heaven will be?

FROM *YouCat*

What is heaven?

Heaven is God's milieu, the dwelling place of the angels and saints, and the goal of creation. With the words "heaven and earth" we designate the whole of created reality.

Heaven is not a place in the universe. It is a condition in the next life. Heaven is where God's will is done without any resistance. Heaven happens when life is present in its greatest intensity and blessedness—a kind of life that we do not find on earth. If with God's help we arrive someday in heaven, then waiting for us will be "what no eye has seen, nor ear heard, nor the heart of man conceived, what God has prepared for those who love him" (1 Cor 2: 9). (*YouCat* 52)

Focus Question 29:

What is the *Parousia*?

Focus Question 30:

What is the General Judgment?

Focus Question 31:

What is the resurrection of the body?

VOCABULARY

PAROUSIA

Greek term for the Second Coming of Christ, who will come for the Final Judgment at the end of time.

Man is the bodily rational creature who seeks happiness. We are made for happiness and all our desires to be happy are perfectly fulfilled in Heaven. Some of the sources of the happiness of Heaven are:

- ✠ the Beatific Vision: seeing God, each of the three Persons of God, and experiencing God's infinite goodness, truth, and beauty;
- ✠ being with the Blessed Virgin, the angels, and all the saints;
- ✠ loving others to our full capacity and being fully loved;
- ✠ rejoicing in one another's good; and
- ✠ receiving back one's body, now glorified, at the time of the General Judgment.

In sum, "The Faithful should be deeply impressed that the happiness of the saints is full to overflowing of all those pleasures which can be enjoyed or even desired in this life, whether they regard the powers of the mind or of the perfection of the body."[10]

We cannot succeed in imagining Heaven because of our current limitations. It is hard to conceive of something we can enjoy forever without getting bored, or disappointed, or frustrated. This is why St. Paul said, "no eye has seen, nor ear heard, nor the heart of man conceived, what God has prepared for those who love him" (1 Cor 2: 9).

The General Judgment

The Second Coming of the Lord is also known as the *Parousia*, a Greek word meaning "apparition" or "presence." At the *Parousia*, Christ will appear to everyone in power and majesty as judge. He will fully establish the Kingdom which was inaugurated at the Incarnation.

At the General Judgment, God's majesty, wisdom, justice, and mercy will become fully evident. We will see why God sometimes allows the good to suffer and the wicked to prosper. We will also see all the good and bad effects of everyone's actions throughout human history. In addition, souls will be reunited to their now immortal glorified bodies in the resurrection. At this point Christ will tell the good to come into the Kingdom of Heaven while sending the wicked into "the eternal fire prepared for the devil and his angels" (Mt 25: 41).

From the viewpoint of salvation history, the Second Coming marks the ultimate triumph of Christ over sin and death. This triumph was first seen in Christ's Resurrection and Ascension, and can be shared now through sanctifying grace. But it will be fully revealed at the end of the world.

> The Last Judgment will come when Christ returns in glory. Only the Father knows the day and the hour; only he determines the moment of its coming. Then through his Son Jesus Christ he will pronounce the final word on all history. We shall know the ultimate meaning of the whole work of creation and of the entire economy of salvation and understand the marvelous ways by which his Providence led everything towards its final end. The Last Judgment will reveal that God's justice triumphs over all the injustices committed by his creatures and that God's love is stronger than death.[11] (CCC 1040)

> At the end of time, the Kingdom of God will come in its fullness. After the universal judgment, the righteous will reign forever with Christ, glorified in body and soul. The universe itself will be renewed:

> > The Church...will receive her perfection only in the glory of heaven, when will come the time of the renewal of all things.

At that time, together with the human race, the universe itself, which is so closely related to man and which attains its destiny through him, will be perfectly re-established in Christ.[12] (CCC 1042)

CONCLUSION

Some people are uncomfortable thinking about what happens after death. Some are frightened by the prospect of Hell, an eternity of pain and unhappiness; some are even scared of Heaven, fearing that eternity of any kind can become boring at the very least. Some choose to deny belief in Hell, or in the afterlife altogether.

The thought of Hell is distressing, but we can take comfort in knowing we were created for Heaven, for communion with God, for eternal happiness. We

ST. MICHAEL THE ARCHANGEL

Although there are hundreds of references to angels in the Bible, the Archangel St. Michael is one of only three who are identified by name (the others are the archangels Sts. Gabriel and Raphael). It may be surprising that angels are hailed as saints and exemplary members of the Church, since as heavily creatures they have always known the revealed nature of God. But the Church is the heavenly assembly of *all* those who have received salvation in Christ, and the first among these are the angels.

Within Scripture, the most dramatic depiction of St. Michael is found in the Book of Revelation, where we see him leading the holy angels in battle against the Devil.

> Now war arose in heaven, Michael and his angels fighting against the dragon; and the dragon and his angels fought, but they were defeated and there was no longer any place for them in heaven. And the great dragon was thrown down, that ancient serpent, who is called the Devil and Satan, the deceiver of the whole world. (Rev 12: 7-9)

As leader of the angelic armies, St. Michael has often been invoked by the Church as her protector against the opposition of the Devil. In 1886, Pope Leo XIII wrote a prayer to St. Michael and encouraged all members of the Pilgrim Church on earth to ask for his supernatural assistance and defense:

> St. Michael the Archangel, defend us in battle;
> be our protection against the wickedness and snares
>   of the Devil.
> May God rebuke him, we humbly pray:
> And do thou, O prince of the heavenly host,
> by the power of God,
> cast into Hell Satan and all the evil spirits
> who prowl about the world seeking the ruin of souls.

FROM *YouCat*

Why do we believe in the resurrection of the "body"?

In Jesus Christ, God himself took on "flesh" (INCARNATION) in order to redeem mankind. The biblical word "flesh" characterizes man in his weakness and mortality. Nevertheless, God does not regard human flesh as something inferior. God does not redeem man's spirit only; he redeems him entirely, body and soul.

God created us with a body (flesh) and a soul. At the end of the world he does not drop the "flesh" like an old toy. On the "Last Day" he will remake all creation and raise us up in the flesh—this means that we will be transformed but still experience ourselves in *our element*. For Jesus, too, being in the flesh was not just a phase. When the risen Lord showed himself, the disciples saw the wounds on his body. (*YouCat* 153)

St. Michael by Giordano.
"Be our protection against the wickedness and snares of the Devil."

CLOSURE

Write a paragraph explaining either the Communion of Saints or the Last Things.

ALTERNATIVE ASSESSMENT

The doctrines of the Communion of Saints and the Last Things are part of Divine Revelation. We believe them because God has revealed them and God does not deceive.

Have a class discussion on to what extent you think these various doctrines are reasonable.

have no concept of what it would be like to exist outside of time, no clue as to the perfect joy of seeing God face to face that awaits us. We can trust that what God has in store for us is beyond our wildest imagination.

We also know that the grace of redemption is ours if we only respond to it. If we respond to the call of Christ and live according to his will, embracing his moral law and seeking holiness, we will indeed reach our heavenly goal. We will fulfill the purpose for which God created us in his image and likeness. We need not fear the judgment of God if we strive to be faithful to him.

Along the way, we can turn to the saints in Heaven to pray on our behalf and help us join the ranks of those who are saved. We do indeed, as we pray in the Creed at Mass, "look forward to the resurrection of the dead, and to the life of the world to come."

DISCUSSION QUESTIONS

1. What are the three states or conditions in which the Church currently exists?

2. What is the Communion of Saints?

3. What are the four meanings of the word "saint"?

4. Why are the saints models of Christian living?

5. What is intercessory prayer?

6. What are the Last Things?

7. What does the moment of death mean in terms of salvation?

8. What is the Particular Judgment?

9. Why are the souls in Purgatory both joyful and suffering?

10. What is Hell?

11. What is Heaven?

12. What is the *Parousia*?

13. What is the General Judgment?

14. What is the resurrection of the body?

The Last Judgment Polyptych, Center Panel by Weyden.
Archangel St. Michael holds a scale with which he weighs souls.

ENDNOTES – CHAPTER 13

1. *Catechism of St Pius X,* no.149; cf. CCC 954-955.
2. Cf. *LG* 40, 48-51.
3. John Paul II, *CL* 16, 3.
4. *CL* 17, 3.
5. Cf. 2 Tm 1: 9-10.
6. Cf. Council of Lyons II (1274): DS 857-858; Council of Florence (1439): DS 1304-1306; Council of Trent (1563): DS 1820.
7. Cf. Benedict XII, *Benedictus Deus* (1336): DS 1000-1001; John XXII, *Ne super his* (1334): DS 990.
8. Cf. Benedict XII, *Benedictus Deus* (1336): DS 1002.
9. St. John of the Cross, *Dichos* 64.
10. *Catechism of the Council of Trent,* 1.12.12.
11. Cf. Sg 8: 6.
12. *LG* 48; cf. Acts 3: 21; Eph 1: 10; Col 1: 20; 2 Pt 3: 10-13.

The Church
Sacrament of Salvation

Chapter 14
Mary, Mother of the Church and Our Mother

Blessed are we if we, like Mary, the "Woman," hear the Word of God and keep it.

OPENING ACTIVITY

Pray the Litany of Loreto, perhaps having each student read one of the points, while everyone responds.

BASIC QUESTIONS

This chapter attempts to answer the following basic questions:

✖ Who is the "woman" of the *Protoevangelium*?

✖ How can Mary be the Mother of God?

✖ What is Mary's Immaculate Conception?

✖ What is Mary's Assumption?

✖ How is Mary the Mother of the Church?

✖ Why is Mary the Help of Christians?

✖ What is the Queenship of Mary?

KEY IDEAS

The key ideas of this chapter are:

✖ Mary is the woman spoken about in the *Protoevangelium* in Genesis.

✖ Mary is the Mother of God because her Son is the Second Person of the Blessed Trinity.

✖ The Immaculate Conception is the dogma that from the moment of her conception, Mary was preserved from Original Sin.

✖ The Assumption is the dogma that the Blessed Virgin Mary was taken up body and soul into Heaven at the end of her life on earth.

✖ Mary is the Mother of the Church because she is the Mother of Christ whose Body is the Church and because Christ made all his disciples children of Mary when he gave her and St. John to each other.

✖ As a good Mother, Mary is always concerned for her children and intercedes for them; thus, she is the Help of Christians.

✖ Mary as the Mother of Christ.

CHAPTER 14
Mary, Mother of the Church and Our Mother

Review of Chapter 13:

✖ The Communion of Saints includes all the faithful on earth, in Purgatory, and in Heaven.

✖ The faithful on earth can intercede in prayer for those in Purgatory, and those in Heaven and Purgatory can pray for those on earth.

✖ At his Second Coming, Christ will judge the living and the dead. The bodies of the dead will rise and be reunited with their souls.

✖ Heaven is the state of perfect communion and eternal happiness with God.

✖ Purgatory is a temporary state for those who will go to Heaven but require purification.

✖ Hell is the abode of those who definitively reject God and his offer of eternal life.

In this chapter, we will study the person of the Blessed Virgin Mary, the Mother of God, her role in redemption, and her relationship with the Church.

THE WOMAN

The Church is a fellowship or assembly of people, the People of God. She is the communion of saved persons united to one other and to God through the God-Man Jesus Christ. She is the people God gathers to himself.

One of the key persons in the Church is the Blessed Virgin Mary. We have encountered Our Lady many times in this series and will continue to do so. One reason is that there is a real connection uniting Christ, Mary, the Church as a whole, and each individual Christian.

God deliberately chose a specific woman, the Blessed Virgin Mary, to be the Mother of the Redeemer. In fact, God chose Mary for this special role from the very beginning. The reference in the *Protoevangelium* in the Book of Genesis to the "woman" whose "seed" would "bruise the head" of the serpent refers to the Virgin Mary, who is considered the "New Eve" because of her perfect obedience to God.

In the New Testament, we encounter subtle references to Mary associated with this "woman." In St. John's Gospel, we hear Christ referring to his Mother as "woman" at the wedding at Cana as he is beginning his redemptive mission (cf. Jn 2: 4). We hear him address her this way again as she stands at the foot of the Cross as he is completing this mission (cf. Jn 19: 26-27). Finally, in the Book of Revelation, St. John describes the "woman" as a queen, "clothed with the sun, with the moon under her feet, and on her head a crown of twelve stars" (Rev 12: 1).

Just as the story of salvation history begins with three characters—Adam, Eve, and the serpent—it ends with Christ, the New Adam; the Woman, Mary, the New Eve; and Satan, defeated by the Cross.

Annunciation (detail) by Gentileschi.
The doctrine of Mary's divine Motherhood originates in the mystery of the Incarnation.

Focus Question 1:
What is the Church?

Focus Question 2:
Who is the woman in the *Protoevangelium*?

Focus Question 3:
When are the three times that St. John's writings refer to the Virgin Mary as "woman"?

Focus Question 4:
What on Mary's part made the Incarnation happen?

Focus Question 5:
Why is Mary the Mother of God?

Focus Question 6:
What truth does the title Mother of God protect?

Focus Question 7:
Who is the *Theotokos* and what does this title mean?

MOTHER OF GOD

When the Archangel Gabriel announced that Mary would give birth to "the Son of the Most High" and that "with God nothing will be impossible," Mary responded, "Behold, I am the handmaid of the Lord; let it be done to me according to your word" (Lk 1: 28-38).[1] In giving her consent to God's message, Mary became the Mother of God (cf. CCC 494).

We call Mary the Mother of God because her Son is God: Jesus Christ is the Second Person of the Blessed Trinity, God the Son. Mary gave Christ his human nature. However, we do not speak of motherhood in relation to nature, but in relation to a person, and Christ is a Person with two natures, human and divine. Since the Person she gave birth to is God, she is rightly called the Mother of God. The title "Mother of God" honors Mary, but its primary purpose is to defend the truth that Jesus Christ is really God the Son.

From the Church's earliest centuries, the faithful have revered Mary as the Mother of God. For example, Greek-speaking Christians called her *Theotokos* or "Bearer of God." In doing so, they were following the example of Mary's cousin St. Elizabeth, who at the Visitation referred to Mary as "the mother of my Lord" (Lk 1: 43).

The doctrine of Mary's divine Motherhood originates in the mystery of the Incarnation. Although the Son possesses his divine nature from all eternity, it is from Mary that he receives his human nature, thus making him both fully human and fully divine.

Mary is truly Christ's Mother, but her Motherhood is different from that of any other mother, for she conceived her Son not through conjugal relations but by the consent of her will. Thus, when one of Christ's listeners cried out,

Virgin and Child (detail) by Fra Angelico.
Greek-speaking Christians called her *Theotokos* or "Bearer of God."

Focus Question 8:

How is Christ's response to the woman who praises Mary's womb a compliment?

Focus Question 9:

How can everyone be a *theotokos*?

GUIDED EXERCISE

Conduct a think/pair/share on the following questions:

- When we say *amen* to God, how is that like an Annunciation?

- When we do apostolate, how is that a kind of Christmas?

VOCABULARY

FIAT

Mary's response of consent at the Annunciation; a Latin word meaning "let it be done."

THEOTOKOS

Greek for "Bearer of God," often translated "Mother of God." Used since the early centuries of the Church, this title of Mary was defended by the Third Ecumenical Council, held at Ephesus in AD 431.

Christ desired that Mary be fully united to him from the first instant of her human existence.

"Blessed is the womb that bore you," Christ calls our attention not to the fact of Mary's biological Motherhood, but to its cause: "Blessed rather are those who hear the word of God and keep it" (Lk 11: 27-28).

In saying this, Christ gives Mary the highest compliment. Christ's Mother heard the word of God and kept it perfectly. As she said to Gabriel, "Let it be done to me according to your word" (Lk 1: 38). Mary was in perfect communion with God. Yet, all who hear the word of God and keep it become themselves bearers of the Word. In this way, the Church is and each member of the Church can be a *theotokos*, a Christ-bearer.

Mary gave her consent to the Father and so received the Word made flesh within her womb. The Church gives her consent to the Father and receives the Word made flesh in the Eucharist. As Pope Bl. John Paul II wrote, "There is a profound analogy between the *Fiat* ["Let it be done"], which Mary said

The Immaculate Conception by Tiepolo.
The holiness that Christ gives the Church is the same as that which his Blessed Mother received at her conception.

in reply to the angel, and the *Amen* which every believer says when receiving the Body of the Lord."[2] By the power of the Holy Spirit, Christ dwells within the Church as once he dwelt within Mary, and therefore both are truly bearers of the Word. Thus, every time one of us says *amen* to God, it is a kind of Annunciation.

THE IMMACULATE CONCEPTION

When the Archangel Gabriel appeared to Mary, announcing that she would be the Mother of the Messiah, he said, "Hail, full of grace, the Lord is with you!" (Lk 1:28). The Church has always understood this greeting, "full of grace," as a revelation that Christ preserved Mary from the effects of Original Sin. This doctrine is called the Immaculate Conception.

> "The most Blessed Virgin Mary was, from the first moment of her conception, by a singular grace and privilege of almighty God and by virtue of the merits of Jesus Christ, Savior of the human race, preserved immune from all stain of original sin."[3] (CCC 491)

We know that because of Adam and Eve's disobedience, all mankind is affected by Original Sin, the deprivation of the holiness and communion with God that our first parents originally possessed. Christ restores this graced communion to us through Baptism. For Mary, however, Christ desired that she be fully united to him from the first instant of her human existence.

The Immaculate Conception helps us see the fullness of salvation that Christ offers to the world. Indeed, the holiness that Christ gives the Church is the same as that which his Blessed Mother received at her conception. Mary is the first and greatest of us who have been chosen by God "before the foundation of the world, that we should be holy and blameless before him" (Eph 1:4).

The Immaculate Conception also reveals our need for God's grace so that we may faithfully respond to his call. It was through the grace of Christ that Mary was immaculately conceived, that she remained sinless throughout her life, and that she was able to give her consent to all that God would ask of her. "In...order for Mary to give the free assent of her faith to the announcement of her vocation, it was necessary that she be wholly borne by grace" (CCC 490).

Sin had entered the world through the disobedience of Adam and Eve. Sin was destroyed by the obedience of Christ and Mary. This is why we recognize Mary as the New Eve, joined by the power of the Holy Spirit to Christ, the New Adam. The marriage of Adam and Eve was a sign of God's graced communion with man. The spiritual union of the New Adam and Eve is the perfect realization of that communion. This communion renders Mary holy and immaculate from the moment of her conception, just as it renders the Church—the spotless Bride of Christ—holy and immaculate from the moment of her institution. This also applies to each member of the Church in what St. Paul calls a "profound mystery" (Eph 5:32):

> **Christ loved the church and gave himself up for her, that he might sanctify her, having cleansed her by the washing of water with the word, that he might present the church to himself in splendor, without spot or wrinkle or any such thing, that she might be holy and without blemish. (Eph 5:25-27)**

Christ made Mary to be "without spot or wrinkle" at the moment of her conception. Through the course of our lives—and even beyond in the purification of Purgatory—we undergo the process of sanctification which Mary received all at once.

Focus Question 10:
What doctrine does "full of grace" reveal?

Focus Question 11:
What is the Immaculate Conception?

Focus Question 12:
Why did God give Mary this singular grace?

Focus Question 13:
How does the Immaculate Conception relate to the experience of the Church?

The Presentation of the Virgin (detail) by Carpaccio. Mary is the first and greatest of us who have been chosen by God.

Focus Question 14:
What happened at the end of Mary's earthly life?

Focus Question 15:
How will the saved be like Mary?

THE ASSUMPTION
OF THE BLESSED VIRGIN MARY

The Immaculate Conception of Mary preserved the Blessed Mother from the effects of the Fall. From the first moment of her conception, Mary was kept free from the spiritual death and decay of Original Sin, and by God's grace and her cooperation she remained sinless her entire life. Thus, it follows that Mary was free from the inherited punishment for Original Sin: physical death.

> Finally the Immaculate Virgin, preserved free from all stain of original sin, when the course of her earthly life was finished, was taken up body and soul into heavenly glory, and exalted by the Lord as Queen over all things, so that she might be the more fully conformed to her Son, the Lord of lords and conqueror of sin and death.[4]

Mary did not "die" per se, since death is defined in Christianity as the separation of the soul from the body. Both went directly to Heaven. Mary became the first person to fully share in Christ's Resurrection.

Through the Sacraments, we participate in Christ's heavenly glory while on our earthly pilgrimage, so the Church is already "risen with Christ." For us, this spiritual resurrection anticipates a final, bodily resurrection.

Mary, however, experienced this bodily resurrection in her Assumption. Because of her unique vocation as the Mother of God, she received in advance what is promised to all of us at the end of history, namely, a resurrected body and entrance into heavenly glory.

Assumption of the Virgin by Sallaert.
The Immaculate Virgin was taken up body and soul into heavenly glory.

Mary became the first person to fully share in Christ's Resurrection.

Coronation of the Virgin (detail) by Veronese.
Mary is the Mother of Christ and also the Mother of the Mystical Body of Christ, his Church.

MARY, MOTHER OF THE CHURCH

Through Mary's consent to God's invitation, the Second Person of the Blessed Trinity became Incarnate, which literally means "in-fleshed," in her womb. Mary is the Mother of Christ, including his "flesh" or body. The Mystical Body of Christ is his Church. Thus, Mary also has the rightful title of "Mother of the Church." Because Mary said "yes" to being the Mother of Christ, each of us has the opportunity to receive supernatural life in him.

Mary is much more than just the "cause" of Christ coming into the world. She participated in Christ's Redemption by joining her life and sufferings completely to those of her Son. The Blessed Virgin was:

> The generous associate and humble handmaid of the Lord. She conceived, brought forth and nourished Christ. She presented Him to the Father in the temple, and was united with Him by compassion as He died on the Cross. In this singular way she cooperated by her obedience, faith, hope and burning charity in the work of the Savior in giving back supernatural life to souls. Wherefore she is our mother in the order of grace.[5]

Christ also explicitly made Mary to be the Mother of the members of the Church. And he made the members of the Church to be her children.

> When Jesus saw his mother, and the disciple whom he loved standing near, he said to his mother, "Woman, behold, your son!" Then he said to the disciple, "Behold, your mother!" And from that hour the disciple took her to his own home. (Jn 19: 25-27)

In this scene, "the disciple whom Jesus loved" represents all of Christ's faithful, the members of his Church. With his mutual introduction of Mother and son, Christ designates his own Mother, Mary, as the Mother of the Church. She who gave birth to the Body of Christ is likewise the Mother of the Mystical Body of Christ. Just as Eve was the physical mother of all human beings who would one day be born into physical life on earth, Mary is the spiritual Mother of all human beings who are born into eternal life in Heaven.

Focus Question 16:
Why is Mary, by being the Mother of Christ, also the Mother of the Church?

Focus Question 17:
Why is Mary our Mother in the order of grace?

Focus Question 18:
When did Christ name Mary as Mother of the Church and the members of the Church as her children?

Focus Question 19:
How does Christ tie Mary to Eve?

GUIDED EXERCISE

Free write on the following questions in order to understand its answer better:

- What is the interconnection between Eve, the Church, and Mary?

Through the Sacraments, we participate in Christ's heavenly glory.

Focus Question 20:
How is Mary a perfect Mother?

Focus Question 21:
How do we talk to Mary our Mother?

Focus Question 22:
What is Mary's "glory"?

St. Roch Asking the Virgin Mary to Heal Victims of the Plague (detail) by David.
Each of us can have an intimate mother-child relationship with Mary.

MARY, HELP OF CHRISTIANS

Mary is the Mother of Christ and of the Church, so her concern is for all her children united in Christ. Mary will never lose patience with her children or reject them, no matter what they do. Her union with Christ in holiness is so complete that she loves us with a truly unconditional and everlasting love.

Like St. John, we can take Mary into our "home" (Jn 19: 27). Each of us can have an intimate mother-child relationship with Mary. We can speak with her, and ask for her help. Because Mary is always in Christ's presence, we have in her an advocate who sees God face-to-face and brings our petitions to him.

We are able to establish a personal relationship with Mary through prayer. Christians have developed many popular devotions to foster prayer with Mary. The Rosary, which we can pray daily, recounts the main events of the life of our Lord and Mary. The *Memorare*, Hail Holy Queen, and *Angelus* are traditional Marian prayers by which we can speak with Mary and keep her in mind throughout our day.

QUEEN OF HEAVEN

In the Book of Revelation, we find a striking description of Mary's heavenly enthronement as Queen of Heaven and Earth:

> And a great sign appeared in heaven, a woman clothed with the sun, with the moon under her feet, and on her head a crown of twelve stars....She brought forth a male child, one who is to rule all the nations. (Rev 12: 1, 5)

We can see in this image of the "woman clothed with the sun" the fullness of glory that Christ bestowed upon his Blessed Mother in Heaven after her Assumption. What is this glory, expressed through images of the heavenly bodies of sun, moon, and stars? It is Mary's communion with God, "The true light that enlightens every man" that came into the world through her *fiat* (Jn 1: 9).

Immaculate Conception (detail)
by Murillo.
We are able to establish a personal relationship with Mary through prayer.

MARY AS MOTHER OF THE CHURCH

Pope Bl. John Paul II was known, among other things, for his deep devotion to the Blessed Virgin Mary. In a general audience on September 17, 1997, he gave the following catechesis about the role of Mary as Mother of the Church, a title ascribed to her with greater fervor in recent centuries:

lthough the title "Mother of the Church" was only recently attributed to Mary, it expresses the Blessed Virgin's maternal relationship with the Church as shown already in several New Testament texts.

Since the Annunciation, Mary was called to give her consent to the coming of the messianic kingdom, which would take place with the formation of the Church.

When at Cana Mary asked the Son to exercise his messianic power, she made a fundamental contribution to implanting the faith in the first community of disciples, and she co-operated in initiating God's kingdom, which has its "seed" and "beginning" in the Church (cf. *LG* 5).

On Calvary, Mary united herself to the sacrifice of her Son and made her own maternal contribution to the work of salvation, which took the form of labour pains, the birth of the new humanity.

In addressing the words "Woman, behold your son" to Mary, the Crucified One proclaims her Motherhood not only in relation to the Apostle John but also to every disciple. The Evangelist himself, by saying that Christ had to die "to gather into one the children of God who are scattered abroad" (Jn 11: 52), indicates the Church's birth as the fruit of the redemptive sacrifice with which Mary is maternally associated.

The Evangelist St. Luke mentions the presence of Christ's Mother in the first community of Jerusalem (Acts 1: 14). In this way he stresses Mary's maternal role in the newborn Church, comparing it to her role in the Redeemer's birth. The maternal dimension thus becomes a fundamental element of Mary's relationship with the new People of the redeemed....

According to St. Irenæus, Mary "became a cause of salvation for the whole human race" (*Haer.* 3, 22, 4; PG 7, 959), and the pure womb of the Virgin "regenerates men in God" (*Haer.* 4, 33, 11; PG 7, 1080). This is reechoed by St. Ambrose, who says: "A Virgin has begotten the salvation of the world, a Virgin has given life to all things" (*Ep.* 63, 33; PL 16, 1198), and by other Fathers who call Mary "Mother of salvation" (Severian of Gabala, *Or. 6 in mundi creationem*, 10; PG 54, 4; Faustus of Riez, *Max. Bibl. Patrum,* VI. 620-621).

In the Middle Ages, St. Anselm addressed Mary in this way: "You are the mother of justification and of the justified, the Mother of reconciliation and of the reconciled, the mother of salvation and of the saved" (*Or.* 52, 8; PL 158, 957), while other authors attribute to her the titles "Mother of grace" and "Mother of life."

The title "Mother of the Church" thus reflects the deep conviction of the Christian faithful, who see in Mary not only the Mother of the Person of Christ, but also of the faithful. She who is recognized as Mother of salvation, life and grace, Mother of the saved and Mother of the living, is rightly proclaimed Mother of the Church.

The Granduca Madonna by Raphael.

Mother of God
Mother of the Church
Mother of Grace
Mother of Life

St. Luke stressed Mary's maternal role in the newborn Church in Acts 1: 14:

"All these with one accord devoted themselves to prayer, together with the women and Mary the Mother of Jesus, and with his brothers."

Focus Question 23:

How is Mary the archetype, or perfect model, on which the Church is patterned?

Focus Question 24:

Who is the enemy of the Church?

Focus Question 25:

What is the condition that the Church on earth endures?

GUIDED EXERCISE

Free write for a few minutes on how Rev 12: 1, 5 refers to Mary and Christ.

CLOSURE

Write a paragraph summarizing how Mary is the Mother of God, of the Church, and of every Christian.

ALTERNATIVE ASSESSMENT

After reviewing some of the titles which praise Mary in the Litany of Loreto, write an original title for Mary and then explain how that title pertains to her.

For example:

Mother of Charity, *pray for us.*

Mary is the Mother of Charity because charity means love, God is love, Jesus is God, and Mary is Jesus' Mother. By saying yes to God, Mary brought Love to fallen humanity.

This same glorious communion awaits every member of the Church at the end of time. What God has done for Mary, he will do for the rest of her children. We, too, will enter into the glory of communion with him. We, too, will be enthroned in Heaven. Thus, Mary is the archetype, or perfect model, on which the Church is patterned.

The Church has already entered into the fullness of heavenly glory through Mary, her most favored daughter. On earth the Church labors to bring forth new sons and daughters of the Father. The Church is opposed at all times by the Devil, the "ancient serpent," who wants to overcome the Church as once he overcame Eve. But even in the face of persecution, the Pilgrim Church is filled with hope because Christ has already won the battle by his Resurrection.

Following the pattern of Christ who endured death on the Cross, and Mary, whose heart was also pierced as if with a sword (cf. Lk 2: 35), Christians enter glory through the suffering of love.

CONCLUSION

The Virgin Mary is unique among all human persons, conceived without sin and assumed body and soul into Heaven. "Blessed art thou among women," we pray in the Hail Mary, echoing the words of her cousin Elizabeth as she greeted Mary during her visit. She is the Mother of God, the Mother of the Church, and the Mother of all members of the faithful. We can and ought to turn to her in prayer as a great intercessor, a mediator before her Son Jesus, and as a model of humility and obedience to the will of God.

DISCUSSION QUESTIONS

1. What is the meaning of "the woman" in salvation history?

2. Why is Mary the Mother of God?

3. Who is the *Theotokos* and what does this title mean?

4. What is the Immaculate Conception?

5. What happened at the end of Mary's earthly life?

6. Why is Mary, by being the Mother of Christ, also the Mother of the Church?

7. When did Christ name Mary as Mother of the Church and the members of the Church as her children?

8. How is Mary a perfect Mother?

9. How is Mary the archetype, or perfect model, on which the Church is patterned?

ENDNOTES – CHAPTER 14

1. Cf. Rom 1: 5; cf. *LG* 56.
2. *Ecclesia de Eucharistia*, 34.
3. Pius IX, *Ineffabilis Deus*, 1854: DS 2803.
4. *LG* 59; cf. Pius XII, *Munificentissimum Deus* (1950): DS 3903; cf. Rev 19: 16.
5. *LG* 61.

The Church
Sacrament of Salvation

Chapter 15
Challenges to the Church

The Catholic Church is the Church established by Christ for the salvation of many.

CHAPTER 15
Challenges to the Church

OPENING ACTIVITY

Incorporate a reading of the first paragraph of *Lumen Gentium* from the Second Vatican Council into the class's Opening Prayer.

Christ is the Light of nations. Because this is so, this Sacred Synod gathered together in the Holy Spirit eagerly desires, by proclaiming the Gospel to every creature, to bring the light of Christ to all men, a light brightly visible on the countenance of the Church. Since the Church is in Christ like a sacrament or as a sign and instrument both of a very closely knit union with God and of the unity of the whole human race, it desires now to unfold more fully to the faithful of the Church and to the whole world its own inner nature and universal mission. This it intends to do following faithfully the teaching of previous councils. The present-day conditions of the world add greater urgency to this work of the Church so that all men, joined more closely today by various social, technical and cultural ties, might also attain fuller unity in Christ.

Then free write for a few minutes on some of the truths mentioned here that you have studied this semester.

Share responses with the group.

BASIC QUESTIONS

This chapter attempts to answer the following basic questions:

✖ Why be a Catholic?

✖ Aren't Catholics just a bunch of hypocritical sinners?

✖ Who needs organized religion anyway?

✖ How does the Catholic Church sustain her unity in an ever-changing world?

Review of Chapter 14:

✖ Mary is properly called the Mother of God because she gave birth to the Son of God, thus giving him his human nature.

✖ Mary is called the Immaculate Conception because, in preparation for her special role, she was conceived without the stain of Original Sin.

✖ Mary remained sinless her entire life. At the end of her earthly life, she was assumed into Heaven body and soul.

✖ Mary is the Mother of the Church, our mediator and intercessor in Heaven. She is also the Queen of Heaven, the "woman clothed with the sun," by virtue of her special place and grace among all creatures.

This final chapter of *The Church* raises and attempts to answer some common objections people have in regard to what the Church teaches about herself.

It is a chapter on *apologetics*—the art of showing people that what the Church teaches:

✖ can be proven

✖ is logical

✖ has philosophical, biblical, and historical foundations

✖ can be shown to be reasonable.

APOLOGETICS

Apologetics enables people to take what the Church teaches seriously, rather than just dismiss Church teaching. This can help them be receptive to God's grace, moving them closer to an act of faith. When a supernatural truth is proposed to a person, and that truth is shown to be not unreasonable, and supernatural grace is gently urging the person to accept it, then that person can make an informed, and thus truly free, choice to say, "I believe."

For example, when the Church teaches that Mary is the Mother of the Church, apologetics (that is, reasoning and evidence) can remove the barriers to accepting the claims that there could be such a thing as the Church, and that it can have a kind of mother, and that its mother could be Mary. When someone who does not have faith can say, "I see what you Catholics mean when you say Mary is the Mother of the Church," the work of apologetics is done. But this is not yet faith, but merely understanding.

Faith is when a person freely says, for example, "I believe Mary is the Mother of the Church." This human act of the will is supported by God's grace. God's grace surrounds, so to speak, this act of faith: grace inclines one to make it *before* it is made, helps one to actually make it *when* it is made, and assists one to hold to it *after* it is made. Then, one can not only intellectually believe that Mary is the Mother of the Church, but that belief can begin to have an effect on how one lives.

The fullness of the truth and the means of salvation subsist in the Catholic Church alone.

We will examine four questions that apologetics regularly engage.

1. Why do I have to be Catholic? Aren't all religions equal?

You *do not* "have to be a Catholic." God created you with a rational intellect and a free will. You are free to do as you think best, but you are personally responsible for your judgments and actions.

The best reason for being a Catholic is that you think what the Church teaches is true. You *should* be a Catholic if you are convinced the Catholic Faith is true.

The Catholic Faith makes the claim that it is the one true Church founded by Christ. The claim is that God became a human being to save us from our sins and gives us the opportunity of enjoying everlasting life and happiness. Christ created his one, holy, catholic, and apostolic Church to be the visible means by which his salvation would be made available to humanity until the end of time.

The Church does not claim that there is no truth anywhere else. In fact, she teaches that there are elements of truth and goodness in practically every human undertaking, including organized religions. For example, our separated brethren in Orthodoxy and Protestantism revere the Sacred Scriptures and possess some or all of the Sacraments. However, the fullness of the truth and the means of salvation subsist in the Catholic Church alone. In the Catholic Church are found:

※ the Faith, which Christ and the Holy Spirit taught the Apostles;

※ the hierarchical structure Christ established through Holy Orders;

※ the Seven Sacraments by which we receive grace;

※ the Magisterium which infallibly guards the truth;

※ and the fullness of the Deposit of Faith, i.e., Sacred Scripture and Sacred Tradition, by which God reveals himself.

Christ willed that the Catholic Church be his Sacrament of Salvation, the sign and the instrument of the communion of God and man. We are made to be in communion, that is, in intimate fellowship with one another and God, and the Catholic Church is the way that this friendship can be established and grow.

Focus Question 8:

What does the Church say about the salvation of people outside her visible body?

Focus Question 9:

Why should Catholics try to spread the Faith?

FROM *YouCat*

How does the Church view other religions?

The CHURCH respects everything in other religions that is good and true. She respects and promotes freedom of religion as a human right. Yet she knows that Jesus Christ is the sole redeemer of all mankind. He alone is "the way, and the truth, and the life" (Jn 14: 6).

Whoever seeks God is close to us Christians....The Church teaches that all men who by no fault of their own do not know Christ and his Church but sincerely seek God and follow the voice of their conscience can attain eternal salvation. However, anyone who has recognized that Jesus Christ is "the way, and the truth, and the life" but is unwilling to follow him cannot find salvation by other paths. This is what is meant by the saying, *Extra ecclesiam nulla salus* (outside of the Church there is no salvation). (*YouCat* 136)

Focus Question 10:

What is hypocrisy?

Focus Question 11:

What is scandal?

Focus Question 12:

Why are some people happy to discover sinful Catholics?

Christ established his Church as a visible organization through which he communicates his grace, truth, and salvation. Through the Magisterium of the Church, which infallibly interprets the Deposit of Faith, you can find true answers to your questions about life, suffering, death, happiness, love, and so on. Through the Church's Sacraments, you can also receive the grace you need to become morally good and more and more fit for Heaven.

Some people defend the idea that all religions are equally good because they look at the great number of religions, sects, and denominations in the world, realize that they cannot all be true, and do not want to see the good people in other religious bodies "lost" if they are in the wrong religion.

The Church teaches that this is a false worry. Those who through no fault of their own do not know Christ or the Catholic Church are not excluded from salvation. In a way known to God, all people are offered the possibility of salvation through the Church.

So people can be saved by the Church who have never heard of the Church. People can even be saved who erroneously think the Catholic Church is false or evil, provided they are not to blame for their errors. This does not mean that Catholics should leave these people alone in their errors. Members of the Catholic Church have the duty to evangelize others. Christ commanded the Apostles to go and teach all nations and to baptize them into the Faith. Each Catholic has the right and the obligation to evangelize others. All are called to do apostolate.

In addition, because the Church teaches the truth about the human person and provides the sacramental means of becoming holy, we want others to share in these goods. These are all reasons why we should want to be Catholic and why we should want others to join us.

2. Isn't the Church hypocritical telling other people to be holy and avoid sin when many Catholics, including clergy, are guilty of terrible wrongs?

Lots of people, including some members of the clergy, are hypocritical. Hypocrisy is espousing something as good while deliberately doing the opposite. It is pretending to be virtuous when one really is not.

When Catholics, including clergy, who are supposed to be committed to doing good, and who put on a face of goodness while secretly doing evil, are exposed for what they really are, people are scandalized. To be scandalized is to be made to "stumble" when it comes time to accept the truth of the Catholic Faith. As Christ said very severely about adults who scandalize children, "Whoever causes one of these little ones who believe in me to sin, it would be better for him if a great millstone were hung round his neck and he were thrown into the sea" (Mk 9: 42).

Sometimes people compare a particular nonbeliever to a particular Christian, observe that the nonbeliever seems "holier" than the believer, and conclude that being a Christian is pointless. What we do not know is how much better the nonbeliever would be if he were a Christian and how much worse the Christian would be if he were a nonbeliever.

Also, some people have blinders on when it comes to the Catholic Church and sin. They notice sin when it is committed by a Catholic, especially a member of the clergy, but are oblivious when it comes to the same sin in others. It is as though they want to discredit the Catholic Faith, sometimes in order to be free of the moral demands it makes on them.

Pope Bl. John Paul II Blesses 83,000 People of God in Giants Stadium, 1995.
Christ commanded the Apostles to go and teach all nations.
All are called to do apostolate.

When it comes to morality, the Church simply teaches what Christ has told her about the necessity of avoiding sin and living a holy life. As Christ said in the Beatitudes, only the pure of heart will see God (cf. Mt 5: 8). God calls everyone to holiness of life, and he wants us to sanctify our ordinary lives here on earth. Unless we are completely purified—either in this life or in Purgatory—we cannot enter Heaven. The Church claims that her teachings on faith and morals are *infallible*, that is, preserved from error. The Church never has claimed that any of her members—except perhaps the Blessed Virgin—is *impeccable*, that is, unable to sin. The saints are people who sinned but kept trying to be holy.

Failure by members of the Church to live out what God has taught does not invalidate the truth of those teachings. Despite the sins of the fallible and weak members of the Pilgrim Church, the Church herself remains holy. Why? The Church is animated and guided by the Holy Spirit. Her head, Jesus Christ, is perfectly holy. Mary, the Mother of the Church, is perfectly holy. The saints—canonized or not—are holy. The means of salvation, the Sacraments, are holy.

God came to save every one of us from our sins and to transform us into holy persons so we can be happy in communion with God—and with the rest of the saved—forever.

3. Who needs organized religion? Isn't it better to worship God in my own way, when and how I want?

Since God is completely good and all-knowing, then it is better to worship God the way he wants, when and how he wants. We can see in the Old and New Testaments how God himself taught people how to worship him. For example, God gave Moses specific instructions on how the Chosen People were to celebrate the original and subsequent Passover meals. Later, God provided directions for building the Tabernacle and Ark of the Covenant.

Focus Question 13:
Where does the Catholic Church get her moral teachings?

Focus Question 14:
Why is holiness necessary?

Focus Question 15:
How common is sin among members of the Catholic Church and human beings in general?

Focus Question 16:
What is the difference between *infallible* and *impeccable*?

Focus Question 17:
What is holy about the Church?

GUIDED EXERCISE

Based on C.S. Lewis's insight about the nice atheist and the grouchy Christian, free write for a few minutes on this question:

✠ Why should we not idly speculate about the saintliness or sinfulness of the people around us?

FROM *YouCat*

Why is "not practicing what you preach" such a serious deficiency in a Christian?

Agreement between one's life and one's witness is the first requirement for proclaiming the Gospel. Not practicing what you profess is therefore HYPOCRISY, a betrayal of the Christian duty to be "salt of the earth" and "light of the world."

Paul was the one who reminded the Church in Corinth: "You show that you are a letter from Christ...written not with ink but with the Spirit of the living God, not on tablets of stone but on tablets of human hearts" (2 Cor 3: 3). Christians themselves, not the things they say, are Christ's "letters of recommendation" (2 Cor 3: 2) to the world. (*YouCat* 347)

Focus Question 18:
Why does God know better than I do how to best worship him?

At the Last Supper, Christ transformed the Passover meal into what we call the Liturgy of the Eucharist and told his Apostles to continue its celebration.

God wants to bring the human race into communion with Christ through the Church he created. God desires us to come to him as members of his family, his new people, so he established the Church to accomplish that purpose. The primary form of worship Christ has given the Church is the Eucharist, which is officially celebrated on the day of the week that Christ rose from the dead. This gives a how and a when for the worship of God.

Furthermore, Christ taught his Apostles the fullness of truth. These teachings are preserved and applied by the bishops of the Church through Apostolic Succession by means of the Magisterium of the Church. Christ also empowered his Apostles, and their successors, to act *in persona Christi capitis*, "in the Person of Christ the Head." Their powers to celebrate the Sacraments come from Christ by virtue of Holy Orders. On one's own, outside the Catholic Faith, one does not have these things. Therefore, the organized religion, which is the Catholic Church, is necessary.

Because human beings are social creatures by nature, we need each other's encouragement, support, and example. We begin life knowing nothing, having yet to acquire any ideas from sense experience and reasoned reflection, and able to do almost nothing. Almost everything we know we have been told or taught by someone else. All our work is highly interdependent. Depending on our stage in life, we are either being taken care of, learning to care of ourselves, or taking care of others. If it were not for others, one might not know enough about God to want to experience him on one's own. Without the help of others, one might not ever get around to paying attention to God.

This does not mean there is no personal dimension to our relationship with God. We can and should develop a personal friendship with God through a life of prayer, which is conversation with God. Worship of God also has both a personal dimension and a communal dimension: personal, private worship is encouraged to complement communal worship. Every time I experience truth, goodness, and beauty in the created world, I can make an interior act of adoration of God, who is infinite truth, goodness, and beauty. But the

Because human beings are social creatures by nature, we need each other's encouragement, support, and example.

Sermon of St. Mark in Alexandria by Bellini.
The unity of the Church is also sustained through the common celebration of worship and of the Sacraments.

Focus Question 22:
How does the apostolic nature of the Church foster unity?

Focus Question 23:
How do the Mass and the Sacraments foster Church unity?

Focus Question 24:
How is the Catholic Church "catholic"?

Church also offers us authentic communal worship when we unite ourselves with Christ's self-offering in the Mass. If I were totally on my own when it comes to God, I would be making up my own religion rather than practicing the one Christ has himself given the Church.

4. How can the Catholic Church sustain the unity of her members in an ever-changing and diverse world?

In the Church there are twenty-one Eastern Catholic Churches and one Western Church. In addition, there are seven major rites used in liturgical worship and many legitimate variations within them. The Church has existed in many different cultures over the past two thousand years and has both affected those societies and been influenced by them.

The Church is able to sustain her unity because she has the Apostolic teaching office of the Pope and bishops to direct her, guided by the Holy Spirit. The Pope and bishops are the successors in every age to St. Peter and the Apostles. In the early Church, whenever a question came up in regard to the orthodox Faith, the answer was always another question: *What did the Apostles teach?* The same is true today. The Church teaches what the Apostles were taught by Christ.

The unity of the Church is also sustained through the common celebration of worship and of the Sacraments. Although the rites may vary greatly, underneath is the same Mass as at the Last Supper. St. Justin Martyr's description of Christian worship on the "day of the sun" should be very familiar to present-day Catholics.

Without these real means of unity, Christian congregations tend to either fracture into smaller and smaller groups, like the thousands of Protestant denominations, or become solidified into local or national churches: e.g., Lutheranism among the Scandinavians, Anglicanism among the English, Greek Orthodoxy in Greece, Russian Orthodoxy in Russia, and so on. On the other hand, the one Catholic Church is spread across and united throughout the world.

The Pope and bishops are the successors in every age to St. Peter and the Apostles.

Focus Question 25:

What was the essence of what God gave St. Josemaria to teach?

St. Josemaria Escriva.
He helped lay people live their call to holiness in a secular world.

CLOSURE

In your own words and in one paragraph, summarize one of the ways described in this chapter that apologetics can defend and promote the Church.

ALTERNATIVE ASSESSMENT

As a class, brainstorm objections to what the Church teaches about herself.

Then choose one and write an apologetical paragraph answering the objection.

ST. JOSEMARIA ESCRIVA, FOUNDER OF OPUS DEI

t. Josemaria Escriva was born on January 9, 1902, in northern Spain. From an early age, Josemaria felt God was calling him to something, but he had no idea what. He began to pray that God would reveal his plan to him.

Josemaria thought he could best prepare for God's call by becoming a priest. After his ordination he pursued doctoral studies in civil law, tutored and taught university students, and served as chaplain in a hospital for the poor in Madrid. He also began work among the poor, sick, and dying. He asked them to offer their sufferings for a special intention he had. He continued to pray unceasingly to know what mission God was asking of him and for the strength to carry it out once he did.

On October 2, 1928, while he was on a retreat, Fr. Escriva finally understood what God was wanting of him. He was to help lay people live their call to holiness in the secular world through the sanctification of ordinary work. Whatever your work is, just do it as well as you can as a service to others and an offering to God. St. Josemaria dedicated the rest of his life to the establishment of what would later be named Opus Dei.

Today, Opus Dei is present in many countries around the world and operates universities, colleges, hospitals, trade schools, and many educational and cultural programs.

St. Josemaria Escriva died in Rome on June 26, 1975. Pope Bl. John Paul II declared him a saint on October 6, 2002.

DISCUSSION QUESTIONS

1. What is apologetics?
2. What is the best reason to be Catholic?
3. What does the Church say about the salvation of people outside her visible body?
4. Why should Catholics try to spread the Faith?
5. Why are some people happy to discover sinful Catholics?
6. Why is holiness necessary?
7. What form of communal worship has Christ given the Church?
8. Does God provide human beings with instructions on how to worship him?
9. How does the apostolic nature of the Church foster unity?
10. How do the Mass and the Sacraments foster Church unity?

ART AND PHOTO CREDITS

Cover

St. Peter's Basilica, Ordination of Twenty-nine Deacons by Pope Benedict XVI, April 27, 2008; ©L'Osservatore Romano

Front Pages

iii *See* Cover Credit

iv *Christ Handing the Keys to St. Peter*, Peter Paul Rubens; Gemäldegalerie, Berlin, Germany

ix *Second Vatican Council*, St. Peter's Basilica, Vatican; Archivo Oronoz

x *Madonna with the Fish (of Tobias)*, Raphael; Museo del Prado, Madrid, Spain

Chapter 1

1 *St. Peter's Basilica*, "Good Shepherd" Sunday Mass, May 7, 2006; ©L'Osservatore Romano

2 *Mass* at St. Paul of the Cross Church, Park Ridge, IL; Julie Koenig, Photographer

3 *St. Peter's Basilica and Square, Canonization of St. Josemaria Escriva*; Wojciech Dubis, photographer; MTF Archives

4 *M78 Reflection Nebula in the Constellation Orion*; Martin Pugh/NASA

5 left: *The Creation*, James Tissot; The Jewish Museum, New York

right: *Creation of the Animals*, (detail from the Grabow Altarpiece), Master Bertram; Kunsthalle, Hamburg, Germany

6 left: *Creation of Adam* (detail), Michelangelo; Sistine Chapel, Vatican

right: *The Creation*, Ceiling Mosaic, Baptistry of St. John, Florence, Italy

7 *Adam and Eve's Life of Toil*, (detail from the Grabow Altarpiece), Master Bertram; Kunsthalle, Hamburg, Germany

8 *The Fall of Man* (detail), Hendrik Goltzius; National Gallery of Art, Washington, DC

9 *Bl. William Joseph Chaminade*, MTF Archives

10 *The Expulsion of Adam and Eve from Paradise*, Benjamin West; National Gallery of Art, Washington, DC

Chapter 2

11 *Separation of the Earth from the Waters* (detail), Michelangelo; Sistine Chapel, Vatican

12 *The Garden of Eden*, Erastus Salisbury Field; Shelburne Museum, Vermont

13 *Noah Sacrificing After the Deluge*, Benjamin West; The San Antonio Museum Association, Texas

14 left: *Abraham, Sarah, and the Angel*, Jan Provost; Musée du Louvre, Paris, France

right: *The Sacrifice of Isaac*, Caravaggio; Galleria degli Uffizi, Florence, Italy

15 *Joseph and His Brethren Welcomed by Pharaoh*, James Tissot; The Jewish Museum, New York

16 *Moses and the Burning Bush*, Raphael; Raphael's Loggia, Palazzi Pontifici, Vatican

17 *Moses Receives the Tablets of Stone*, João Zeferino da Costa; Museu Dom Joao VI, Rio de Janeiro, Brazil

18 *King David Playing the Zither*, Andrea Celesti; Private Collection

19 *The Idolatry of Solomon* (detail), Sebastiano Conca; Museo del Prado, Madrid, Spain; Archivo Oronoz

20 *Jeremiah Lamenting the Destruction of Jerusalem*, Rembrandt; Rijksmuseum, Amsterdam, Netherlands

Chapter 3

21 *The Last Supper*, Carl H. Bloch; Frederiksborg Palace Chapel, Denmark

23 *Annunciation*, Nicolas Poussin; National Gallery, London

24 *Parable of the Hidden Treasure*, James Tissot; Brooklyn Museum, New York

26 *Calling of the Apostles* (detail), Domenico Ghirlandaio; Sistine Chapel, Vatican

27 *The Last Supper* (detail), Bartolomeo Carducci; Museo del Prado, Madrid, Spain; Archivo Oronoz

28 *Communion of the Apostles* (detail), Luca Signorelli; Museo Diocesano, Cortona, Italy

29 *Noah Releases the Dove*, Stories of Noah Mosaic; Basilica di San Marco, Venice, Italy

30 *The Savior*, Juan de Juanes; Museo del Prado, Madrid, Spain; Archivo Oronoz

31 left: *St. Augustine and St. Monica*, Ary Scheffer; Musée du Louvre, Paris, France

right: *St. Augustine Reading the Epistle of St. Paul*, Benozzo Gozzoli; Apsidal Chapel, Sant'Agostino, San Gimignano, Italy

32 *Moses on Mount Sinai*, Jean-Léon Gérôme; Private Collection

Chapter 4

33 *The Ascension*, Benjamin West; The Berger Collection, Denver Art Museum, Colorado

35 left: *Appearance Behind Locked Doors*, Duccio; Museo dell'Opera del Duomo, Siena, Italy

right: *The Disbelief of Saint Thomas* (detail), James Tissot; Brooklyn Museum, New York

36 *Christ's Charge to Peter*, Raphael; Tapestry Cartoon, Victoria and Albert Museum, London, England

37 *The Ascension*, John Singleton Copley; Museum of Fine Arts, Boston

39 left: *Pentecost*, Adriaen Van Der Werff; Staatsgalerie, Schleissheim Palace, Oberschleissheim, Germany

right: *St. Peter Preaching* (detail), Masolino; Cappella Brancacci, Santa Maria del Carmine, Florence, Italy

41 left: *St. Peter Consecrates Stephen as Deacon* (detail), Fra Angelico; Cappella Niccolina, Palazzi Pontifici, Vatican

right: *Stoning of St. Stephen*, Rembrandt; Musée des Beaux Arts, Lyon, France

42 Appearance on the Mountain in Galilee, Duccio; Museo dell'Opera del Duomo, Siena, Italy

ART AND PHOTO CREDITS

Chapter 5

43 *Apostles Peter and Paul*, El Greco; The Hermitage, St. Petersburg, Russia

45 left: *The Conversion of St. Paul*, Bartolomé Esteban Murillo; Museo del Prado, Madrid, Spain

right: *Ananias Laying Hands on Saul*, Byzantine Mosaic (thirteenth century); Basilica San Giovanni Evangelista, Ravenna, Italy

46 *St. Philip Baptizing the Ethiopian*, alternate title *The Baptism of the Eunuch*, Rembrandt; Private Collection

47 *Baptism of a Centurion* (detail), Michel Corneille; All-Union Art and Technical Institute, Moscow, Russia

48 *Ordaining of the Twelve Apostles*, James Tissot; Brooklyn Museum, New York

49 *St. John the Evangelist*, Vladimir Borovikovsky; The State Russian Museum, St. Petersburg, Russia

50 *Doubting Thomas*, Bernardo Strozzi; Museum of Art, Ponce, Puerto Rico

51 *The Martyrdom of St. Andrew*, Bartolomé Esteban Murillo; Museo del Prado, Madrid, Spain

52 Pentecost, Juan de Flandes; Museo del Prado, Madrid, Spain

Chapter 6

53 *Bernini's Throne of St. Peter*, St. Peter's Basilica; ©L'Osservatore Romano

55 left: *What Is Truth?* (detail), Nikolai Nikolaevich Ge (Gay); Tretyakov Gallery, Moscow, Russia

right: *St. Peter Enthroned with Saints* (detail), Cima da Conegliano; Pinacoteca di Brera, Milan, Italy

56 *Pope Francis and the College of Cardinals*; ©L'Osservatore Romano

57 *Pope Francis in St. Peter's Square*; ©L'Osservatore Romano

bottom right: *Coat of Arms of Pope Francis*; Illustration published by the Vatican

58 *The Martyrdom of St. Ignatius*; MTF Archives

59 *Pope Benedict XVI Ordains Twenty-two Men to the Priesthood*, St. Peter's Basilica, April 29, 2007; ©L'Osservatore Romano

61 *Iconostasis*, St. Joseph the Betrothed Ukrainian Greek Catholic Church, Chicago, IL; Jeremy Atherton, Photographer

62 *Christ Handing the Keys to St. Peter* (detail), Pietro Perugino; Sistine Chapel, Vatican

Chapter 7

63 *Baptism of Christ*, Bartolomé Murillo; Museo Staatliche, Berlin, Germany; Archivo Oronoz

64 *Christ Pantocrator*, Mosaic; Hagia Sophia, Istanbul, Turkey

65 *St. Peter Preaching in the Presence of St. Mark*, Fra Angelico; Museo di San Marco, Florence, Italy

66 *Pope Benedict XVI Administered Baptism to Fourteen Babies*, January 10, 2010, Feast of the Baptism of the Lord, Vatican

67 *The Baptism of Christ* (detail), Jean Baptiste Camille Corot; Church of St. Nicolas-du-Chardonnet, Paris, France

68 *Pentecost*, Jean Restout; Musée du Louvre, Paris

69 *The Last Supper* (detail), Dieric Bouts the Elder; Sint-Pieterskerk, Leuven, Belgium

70 *Sermon on the Mount* (detail), Carl H. Bloch; Frederiksborg Palace Chapel, Denmark

72 *Feed My Lambs* (detail), James Tissot; Brooklyn Museum, New York

73 *St. John Vianney*, Icon; MTF Archives

74 *The Wife of Zebedee Interceding with Christ over Her Sons* (detail), Paolo Veronese; Burghley House at Stamford, Lincolnshire, England

Chapter 8

75 *Adoring Saints, San Pier Maggiore Altarpiece*, Left Main Tier Panel, Jacopo di Cione and workshop; National Gallery, London

77 *Second Vatican Council*, St. Peter's Basilica, Vatican; Archivo Oronoz

78 *Sts. Peter and Paul Present God's Temple*, Byzantine Icon; Scuola Cretese Veneziana; AG Archives

81 *Let the Children Come to Me* (detail), Carl Christian Vogel von Vogelstein; AG Archives

82 *Pope Benedict XVI Greeted by Crowds at the Basilica of the National Shrine of Our Lady of Aparecida*, São Paulo, Brazil; Agência Brasil; Valter Campanato/ABr, photographer

83 *The Good Shepherd*, Philippe de Champaigne; AG Archives

84 *Rest on the Flight to Egypt*, Federico Fiori Barocci; Pinacoteca, Vatican

Chapter 9

85 *Christ Handing the Keys to St. Peter*, Master of the Legend of the Holy Prior; Wallraf-Richartz Museum, Cologne, Germany

87 *Pentecost* (detail), Alvise Vivarini; Gemäldegalerie, Berlin, Germany

89 *The Council of Nicæa*; Church of San Martino, Rome, Italy; Archivo Oronoz

91 *Martin Luther Nailing His Ninety-Five Theses to the Wittenburg Church Door*, Hugo Vogel; Archiv Für Kunst und Geschichte, Berlin, Germany

92 *Pope Paul VI Meets with Patriarch Athenagoras I*; Archivo Oronoz

93 *Pope St. Leo I the Great* (detail), Francisco de Herrera el Mozo; Museo del Prado, Madrid, Spain

94 *Christ and the Samaritan Woman*, Henryk Siemiradzki; Lviv National Art Gallery, Ukraine

Chapter 10

95 *Apostle Peter*, Anton Raphael Mengs; Kunsthistorisches Museum Wien, Austria

97 left: *The Holy Trinity*, Antonio de Pereda; Museum of Fine Arts, Budapest, Hungary

right: [*St. Basil the Great and*] *St. Athanasius* (detail), Alonso Sanchez Coello; Royal Monastery of St. Lawrence of Escorial, Madrid, Spain; Archivo Oronoz

ART AND PHOTO CREDITS

INDEX

INDEX